**Deborah Tannen** is the author of *You Just Don't Understand*, which was on the *New York Times* bestseller list for nearly four years, including eight months at number one, and has been translated into twenty-six languages. Among her books also published by Virago are *The Argument Culture*, *Talking From 9 to 5*, and *That's Not What I Meant!* Deborah Tannen is a professor of linguistics at Georgetown University in Washington, D.C.

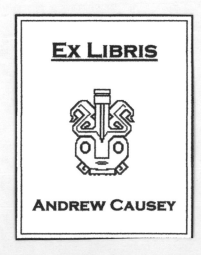

Also by Deborah Tannen

The Argument Culture:
Stopping America's War of Words

Talking from 9 to 5:
Women and Men in the Workplace:
Language, Sex, and Power

You Just Don't Understand:
Women and Men in Conversation

That's Not What I Meant!
How Conversational Style
Makes or Breaks Relationships

# I Only Say This Because I Love You

## How the Way We Talk Can Make or Break Family Relationships Throughout Our Lives

Deborah Tannen

Virago

A *Virago* Book

Published by Virago Press 2002

First published in the United States of America by Random House US



Grateful acknowledgment is made to the following for permission to reprint previously published material:

*Cambridge University Press:* Excerpts from "The Sequential Organization of Closing in Verbal Family Conflict" by Samuel Vuchinich, in *Conflict Talk: Sociolinguistic Investigations of Arguments in Conversations*, edited by Allen Grimshaw. Reprinted with the permission of Cambridge University Press.

*Harmony Music Ltd.:* Excerpt from "Different Tunes" by Peggy Seeger. "Different Tunes" is published by Harmony Music Ltd. for the world, 11 Uxbridge Street, London W8 7TQ. "Different Tunes" is from the CD *Period Pieces*, catalogue no. TCD 1078, released by Rykodisc. Peggy Seeger's website is www.pegseeger.com. Used by permission.

*Alfred A. Knopf, a division of Random House, Inc.:* Excerpt from *Phoenix* by J. D. Dolan. Copyright © 2000 by J. D. Dolan. Used by permission of Alfred A. Knopf, a division of Random House, Inc.

*International Creative Management:* Excerpt from "The Color of Love" by Danzy Senna, which was originally published in the May/June 2000 issue of *O, the Oprah Magazine*. Copyright © 2000 by Danzy Senna. Reprinted by permission of International Creative Management.

A CIP catalogue record for this book is available from the British Library.

ISBN 1 86049 855 8

Printed and bound in Great Britain by
Clays Ltd, St Ives plc

Virago
An imprint of
Time Warner Books UK
Brettenham House
Lancaster Place
London WC2E 7EN

www.virago.co.uk

To my parents

Dorothy and Eli Tannen

for whose loving presence in my life
I am grateful every day

# Contents

Acknowledgments ix
Preface xiii
Author's Note:
"Where Do You Get Your Examples?" xxiii

1. "I Can't Even Open My Mouth": Separating Messages from Metamessages in Family Talk 3

2. "Who Do You Love Best?" Family Secrets, Family Gossip: Taking Sides 29

A Brief Interlude I: "Go Ahead, Treat Me Like a Stranger" 64

3. Fighting for Love: Connection and Control in Family Arguments 67

4. "I'm Sorry, I'm Not Apologizing": Why Women Apologize More Than Men, and Why It Matters 95

5. "She Said," "He Said": Gender Patterns in Family Talk 124

6. "You Guys Are Living in the Past": Talking with Teens 161

A Brief Interlude II: "Call Me by My Rightful Name" 203

7. "I'm Still Your Mother": Mothers and Adult Children 209

8. "Help Me—Get out of My Way": Sisters and Brothers Forever 248

9. In-Laws and Other Strangers: Mixing Families, Mixing Talk 281

Coda: Talking Families 303

Notes 309
References 319
Index 325

# Acknowledgments

WORDS ALWAYS SEEM paltry when I want them to help me thank those who contributed to the making of a book. But words are all I've got, so I will use them to thank, first, those who selflessly read drafts of chapters or of the whole book and offered their comments: Sally Arteseros, A. L. Becker, Karl Goldstein, Paul Gordon, Harriet Grant, Leslie Jacobson, Shari Kendall, Scooter Libby, Richard Lutz, Addie and Al Macovski, Michael Macovski, Patrick O'Malley, Miriam Tannen, Naomi Tannen, and David Wise. David Wise has read drafts of every general-audience book I have written, starting with *That's Not What I Meant!* I am lucky to have such a loyal friend. A. L. Becker, Harriet Grant, Michael Macovski, and Naomi Tannen were *über*-readers, commenting on multiple drafts and providing short-notice answers to specific questions. To all these dear people, for their wisdom and generosity, I am deeply grateful.

When I am writing a book, I find examples and insights in all sorts of conversations—both with people I know well and with people I have just met, both in focused discussions and in chance remarks. I am grateful for these to Emily Anning, John Anning, Caren Anton, Kitty Bayh, A. L. Becker, Darlene Bookoff, Tom Brazaitis, Gay Daly, Gretchen Effler, Elizabeth Esswein, Amitai Etzioni, Ralph Fasold, Crawford Feagin, David Goldman, Karl Goldstein, Alfonso Gomez-Lobo, Harriet Grant, Joan Holmer,

Imelda Idar, Erling Indreeide, Leslie Jacobson, Caleen Sinnette Jennings, Roberta Johnson, David Evan Jones, Christina Kakava, Shari Kendall, Steve Kuhn, Linda Lader, Linda Lehr, Kate Lehrer, Molly Myerowitz Levine, Philip LeVine, Hal Libby, Peter Lowenberg, Phyllis Loy, Addie Macovski, Al Macovski, Joshua Marx, Barbara McGrael, Larry McGrael, Barbara Meade, Sheila Meyer, Susan Morgan, Steve Norring, Manjari Ohala, Michael Ondaatje, Clarence Page, Ilana Papele, Susan Philips, Dan Read, Deborah Schiffrin, Bill Schneider, Pam Sherman, Elinor DesVerney Sinnette, Rami Tal, Karen Tecott, Melissa Tully, Katharine Whitehorn, Karen Wilson, and Haru Yamada.

I would not know how to write a book without teaching related courses. Throughout the years of researching and writing this book, I taught advanced graduate seminars on family communication at Georgetown University. I thank the talented and insightful students who took part in these seminars: Francisco Alves, Najma Al Zidjaly, Cecilia Ayometzi, Anne Berry, Shu-Ching Susan Chen, Sylvia Chou, Mirjana N. Dedaic, Elisa Everts, Cynthia Gordon, Andrew Jocuns, Alexandra Johnston, Ki-tae Kim, Philip LeVine, Mindy McWilliams, Karen Murph, Amanda Neptune, Sigrid Norris, Ingrid de Saint-Georges, Pornpimon Supakorn, Maureen Taylor, Alla Yeliseyeva, and Chiara Zucconi. I have learned something from each one, and all helped me survey the relevant academic literature.

At the same time that I was completing this manuscript I was beginning work on a two-year project supported by the Alfred P. Sloan Foundation (Grant #99-10-7 to me and Shari Kendall) at Georgetown University. That project is designed to examine the role played by talk as women and men meet the challenge of integrating both family and work in their lives. Although the project was still in its early stages as I finished this book, I have used examples from that study here. I am extremely grateful to Kathleen Christensen and the Sloan Foundation; to my co-principal investigator, Shari Kendall, without whom I would never have undertaken the project; and, especially, to the adventuresome families who volunteered to participate by tape-recording their own conversations. I am grateful for their participation in the project and for their permission to use their words in this book. To Cynthia Gordon and Alexandra Johnston, the research assistants who logged in, transcribed, and helped analyze the examples from that project that I use here, I express my gratitude and appreciation.

My thanks go, also, to my agent, Suzanne Gluck, who has been, as always, a wise and steadfast advocate, and to my editor, Kate Medina, whose unflagging enthusiasm and support for the book have been a great gift. My invaluable and unflappable assistant, David Robinson, helped by tracking down sources and people—and by keeping the world at bay when I needed him to.

I am grateful to Georgetown University for providing the intellectual and collegial environment out of which all my writing grows: the students, without whom there would be no university; my colleagues in the linguistics department in general and the sociolinguistics program in particular; and the department's support staff, as well as the university administration.

With fervor, I thank my own family, all of whom make appearances in this book: my nieces and nephews, Micah, Rebekah, Ilana, Eben, Aaron, Josh, and Gabe; my in-laws, Addie and Al Macovski; my sisters, Naomi Tannen and Miriam Tannen, and their husbands, Joe Mahay and Bruce Phipps; my sister-in-law, Nancy Marx, and her husband, Alan; my parents, Dorothy and Eli Tannen, to whom this book, like my first, so many books back, is dedicated: To still have them with me as they enter their tenth decade is a blessing that fills me with awe. As ever and for always, I offer thanks to—and for—my husband and life partner, my family fortress, Michael Macovski. To all these precious members of my family, I hope I have represented you fairly. I know I have written of you with love.

# Preface

IN THE WAKE of bad news, or a spate of the blues, you pick up the telephone and call your sister, your mom, your brother, or your dad. You are looking for comfort—and often you find it. But sometimes you end up frustrated, even snapping.

Why does talk in the family so frequently go in circles, leaving us tied up in knots?

Through talk we create and shape our relationships. Through talk we are comforted; through talk we are hurt. My life's work has been understanding relationships—how they work, how to make them work better—by figuring out the workings of everyday talk. And nowhere is talk more powerful or more troublesome than among members of our family. In this book I turn my attention to conversations that take place in the family—especially among adult family members: adults and older-adult parents; parents and grown-up children; adult sisters and brothers.

The family is a pressure cooker in which relationships roil: The same processes that drive all conversations drive family talk, but the consequences are greater, the reactions more intense, because so much is at stake—our sense of being a right sort of person, our sense that the world is a right sort of place. Here I examine what's going on inside the pressure cooker: how ways of talking contribute to both the special balm and the particular pain that we find in our families. Once you know what's in the pot, and how the pressure of the cooker affects what's in it, you can stir and blend the ingredients in new and different ways.

In *That's Not What I Meant!* I introduced my concept of *conversational style* and showed how understanding the workings of conversation can shed light on relationships—and provide a starting point to improve them. *You Just Don't Understand* focused on the conversational styles of women and men—how they're the same, how they're different, how those differences can cause distress, and how understanding the differences can dispel some of that distress. In *Talking from 9 to 5* I considered, as the original subtitle put it, "how women's and men's conversational styles affect who gets heard, who gets credit, and what gets done at work." Then, in *The Argument Culture*, I moved to public conversations—in the media, politics, law, and education—and our tendency to approach everything as a metaphorical battle.

Now I return to my first love: the language of everyday conversation, and how it works—or fails to work—to create, reinforce, complicate, and improve relationships in the family.

We hear a lot of talk about "family" these days. Politicians pepper their speeches with the phrase "family values." If someone leaving a job or public office gives the explanation "I want to spend more time with my family," no one questions that motive. We excuse behavior we would otherwise not tolerate with the all-forgiving comment, "Well, they're family."

Why does the word carry such weight?

*Family* represents a sense of belonging—a foundation for everything else we are or do. It feels that if we can fit into our families, we can fit into the world. And if our families can see us for who we really are, we can be who we are not only in the family but also in the world. But the coin has another side: If members of our family—those who, presumably, know us best and care the most—are critical, find us wanting, then who will love us?

The more impersonal, complex, and overwhelming the world gets, the more we turn to our families for comfort and belonging. Though it's possible to reject our families completely—and sometimes that becomes necessary—in most cases we want to keep contact, keep the caring. Yet at times we feel frustrated by the very contact we seek.

Sometimes it feels as if the seeds of family love yield a harvest of criticism and judgment rather than (or along with) approval and acceptance. When we talk to family members, we search for signs of love but become attuned to signs of disapproval.

One woman whose daughter called her often but ended up getting annoyed at her each time, protested, "You called me! Why do you call me if you don't like what I say?"

We all keep calling—by telephone, e-mail, or in our hearts—because we want the connection that family affords. That's why we need to find ways to ensure that those conversations more often yield the comfort we seek and less often lead to dismay.

Every relationship is an ambivalent one, a psychologist friend used to say. There are things we treasure, and things that irritate, about each person in our lives, including each person in our families. At times those irritations blossom into arguments—and often the arguments get as tangled as uncontrollable vines. Part of the power of understanding talk in families is the ability to see what makes this happen. With this knowledge we stand a better chance of working things out without working each other over.

## What's in Store

In this book I look at family as a small community of speech, an organic unit that shapes and maintains itself linguistically. Here are some of the key concepts that I develop to uncover the ways that conversations create a family.

Everything we say to each other echoes with meanings left over from our past experience—both our history talking to the person before us at this moment and our history talking to others. This is especially true in the family—and our history of family talk is like a prism through which all other conversations (and relationships) are refracted.

We react not only to the meaning of the words spoken—the *message*—but also to what we think those words say about the relationship—the *metamessage*. Metamessages are unstated meanings we glean based on how someone spoke—tone of voice, phrasing—and on associations we brought to the conversation. You might say that the message communicates word meaning, but the metamessage yields heart meaning. So a crucial step in breaking the gridlock of frustrating conversations is learning to separate messages from metamessages.

An example—perhaps the most persistent and painful example—of message and metamessage in a family is the way that caring and criticizing are intertwined. As a woman named Esther said on hearing the title of this book, "When my mother says, 'I only say this because I love you,' I know she's going to tell me I'm fat." The message is just an observation about Esther's weight. But both Esther and her mother are concerned with metamessages: what her mother's comment says about their relationship. Her mother focuses on one metamessage: I want to help you improve because I care about you. Esther focuses on another: You're criticizing me. And she ends up feeling, I can't get approval from the person whose approval means the most.

The overall meaning that metamessages send can be called *framing*. As the anthropologist Gregory Bateson and the sociologist Erving Goffman used the term, framing is like an instruction sheet, telling us how to interpret the words we hear. (For example, "Have you thought of . . . ," coming from a parent, is often framed as "giving advice." And by giving advice older sisters or brothers are framing themselves as parents or parentlike siblings.)

One of the most powerful ways we have to change conversations, and relationships, for the better is *reframing*. Reframing can be done by talking in a different way to alter the meaning of a whole interaction: You might decide, for example, to stop offering advice and start offering understanding instead. But it can also be done simply by changing the way you interpret what is said: You might decide to regard your sibling's advice as the suggestions of a peer rather than dismissing it with resentment: "You're not my mother." Throughout this book I suggest reframing as a key to understanding—and improving—conversations and relationships.

I use the terms *connection* and *control* to describe the forces that drive all our conversations—how we use talk to get closer to each other or put distance between us; how the words we choose help us gain dominance or show respect. All this takes on extra meaning when the people we're talking to are members of our family, because a family is the most hierarchical institution and also the most connected. The power of parent over child, of an older brother or sister over a younger one, is absolute. At the same time the bond between parent and child, between brothers and sisters, is among the closest imaginable. And these strands of connection and control dovetail and are in constant play.

In talking to family members, we strive to find the right footing on a continuum between closeness and distance. We want to be close enough to feel protected and safe but not so close that we feel overwhelmed and suffocated. I call this the *connection continuum*. At the same time we try to find the right footing on a continuum between hierarchy and equality. Equality is, in a sense, an ideal; all relationships are more or less hierarchical, as one person always has the rank—or the force of personality—to make demands and have them met. One person's wishes or needs impinge on the other's actions, curtailing freedom and independence. That's why I call this the *control continuum*.

Americans tend to think of one person having power or control over another as inherently unsavory, and of two people being close and equal as inherently sweet. But hierarchy or power relations can be comforting and close—think of the comfort of protection that exists between parent and child. At the same time closeness or connection can be cloying, stifling, a threat to individuality—and this, too, is represented most clearly in the relationship between parent and child, especially when children enter their teenage years.

It's a challenge to get it right because words have meaning on both continua. What looks like a control maneuver could just as well be a connection maneuver—or both at once. An important step in understanding conversations (and hence bettering relationships) in the family is learning to see where a particular way of speaking places you on each continuum. If something feels intrusive, like an attempt to control you, consider how it is also a connection maneuver. (An example might be, "Please wait; I want to go with you on your walk, but I won't be ready for another half hour.") If you think you are saying something in the spirit of connection—"because I love you"—consider how it might be coming across as a control maneuver, an attempt to exercise power.

(Think of the request from the perspective of the person who is eager to get going on the walk.)

## Chapter by Chapter

I introduce control and connection maneuvers, along with messages and metamessages, in Chapter 1. Chapter 2 is about another crucial dynamic in family talk—*alignment:* the shifting alliances and conflicts that can make a family feel like a united circle in which all join hands or a circle of dancers you can't get into because you don't know the steps and can't pick up the beat. The idea of alignments captures why we sometimes feel left out in our own families—and how to make readjustments to get back in.

When conflicts arise, as they inevitably do among family members, talk sometimes heats up, gets louder, and turns into arguments. Nothing is more disheartening than finding yourself in the same argument over and over, like being stuck on a carousel that won't stop to let you off. In Chapter 3 I look at family arguments that actually took place, showing the ways of talking that sparked the disputes, then made them escalate, and how the people caught in their grip might have spoken differently, with better results. This is also the chapter in which I introduce the idea of a control continuum and a connection continuum, and look more closely at how these two forces are related to each other and interplay.

Sometimes the most powerful weapons are lying in plain sight—like the underused (but also sometimes overused) verbal act of apologizing. Many arguments result when a woman (a wife, a mother, a sister) is upset because a man (her husband, her father, her brother) refuses to apologize when he did something that caused her pain. At the same time the man is stewing because his wife, daughter, or sister seems to want him to humiliate himself by apologizing when he feels he didn't do anything wrong. In Chapter 4, I sort out what apologies mean to women and men, and show how they can be a tonic to relationships rather than a source of conflict.

From apologizing it's a natural step to the broader question of how gender relations affect everything that happens in a family. In Chapter 5 I look at gender patterns of talk—where they come from and how they affect even so simple a family ritual as the evening meal, when a mother might say to her child, "Tell Daddy what you did today." I showed in *You Just Don't Understand* why talking to someone of the other sex can feel like talking to someone from another world. This is just as true—and especially troubling—when the person you're talking to is a member of your family. Understanding how gender patterns of talk affect family relationships is crucial in finding a common language to bridge those worlds.

Talking to teenagers (or trying to) is an extreme case of the differing worldviews two people in a family can have. Teens are beginning to go out into the world—and it's a different world from the one their parents know. Because of conflicting assumptions about the world and how it works, conversations between teens and the adults they live with can spiral out of control, never getting settled. Chapter 6 considers conversations with teenagers. It also is the chapter in which I explore the concept of framing: how arguments can result from clashing frames, and how reframing can help resolve disputes.

"My relationship with my mother keeps changing," said a man who lost his mother to cancer when he was a young adult. In Chapter 7 I explore some of the changes—and some of the constancies—in conversations with our mothers throughout our lives, even after our mothers are gone. I also consider the special challenge to mothers talking to their adult children. Mothers in particular come to mind when people hear my title *I Only Say This Because I Love You*. As perhaps the most powerful family relationship, the mother-child constellation is a crystal of many sides, each of which reflects an aspect of communication that has reverberations for all other family relationships as well.

It is impossible to talk about mothers without also talking about fathers, since the roles mothers play in the family are inextricably interwoven with the roles of fathers—as when mothers become Communication Central, relaying and mediating information between their husbands and their children. Thus, fathers appear prominently in Chapter 7, and in other chapters as well.

Next, Chapter 8 is about siblings: the sisters and brothers who are our companions and rivals. I am concerned primarily with the adult sibling relationships that so enrich, and so vex, our dealings with family. But I also look at conversations among sisters and brothers growing up, to find the sources of themes that are echoed when we talk to our siblings as adults.

Given the different conversational styles of women and men, and those of different generations, talking at home is like trying to talk across cultures. Sometimes a family involves people who grew up in different countries or different parts of the country, or who come from different social classes, different economic levels, different cultural backgrounds. When two people join their lives, they bring along a host of family members of their own—from previous marriages, or from the family they grew up in. Talking to in-laws can be especially challenging if their backgrounds have resulted in differing conversational styles—speech habits like volubility or taciturnity; directness or indirectness; how loudly or softly, how quickly or slowly, to speak; attitudes toward interruption, asking questions, and joking; and so on. The last chapter shows how conversational style affects families whose members come from vastly, or even slightly, different cultural backgrounds. In that sense it is also a guide to talking with in-laws.

Although this book is mostly about adult family members, family relationships begin in the homes where we grew up, and I also have much to say—throughout the book—about conversations among parents and children, and between siblings growing up.

## All in the Family

In their lives together, families often confront major conflicts caused by illness, abuse, infidelity, alcoholism, incest, and tragic events like the death of a child. I will not deal with these cataclysmic events here: Psychologists are trained to do this. My training is as a linguist, an analyst of conversation. Drawing on this expertise, I focus on the daily strains and verbal exchanges that both constitute and complicate family relationships.

Families take many forms: Children may be raised by one parent, two parents, foster parents, grandparents—even great-grandparents. Aunts and uncles or stepparents move in, move out, or stay for the duration. Families include parents and children who are gay or lesbian. A family can be as small as two people of one generation or as large as ten or more children and three or even four generations living together. I don't address these diversities directly, yet everything I have to say applies to all kinds of families: how the pushes and pulls of conversation reflect and negotiate the pushes and pulls of relationships.

Families also come in all the racial, class, and gender distinctions that people come in. The individuals who people my examples come from a wide range of backgrounds. There are Asian Americans, African Americans, Mexican Americans, and whites; there are middle-class, working-class, and upper-middle-class people; there are lesbian, gay, and straight people. In presenting examples, I don't specify these distinctions. This omission could be seen as contributing to the invisibility of anyone who is not mainstream, but I see it as evidence of the universality of the forces that I describe.

Each of us lives our own life, and no one—not even the people we live with or the person we are closest to—knows what the world looks like from our point of view. The husband who has been away at work does not really know the many burdens his wife is managing in order to provide the "hold" in household—holding things together by doing many tasks at once. At the same time the wife who is angry because her husband tells her on Friday night that he is going to work yet another weekend cannot know the pressure he is under when a report is due on Monday and the statistics he thought were final were just found to be way off. And neither of them can really understand the world of their teenage daughter or son, ruled by the norms, expectations, and reactions of peers.

Precisely because we *can't* really see the world from someone else's point of view, it is crucial that we find ways to talk to each other so we can explain our points of view and work out solutions—or at least compromises—rather than talk in circles, argue about ways of arguing, or let vital issues drop to avoid arguments.

There are few experiences as satisfying as a family conversation that goes well. You can talk to each other about anything, from the deepest concerns to the most trivial daily encounters. Your sense of rhythm, timing, and directness are all in sync; you laugh at the same jokes, find the same topics of interest. You can refer, without explanation, to events that took place when you were a child and to people long gone that you both knew. You speak a private language—a familylect—that only members of your family share.

Understanding how talk works can ensure that more family conversations are satisfying and fewer lead to frustration. There is a gift simply in realizing that you are not alone—that other families are experiencing similar conflicts, comparable strains. Understanding the workings of conversational style in families gives you a language in which to talk about what's going on—and the tools to make sure that talk works for you rather than against you in building the relationships that are so central to your life.

# Author's Note

## "Where Do You Get Your Examples?"

THROUGHOUT THIS BOOK I present conversations to illustrate the workings of talk. I would like to answer in advance the question "Where do you get your examples?"

All my examples come from real conversations that actually took place. In many cases the conversations were captured on tape, and my analyses are based on the transcripts.

Some of the examples I present were recorded by families who participated in a two-year study I am codirecting with Shari Kendall at Georgetown University, with support from the Alfred P. Sloan Foundation. As part of this study, couples who have children living at home and who both work outside the home tape-recorded all the conversations they participated in, together or separately, for a week. The recordings were listened to, logged in, and in some cases transcribed by graduate student research assistants, who also helped identify segments relevant to the themes of this book. The larger study—which was still in its early stages as I completed this book—is designed to examine the role of talk in meeting the challenge of balancing work and family. Here I use only the transcripts of talk at home. Although I occasionally changed minor details to assure anonymity, and eliminated some hesitations and false starts to make the dialogue more readable, these conversations otherwise appear exactly as they occurred.

The speakers themselves have seen and approved my use of their talk.

I have also taken examples from television documentaries that showed families in the privacy of their homes over time. Two of these were shown in the United States by the Public Broadcasting System. For *An American Love Story*, which aired in five two-hour segments in September 1999, the filmmaker Jennifer Fox followed the family of Karen Wilson, Bill Sims, and their two daughters in Queens, New York, over two years beginning in 1992. For *An American Family*, which appeared in twelve weekly hourlong segments in 1973, the filmmakers Alan and Susan Raymond and the producer, Craig Gilbert, filmed the family of William and Pat Loud and their five children in Santa Barbara, California, for seven months. Americans who watched this series will recall that during the filming Pat and Bill Loud decided to divorce and their son Lance came out as gay.

A third television documentary, called *Sylvania Waters*, was filmed in Australia over six months in the home of the New Zealander Noeline Baker, her Australian boyfriend (whom she planned to marry), and her teenage son by a previous marriage. The twelve programs were shown by the Australian Broadcasting Commission in 1992 and by the British Broadcasting Corporation in 1993. The excerpts I analyze appeared in an academic paper published by the Australian researcher David A. Lee of the University of Queensland.

Because the dinner table is a setting at which family members gather and talk, many researchers in the fields of linguistics, sociology, and anthropology have based studies on tape recordings of dinner-table conversations. Their academic articles provide another source for the examples that I draw on. I always identify the researchers and their publications when I borrow their examples. I also try to make clear when the analysis I present is my own interpretation of the authors' examples and when I am recounting the authors' own findings.

During the many years I have been teaching courses in analyzing conversation at Georgetown University, students in my classes have recorded conversations in their own homes and in the homes of friends who are amenable to being taped. For the last two years

I have taught graduate seminars on family communication. I cite transcripts students analyzed in their term papers as well as insights that emerged in class discussion and in the course readings, always with attribution.

I should emphasize that taping is always done with the knowledge and consent of everyone concerned. Although this introduces the possibility that speakers' behavior is influenced by knowing a tape recorder is running, the level of language I am concerned with is not something people tend to focus on, even if they are on their guard. (Their self-censorship is generally aimed at not revealing compromising information.) The give-and-take of interaction in a family, when the tape recorder is running over an extended period of time, tends to take over. Readers can, in the end, judge for themselves whether the conversations they overhear on these pages sound like those they have had in the privacy of their own homes.

Other conversations that appear in this book were not captured on tape but rather reported to me by relatives, friends, or casual acquaintances—either because I specifically asked for their experiences or by chance in the course of our own conversations. In presenting interactions that were reported to me, or that I experienced or overheard, I construct dialogue out of a combination of reported, remembered, and overheard speech much as a novelist invents dialogue. In these cases I often change details to preserve the anonymity of the people involved, though I try hard to get the wording just as it was reported, remembered, or overheard. Here, too, I always show the principals what I have written about them, to make sure that I got it right and that they are comfortable with my use of their lives.

I always specify when examples are taken from transcripts. In the absence of such specification, the dialogue is my creation—but every conversation I thus created is based on a real interaction.

# I Only Say This Because I Love You

ONE

# "I Can't Even Open My Mouth"

## Separating Messages from Metamessages in Family Talk

"DO YOU REALLY need another piece of cake?" Donna asks George.

"You bet I do," he replies, with that edge to his voice that implies, "If I wasn't sure I needed it before, I am darned sure now."

Donna feels hamstrung. She knows that George is going to say later that he wished he hadn't had that second piece of cake.

"Why are you always watching what I eat?" George asks.

"I was just watching out for you," Donna replies. "I only say it because I love you."

Elizabeth, in her late twenties, is happy to be making Thanksgiving dinner for her extended family in her own home. Her mother, who is visiting, is helping out in the kitchen. As Elizabeth prepares the stuffing for the turkey, her mother remarks, "Oh, you put onions in the stuffing?"

Feeling suddenly as if she were sixteen years old again, Elizabeth turns on her mother and says, "*I'm* making the stuffing, Mom. Why do you have to criticize everything I do?"

"I didn't criticize," her mother replies. "I just asked a question. What's got into you? I can't even open my mouth."

The allure of family—which is, at heart, the allure of love—is to have someone who knows you so well that you don't have to explain yourself. It is the promise of someone who cares enough about you to protect you against the world of strangers who do not wish you well. Yet, by an odd and cruel twist, it is the family itself that often causes pain. Those we love are looking at us so close-up that they see all our blemishes—see them as if through a magnifying glass. Family members have innumerable opportunities to witness our faults and feel they have a right to point them out. Often their intention is to help us improve. They feel, as Donna did, "I only say it because I love you."

Family members also have a long shared history, so everything we say in a conversation today echoes with meanings from the past. If you have a tendency to be late, your parent, sibling, or spouse may say, "We have to leave at eight"—and then add, "It's really important. Don't be late. Please start your shower at seven, not seven-thirty!" These extra injunctions are demeaning and interfering, but they are based on experience. At the same time, having experienced negative judgments in the past, we develop a sixth sense to sniff out criticism in almost anything a loved one says—even an innocent question about ingredients in the stuffing. That's why Elizabeth's mother ends up feeling as if she can't even open her mouth—and Elizabeth ends up feeling criticized.

When we are children our family constitutes the world. When we grow up family members—not only our spouses but also our grown-up children and adult sisters and brothers—keep this larger-than-life aura. We overreact to their judgments because it feels as if they were handed down by the Supreme Court and are unassailable assessments of our value as human beings. We bristle because these judgments seem unjust; or because we sense a kernel of truth we would rather not face; or because we fear that if someone who knows us so well judges us harshly we must really be guilty, so we risk losing not only that person's love but everyone else's, too. Along with this heavy load of implications comes a dark resentment that a loved one is judging us at all—and has such power to wound.

"I still fight with my father," a man who had reached a high position in journalism said to me. "He's been dead twenty-one years." I asked for an example. "He'd tell me that I had to comb my hair and dress better, that I'd learn when I grew up that appearance is important." When he said this I noticed that his hair was uncombed, and the tails of his faded shirt were creeping out from the waist of his pants. He went on, "I told him I'd ignore that. And now sometimes when I'm going somewhere important, I'll look in the mirror and think— I'll say to him in my mind, 'See? I *am* a success and it didn't matter.' "

This man's "fights" with his father are about approval. No matter what age we've reached, no matter whether our parents are alive or dead, whether we were close to them or not, there are times when theirs are the eyes through which we view ourselves, theirs the standards against which we measure ourselves when we wonder whether we have measured up. The criticism of parents carries extra weight, even when children are adults.

## I Care, Therefore I Criticize

Some family members feel they have not only a right but an obligation to tell you when they think you're doing something wrong. A woman from Thailand recalls that when she was in her late teens and early twenties, her mother frequently had talks with her in which she tried to set her daughter straight. "At the end of each lecture," the woman says, "my mother would always tell me, 'I have to complain about you because I am your mother and I love you. Nobody else will talk to you the way I do because they don't care.' "

It sometimes seems that family members operate under the tenet "I care, therefore I criticize." To the one who is being told to do things differently, what comes through loudest and clearest is the criticism. But the one offering suggestions and judgments is usually focused on the caring. A mother, for example, was expressing concern about her daughter's boyfriend: He didn't have a serious job, he didn't seem to want one, and she didn't think he was a good prospect for marriage. The daughter protested that her mother disapproved of everyone she dated. Her mother responded indignantly, "Would you rather I didn't care?"

As family members we wonder why our parents, children, siblings, and spouses are so critical of us. But as family members we also feel frustrated because comments we make in the spirit of caring are taken as criticizing.

Both sentiments are explained by the double meaning of giving advice: a loving sign of caring, a hurtful sign of criticizing. It's impossible to say which is right; both meanings are there. Sorting out the ambiguous meanings of caring and criticizing is difficult because language works on two levels: the message and the metamessage. Separating these levels—and being aware of both—is crucial to improving communication in the family.

## The Intimate Critic: When Metamessages Hurt

Because those closest to us have front-row seats to view our faults, we quickly react—sometimes overreact—to any hint of criticism. The result can be downright comic, as in Phyllis Richman's novel *Who's Afraid of Virginia Ham?* One scene, a conversation between the narrator and her adult daughter, Lily, shows how criticism can be the metronome providing the beat for the family theme song. The dialogue goes like this:

LILY: Am I too critical of people?
MOTHER: What people? Me?
LILY: Mamma, don't be so self-centered.
MOTHER: Lily, don't be so critical.
LILY: I knew it. You do think I'm critical. Mamma, why do you always have to find something wrong with me?

The mother then protests that it was Lily who asked if she was too critical, and now she's criticizing her mother for answering. Lily responds, "I can't follow this. Sometimes you're impossibly hard to talk to."

It turns out that Lily is upset because her boyfriend, Brian, told her she is too critical of him. She made a great effort to stop criticizing, but now she's having a hard time keeping her resolve. He gave her a sexy outfit for her birthday—it's expensive and beautiful—but the generous gift made her angry because she took it as criticism of the way she usually dresses.

In this brief exchange Richman captures the layers of meaning that can make the most well-intentioned comment or action a source of conflict and hurt among family members. Key to understanding why Lily finds the conversation so hard to follow—and her mother so hard to talk to—is separating messages from metamessages. The *message* is the meaning of the words and sentences spoken, what anyone with a dictionary and a grammar book could figure out. Two people in a conversation usually agree on what the message is. The *metamessage* is meaning that is not said—at least not in so many words—but that we glean from every aspect of context: the way something is said, who is saying it, or the fact that it is said at all.

Because they do not reside in the words themselves, metamessages are hard to deal with. Yet they are often the source of both comfort and hurt. The message (as I've said) is the word meaning while the metamessage is the heart meaning—the meaning that we react to most strongly, that triggers emotion.

When Lily asked her mother if she was too critical of people, the message was a question about Lily's own personality. But her mother responded to what she perceived as the metamessage: that Lily was feeling critical of *her*. This was probably based on experience: Her daughter had been critical of her in the past. If Lily had responded to the message alone, she would have answered, "No, not you. I was thinking of Brian." But she, too, is reacting to a metamessage—that her mother had made herself the point of a comment that was not about her mother at all. Perhaps Lily's resentment was also triggered because her mother still looms so large in her life.

The mixing up of message and metamessage also explains Lily's confused response to the gift of sexy clothing from her boyfriend. The message is the gift. But what made Lily angry was what she thought the gift implied: that Brian finds the way she usually dresses not sexy enough—and unattractive. This implication is the metamessage, and it is what made Lily critical of the gift, of Brian, and of herself. Metamessages speak louder than messages, so this is what Lily reacted to most strongly.

It's impossible to know whether Brian intended this metamessage. It's possible that he wishes Lily would dress differently; it's also possible that he likes the way she dresses just fine but simply thought this particular outfit would look good on her. That's what makes metamessages so difficult to pinpoint and talk about: They're implicit, not explicit.

When we talk about messages, we are talking about the meanings of words. But when we talk about metamessages, we are talking about relationships. And when family members react to each other's comments, it's metamessages they are usually responding to. Richman's dialogue is funny because it shows how we all get confused between messages and metamessages when we talk to those we are close to. But when it happens in the context of a relationship we care about, our reactions often lead to hurt rather than to humor.

In all the conversations that follow, both in this chapter and throughout the book, a key to improving relationships within the family is distinguishing the message from the metamessage, and being clear about which one you are reacting to. One way you can do this is *metacommunicating*—talking about communication.

## "What's Wrong with French Bread?" Try Metacommunicating

The movie *Divorce American Style* begins with Debbie Reynolds and Dick Van Dyke preparing for dinner guests—and arguing. She lodges a complaint: that all he does is criticize. He protests that he doesn't. She says she can't discuss it right then because she has to take the French bread out of the oven. He asks, "French bread?"

A simple question, right? Not even a question, just an observation. But on hearing it Debbie Reynolds turns on him, hands on hips, ready for battle: "What's wrong with French bread?" she asks, her voice full of challenge.

"Nothing," he says, all innocence. "It's just that I really like those little dinner rolls you usually make." This is like the bell that sets in motion a boxing match, which is stopped by another bell—the one at the front door announcing their guests have arrived.

Did he criticize or didn't he? On the message level, no. He simply asked a question to confirm what type of bread she was preparing. But on the metamessage level, yes. If he were satisfied with her choice of bread, he would not comment, except perhaps to compliment. Still, you might ask, So what? So what if he prefers the dinner rolls she usually makes to French bread? Why is it such a big deal? The big deal is explained by her original complaint: She feels that he is *always* criticizing—always telling her to do things differently than she chose to do them.

The big deal, in a larger sense, is a paradox of family: We depend on those closest to us to see our best side, and often they do. But because they are so close, they also see our worst side. You want the one you love to be an intimate ally who reassures you that you're doing things right, but sometimes you find instead an intimate critic who implies, time and again, that you're doing things wrong. It's the cumulative effect of minor, innocent suggestions that creates major problems. You will never work things out if you continue to talk about the message—about French bread versus dinner rolls—rather than the metamessage—the implication that your partner is dissatisfied with everything you do. (*Divorce American Style* was made in 1967; that it still rings true today is evidence of how common—and how recalcitrant—such conversational quagmires are.)

One way to approach a dilemma like this is to *metacommunicate*—to talk about ways of talking. He might *say* that he feels he can't open his mouth to make a suggestion or comment because she takes everything as criticism. She might *say* that she feels he's always dissatisfied with what she does, rather than turn on him in a challenging way. Once they both understand this dynamic, they will come up with their own ideas about how to address it. For example, he might decide to preface his question with a disclaimer: "I'm not criticizing the French bread." Or maybe he *does* want to make a request—a direct one—that she please make dinner rolls because he likes them. They might also set a limit on how many actions of hers he can question in a day. The important thing is to talk about the metamessage she is reacting to: that having too many of her actions questioned makes her feel that her partner in life has changed into an in-house inspection agent, on the lookout for wrong moves.

## Living with the Recycling Police

"This is recyclable," Helen exclaims, brandishing a small gray cylinder that was once at the center of a roll of toilet paper. There she stops, as if the damning evidence is sufficient to rest her case.

"I know it's recyclable," says Samuel. "You don't have to tell me." He approves of recycling and generally practices it, if not quite as enthusiastically (he would say obsessively) as Helen. But this time he slipped: In a moment of haste he tossed the cardboard toilet paper tube into the wastebasket. Now Helen has found it and wants to know why it was there. "You can't go through the garbage looking for things I threw away," Samuel protests. "Our relationship is more important than a toilet paper carcass."

"I'm not talking about our relationship," Helen protests. "I'm talking about recycling."

Helen was right: She *was* talking about recycling. But Samuel was right, too. If you feel like you're living with the recycling police—or the diet police, or the neatness police—someone who assumes the role of judge of your actions and repeatedly finds you guilty—it takes the joy out of living together. Sometimes it even makes you wish, for a fleeting moment, that you lived alone, in peace. In that sense, Samuel was talking about the relationship.

Helen was focusing on the message: the benefits of recycling. Samuel was focusing on the metamessage: the implication he perceives that Helen is enforcing rules and telling him he broke one. Perhaps, too, he is reacting to the metamessage of moral superiority in Helen's being the more fervent recycler. Because messages lie in words, Helen's position is more obviously defensible. But it's metamessages that have clout, because they stir emotions, and emotions are the currency of relationships.

In understanding Samuel's reaction, it's also crucial to bear in mind that the meaning of Helen's remark resides not just in the conversation of the moment but in the resonance of all the conversations on the subject they've had in their years together—as well as the conversations Samuel had before that, especially while growing up in his own family. Furthermore, it's her *repeatedly* remarking on what he does or does not recycle that gives Samuel the impression that living with Helen is like living with the recycling police.

## Give Me Connection, Give Me Control

There is another dimension to this argument—another aspect of communication that complicates everything we say to each other but that is especially powerful in families. That is our simultaneous but conflicting desires for connection and for control.

In her view Helen is simply calling her husband's attention to a small oversight in their mutual pursuit of a moral good—an expression of their connection. Their shared policy on recycling reflects their shared life: his trash is her trash. But Samuel feels that by installing herself as the judge of his actions, she is placing herself one-up. In protest he accuses, "You're trying to control me."

Both connection and control are at the heart of family. There is no relationship as close—and none as deeply hierarchical—as the relationship between parent and child, or between older and younger sibling. To understand what goes on when family members talk to each other, you have to understand how the forces of connection and control reflect both closeness and hierarchy in a family.

"He's like family," my mother says of someone she likes. Underlying this remark is the assumption that *family* connotes closeness, being connected to each other. We all seek connection: It makes us feel safe; it makes us feel loved. But being close means you care about what those you are close to think. Whatever you do has an impact on them, so you have to take their needs and preferences into account. This gives them power to control your actions, limiting your independence and making you feel hemmed in.

Parents and older siblings have power over children and younger siblings as a result of their age and their roles in the family. At the same time, *ways of talking create power.* Younger siblings or children can make life wonderful or miserable for older siblings or parents by what they say—or refuse to say. Some family members increase their chances of getting their way by frequently speaking up, or by speaking more loudly and more forcefully. Some increase their influence by holding their tongues, so others become more and more concerned about winning them over.

"Don't tell me what to do. Don't try to control me" are frequent protests within families. It is automatic for many of us to think in terms of power relations and to see others' incursions on our freedom as control maneuvers. We are less likely to think of them as connection maneuvers, but they often are that, too. At every moment we're struggling not only for control but also for love, approval, and involvement. What's tough is that the *same* actions and comments can be either control maneuvers or connection maneuvers—or, as in most cases, both at once.

## Control Maneuver or Connection Maneuver?

"Don't start eating yet," Louis says to Claudia as he walks out of the kitchen. "I'll be right there."

Famished, Claudia eyes the pizza before her. The aroma of tomato sauce and melted cheese is so sweet, her mouth thinks she has taken a bite. But Louis, always slow-moving, does not return, and the pizza is cooling. Claudia feels a bit like their dog Muffin when she was being trained: "Wait!" the instructor told Muffin, as the hungry dog poised pitifully beside her bowl of food. After pausing long enough to be convinced Muffin would wait forever, the trainer would say, "Okay!" Only then would Muffin fall into the food.

Was Louis intentionally taking his time in order to prove he could make Claudia wait no matter how hungry she was? Or was he just eager for them to sit down to dinner together? In other words, when he said, "Don't start eating yet," was it a control maneuver, to make her adjust to his pace and timing, or a connection maneuver, to preserve their evening ritual of sharing food? The answer is, it was both. Eating together is one of the most evocative rituals that bond individuals as a family. At the same time, the requirement that they sit down to dinner together gave Louis the power to make Claudia wait. So the need for connection entailed control, and controlling each other is in itself a kind of connection.

Control and connection are intertwined, often conflicting forces that thread through everything said in a family. These dual forces explain the double meaning of caring and criticizing. Giving advice, suggesting changes, and making observations are signs of caring when looked at through the lens of connection. But looked at through the lens of control, they are put-downs, interfering with our desire to manage our own lives and actions, telling us to do things differently than we choose to do them. That's why caring and criticizing are tied up like a knot.

The drives toward connection and toward control are the forces that underlie our reactions to metamessages. So the second step in improving communication in the family—after distinguishing between message and metamessage—is understanding the double meaning of control and connection. Once these multiple layers are sorted out and brought into focus, talking about ways of talking—metacommunicating—can help solve family problems rather than making them worse.

## Small Spark, Big Explosion

Given the intricacies of messages and metamessages, and of connection and control, the tiniest suggestion or correction can spark an explosion fueled by the stored energy of a history of criticism. One day, for example, Vivian was washing dishes. She tried to fix the drain cup in an open position so it would catch debris and still allow water to drain, but it kept falling into the closed position. With a mental shrug of her shoulders, she decided to leave it, since she didn't have many dishes to wash and the amount of water that would fill the sink wouldn't be that great. But a moment later her husband, Mel, happened by and glanced at the sink. "You should keep the drain open," he said, "so the water can drain."

This sounds innocent enough in the telling. Vivian could have said, "I tried, but it kept slipping in, so I figured it didn't matter that much." Or she could have said, "It's irritating to feel that you're looking over my shoulder all the time, telling me to do things differently from the way I'm doing them." This was, in fact, what she was feeling—and why she experienced, in reaction to Mel's suggestion, a small eruption of anger that she had to expend effort to suppress.

Vivian was surprised at what she did say. She made up a reason and implied she had acted on purpose: "I figured it would be easier to clean the strainer if I let it drain all at once." This thought *had* occurred to her when she decided not to struggle any longer to balance the drain cup in an open position, though it wasn't true that she did it on purpose for that reason. But by justifying her actions, Vivian gave Mel the opening to argue for his method, which he did.

"The whole sink gets dirty if you let it fill up with water," Mel said. Vivian decided to let it drop and remained silent. Had she spoken up, the result would probably have been an argument.

Throughout this interchange Vivian and Mel focused on the message: When you wash the dishes, should the drain cup be open or closed? Just laying out the dilemma in these terms shows how ridiculous it is to argue about. Wars are being fought; people are dying; accident or illness could throw this family into turmoil at any moment. The position of the drain cup in the sink is not a major factor in their lives. But the conversation wasn't really about the message—the drain cup—at least not for Vivian.

Mel probably thought he was just making a suggestion about the drain cup, and in the immediate context he was. But messages always bring metamessages in tow: In the context of the history of their relationship, Mel's comment was not so much about a drain cup as it was about Vivian's ability to do things right and Mel's role as judge of her actions.

This was clear to Vivian, which is why she bristled at his comment, but it was less clear to Mel. Our field of vision is different depending on whether we're criticizing or being criticized. The critic tends to focus on the message: "I just made a suggestion. Why are you so touchy?" The one who feels criticized, however, is responding to the metamessage, which is harder to explain. If Vivian had complained, "You're always telling me how to do things," Mel would surely have felt, and might well have said, "I can't even open my mouth."

At the same time, connection and control are in play. Mel's assumption that he and Vivian are on the same team makes him feel comfortable giving her pointers. Furthermore, if a problem develops with the sink's drainage, he's the one who will have to fix it. Their lives are intertwined; that's where the connection lies. But if Vivian feels she can't even wash dishes without Mel telling her to do it differently, then it seems to her that he is trying to control her. It's as if she has a boss to answer to in her own kitchen.

Vivian might explain her reaction in terms of metamessages. Understanding and respecting her perspective, Mel might decide to limit his suggestions and corrections. Or Vivian might decide that she is overinterpreting the metamessage and make an effort to focus more on the message, taking some of Mel's suggestions and ignoring others. Once they both understand the metamessages as well as the messages they are communicating and reacting to, they can metacommunicate: talk about each other's ways of talking and how they might talk differently to avoid hurt and recriminations.

## "Wouldn't You Rather Have Salmon?"

Irene and David are looking over their menus in a restaurant. David says he will order a steak. Irene says, "Did you notice they also have salmon?"

This question exasperates David; he protests, "Will you please stop criticizing what I eat?"

Irene feels unfairly accused: "I didn't criticize. I just pointed out something on the menu I thought you might like."

The question "Did you notice they also have salmon?" is not, on the message level, a criticism. It could easily be friendly and helpful, calling attention to a menu item her husband might have missed. But, again, conversations between spouses—or between any two people who have a history—are always part of an ongoing relationship. David knows that Irene thinks he eats too much red meat, too much dessert, and, generally speaking, too much.

Against the background of this aspect of their relationship, any indication that Irene is noticing what he is eating is a reminder to David that she disapproves of his eating habits. That's why the question "Do you really want to have dessert?" will be heard as "You shouldn't have dessert," and the observation "That's a big piece of cake" will communicate "That piece of cake is too big," regardless of how they're intended. The impression of disapproval comes not from the message—the words spoken—but from the metamessage, which grows out of their shared history.

It's possible that Irene really was not feeling disapproval when she pointed out the salmon on the menu, but it's also possible that she was and preferred not to admit it. Asking a question is a handy way of expressing disapproval without seeming to. But to the extent that the disapproval comes through, such indirect means of communicating can make for more arguments, and more hurt feelings on both sides. Irene sees David overreacting to an innocent, even helpful, remark, and he sees her hounding him about what he eats and then denying having done so. Suppose he had announced he was going to order salmon. Would she have said, "Did you notice they also have steak?" Not likely. It is reasonable, in this context, to interpret any alternative suggestion to an announced decision as dissatisfaction with that decision.

Though Irene and David's argument has much in common with the previous examples, the salmon versus steak decision is weightier than French bread versus dinner rolls, recycling, or drain cups. Irene feels that David's health—maybe even his life—is at stake. He has high cholesterol, and his father died young of a heart attack. Irene has good reason to want David to eat less red meat. She loves him, and his health and life are irrevocably intertwined with hers. Here is another paradox of family: A blessing of being close is knowing that someone cares about you: cares what you do and what happens to you. But caring also means interference and disapproval.

In other words, here again is the paradox of connection and control. From the perspective of control, Irene is judging and interfering; from the perspective of connection, she is simply recognizing that her life and David's are intertwined. This potent brew is family: Just knowing that someone has the closeness to care and the right to pass judgment—and that you care so much about that judgment—creates resentment that can turn into anger.

## Crying Literal Meaning: How Not to Resolve Arguments

When Irene protested, "I didn't criticize," she was crying literal meaning: taking refuge in the message level of talk, ducking the metamessage. All of us do that when we want to avoid a fight but still get our point across. In many cases this defense is sincere, though it does not justify ignoring or denying the metamessage someone else may have perceived. If the person we're talking to believes it wasn't "just a suggestion," keeping the conversation focused on the message can result in interchanges that sound like a tape loop playing over and over. Let's look more closely at an actual conversation in which this happened—one that was taped by the people who had it.

Sitting at the dining room table, Evelyn is filling out an application. Because Joel is the one who has access to a copy machine at work, the last step of the process will rest on his shoulders. Evelyn explains, "Okay, so you'll have to attach the voided check here, after you make the Xerox copy. Okay?" Joel takes the papers, but Evelyn goes on: "Okay just— Please get that out tomorrow. I'm counting on you, hon. I'm counting on you, love."

Joel reacts with annoyance: "Oh, for Pete's sake."

Evelyn is miffed in turn: "What do you mean by that?"

Joel turns her words back on her: "What do *you* mean by that?"

The question "What do you mean by that?" is a challenge. When communication runs smoothly, the meanings of words are self-evident, or at least we assume they are. (We may discover later that we misinterpreted them.) Although "What do you mean?" might be an innocent request for clarification, adding "by that" usually signals not so much that you didn't understand what the other person meant but that you understood—all too well—the *implication* of the words, and you didn't like it.

Evelyn cries literal meaning. She sticks to the message: "Oh, honey, I just mean I'm *counting* on you."

Joel calls attention to the metamessage: "Yes, but you say it in a way that suggests I can't be counted on."

Evelyn protests, accurately, "I never said that."

But Joel points to evidence of the metamessage: "I'm talking about your *tone*."

I suspect Joel was using *tone* as a catchall way of describing the metamessage level of talk. Moreover, it probably wasn't only the way Evelyn spoke—her tone—that he was reacting to but the fact that Evelyn said it at all. If she really felt she could count on him, she would just hand over the task. "I'm counting on you" is what people say to reinforce the importance of doing something when they believe extra reinforcement is needed. Here, the shared history of the relationship adds meaning to the metamessage as well. Joel has reason to believe that Evelyn feels she can't count on him.

Later in the same conversation, Joel takes a turn crying literal meaning. He unplugs the radio from the wall in the kitchen and brings it into the dining room so they can listen to the news. He sets it on the table and turns it on.

"Why aren't you using the plug?" Evelyn asks. "Why waste the batteries?" This sparks a heated discussion about the relative importance of saving batteries. Evelyn then suggests, "Well, we could plug it in right here," and offers Joel the wire.

Joel shoots her a look.

Evelyn protests, "Why are you giving me a dirty look?"

And Joel cries literal meaning: "I'm not!" After all, you can't prove a facial expression; it's not in the message.

"You are!" Evelyn insists, reacting to the metamessage: "Just because I'm handing this to you to plug in."

I have no doubt that Joel did look at Evelyn with annoyance or worse, but not because she handed him a plug—that would be literal meaning, too. He was surely reacting to the metamessage of being corrected, of her judging his actions. For her part, Evelyn probably felt Joel was irrationally refusing to plug in the radio when an electrical outlet was staring them in the face.

How to sort through this jumble of messages and metamessages? The message level is a draw. Some people prefer the convenience of letting the radio run on batteries when it's moved from its normal perch to a temporary one. Others find it obviously reasonable to plug the radio in when there's an outlet handy, to save batteries. Convenience or frugality, take your pick. We all do. But when you live with someone else—caution! It may seem natural to suggest that others do things the way you would do them, but that is taking account only of the message. Giving the metamessage its due, the expense in spirit and goodwill is more costly than batteries. Being corrected all the time is wearying. And it's even more frustrating when you try to talk about what you believe they implied and they cry literal meaning—denying having "said" what you know they communicated.

Consider, too, the role of connection and control. Telling someone what to do is a control maneuver. But it is also a connection maneuver: Your lives are intertwined, and anything one person does has an impact on the other. In the earlier example, when Evelyn said, "I'm counting on you," I suspect some readers sympathized with Joel and others with Evelyn, depending on their own experience with people they've lived with. Does it affect your reaction to learn that Joel forgot to mail the application? Evelyn had good reason, based on years of living with Joel, to have doubts about whether he would remember to do what he said he would do.

Given this shared history, it might have been more constructive for Evelyn to admit that she did not feel she could completely count on Joel, rather than cry literal meaning and deny the metamessage of her words. Taking into account Joel's forgetfulness—or maybe his being overburdened at work—they could devise a plan: Joel might write himself a reminder and place it strategically in his briefcase. Or Evelyn might consider mailing the form herself, even though that would mean a trip to make copies. Whatever they decide, they stand a better chance of avoiding arguments—and getting the application mailed on time—if they acknowledge their metamessages and the reasons motivating them.

## Who Burned the Popcorn?

Living together means coordinating so many tasks, it's inevitable that family members will have different ideas of how to perform those tasks. In addition, everyone makes mistakes; sometimes the dish breaks, you forget to mail the application, the drain cup falls into the closed position. At work, lines of responsibility and authority are clear (at least in principle). But in a family—especially when adults are trying to share responsibilities and authority—there are fewer and fewer domains that belong solely to one person. As couples share responsibility for more and more tasks, they also develop unique and firm opinions about how those tasks should be done—and a belief in their right to express their opinions.

Even the most mundane activity, such as making popcorn (unless you buy the microwave type or an electric popper), can spark conflict. First, it takes a little doing, and people have their own ideas of how to do it best. Second, popcorn is often made in the evening, when everyone's tired. Add to that the paradox of connection and control—wanting the person you love to approve of what you do, yet having someone right there to witness and judge mistakes—and you have a potful of kernels sizzling in oil, ready to pop right out of the pot.

More than one couple have told me of arguments about how to make popcorn. One such argument broke out between another couple who were taping their conversations. Since their words were recorded, we have a rare opportunity to listen in on a conversation very much like innumerable ones that vanish into air in homes all around the country. And we have the chance to think about how it could have been handled differently.

The seed of trouble is planted when Molly is in the kitchen and Kevin is watching their four-year-old son, Benny. Kevin calls out, "Molly! Mol! Let's switch. You take care of him. I'll do whatever you're doing."

"I'm making popcorn," Molly calls back. "You always burn it."

Molly's reply is, first and foremost, a sign of resistance. She doesn't want to switch jobs with Kevin. Maybe she's had enough of a four-year-old's company and is looking forward to being on her own in the kitchen. Maybe she is enjoying making popcorn. And maybe her reason is truly the one she gives: She doesn't want Kevin to make the popcorn because he always burns it. Whatever her motivation, Molly resists the switch Kevin proposes by impugning his ability to make popcorn. And this comes across as a call to arms.

Kevin protests, "No I don't! I never burn it. I make it perfect." He joins Molly in the kitchen and peers over her shoulder. "You making popcorn? In the big pot?" (Remember this line; it will become important later.)

"Yes," Molly says, "but you're going to ruin it."

"No I won't," Kevin says. "I'll get it just right." With that they make the switch. Kevin becomes the popcorn chef, Molly the caretaker. But she is not a happy caretaker.

Seeing a way she can be both caretaker and popcorn chef, Molly asks Benny, "You want to help Mommy make popcorn? Let's not let Daddy do it. Come on."

Hearing this, Kevin insists, "I know how to make popcorn!" Then he ups the ante: "I can make popcorn better than you can!" After that the argument heats up faster than the popcorn. "I cook every kernel!" Kevin says.

"No you won't," says Molly.

"I will too! It's never burned!" Kevin defends himself. And he adds, "It always burns when you do it!"

"Don't make excuses!"

"There's a trick to it," he says.

And she says, "I know the trick!"

"No you don't," he retorts, " 'cause you always burn it."

*"I do not!"* she says. "What are you, crazy?"

It is possible that Kevin is right—that Molly, not he, is the one who always burns the popcorn. It is also possible that Molly is right—that he always burns the popcorn, that she doesn't, and that he has turned the accusation back onto her as a self-defense strategy. Move 1: I am not guilty. Move 2: You are guilty.

In any case, Kevin continues as popcorn chef. After a while Molly returns to the kitchen. "Just heat it!" she tells Kevin. "Heat it! No, I don't want you—"

"It's going, it's going," Kevin assures her. "Hear it?"

Molly is not reassured, because she does not like what she hears. "It's too slow," she says. "It's all soaking in. You hear that little—"

"It's not soaking in," Kevin insists. "It's fine."

"It's just a few kernels," Molly disagrees.

But Kevin is adamant: "All the popcorn is being popped!"

Acting on her mounting unease about the sounds coming from the popping corn, Molly makes another suggestion. She reminds Kevin, "You gotta take the trash outside."

But Kevin isn't buying. "I can't," he says. "I'm doing the popcorn." And he declines Molly's offer to watch it while he takes out the trash.

In the end Molly gets to say, "See, what'd I tell you?" But Kevin doesn't see the burned popcorn as a reason to admit fault. Remember his earlier question, "In the big pot?" Now he protests, "Well, I never *use* this pot. I use the other pot."

Molly comes back, "It's not the pot! It's you!"

"It's the pot," Kevin persists. "It doesn't heat up properly. If it did, then it would get hot." But pots can't really be at fault; those who choose pots can. So Kevin accuses, "You should have let me do it from the start."

"You *did* it from the start!" Molly says.

"No, I didn't," says Kevin. "You chose this pan. I would've chosen a different pan." So it's the pot's fault, and Molly's fault for choosing the pot.

This interchange is almost funny, especially for those of us—most of us, I'd bet—who have found ourselves in similar clashes.

How could Kevin and Molly have avoided this argument? Things might have turned out better if they had talked about their motivations: Is either one of them eager to get a brief respite from caring for Benny? If so, is there another way they can accomplish that goal? (Perhaps they could set Benny up with a task he enjoys on his own.) With this motivation out in the open, Molly might have declined to switch places when Kevin proposed it, saying something like, "I'm making popcorn. I'm enjoying making it. I'd rather not switch." The justification Molly used, "You always burn it," may have seemed to her a better tactic because it claims her right to keep making popcorn on the basis of the family good rather than her own preference. But the metamessage of incompetence can come across as provocative, in addition to being hurtful.

It's understandable that Kevin would be offended to have his popcorn-making skills impugned, but he would have done better to avoid the temptation to counterattack by insisting he does it better, that it's Molly who burns it. He could have prevented the argument rather than escalate it if he had metacommunicated: "You can make the popcorn if you want," he might have said, "but you don't have to say I can't do it." For both Molly and Kevin—as for any two people negotiating who's going to do what—metacommunicating is a way to avoid the flying metamessages of incompetence.

## "I Know a Thing or Two"

One of the most hurtful metamessages, and one of the most frequent, that family talk entails is the implication of incompetence—even (if not especially) when children grow up. Now that we're adults we feel we should be entitled to make our own decisions, lead our own lives, imperfect though they may be. But we still want to feel that our parents are proud of us, that they believe in our competence. That's the metamessage we yearn for. Indeed, it's because we want their approval so much that we find the opposite metamessage—that they don't trust our competence—so distressing.

Martin and Gail knew that Gail's mother tended to be critical of whatever they did, so they put off letting her see their new home until the purchase was final. Once the deal was sealed they showed her, with pride, the home they had chosen while the previous owner's furniture was still in it. They were sure she would be impressed by the house they were now able to afford, as well as its spotless condition. But she managed to find something to criticize—even if it was invisible: "They may've told you it's in move-in condition," she said with authority, "but I know a thing or two, and when they take those pictures off the wall, there will be holes!" Even though they were familiar with her tendency to find fault, Gail and Martin were flummoxed.

The aspect of the house Gail's mother found to criticize was profoundly insignificant: Every home has pictures on the wall, every picture taken down leaves holes, and holes are easily spackled in and painted over. It seems that Gail's mother was really reaching to find *something* about their new home to criticize. From the perspective of control, it would be easy to conclude that Gail's mother was trying to take the role of expert in order to put them down, or even to spoil the joy of their momentous purchase. But consider the perspective of connection. Pointing out a problem that her children might not have noticed shows that she can still be of use, even though they are grown and have found this wonderful house without her help. She was being protective, watching out for them, making sure no one pulled the wool over their eyes.

Because control and connection are inextricably intertwined, protection implies incompetence. If Gail and Martin need her mother's guidance, they are incapable of taking care of themselves. Though Gail's mother may well have been reacting to—and trying to overcome—the metamessage that they don't need her anymore, the metamessage they heard is that she can't approve wholeheartedly of anything they do.

## "She Knew What Was Right"

In addition to concern about their children's choice of home, parents often have strong opinions about adult children's partners, jobs, and—especially—how they treat their own children. Raising children is something at which parents self-evidently have more experience, but metamessages of criticism in this area, though particularly common, are also particularly hurtful, because young parents want so much to be good parents.

A woman of seventy still recalls the pain she felt when her children were small and her mother-in-law regarded her as an incompetent parent. It started in the first week of her first child's life. Her mother-in-law had come to help—and didn't want to go home. Finally, her father-in-law told his wife it was time to leave the young couple on their own. Unconvinced, she said outright—in front of her son and his wife—"I can't trust them with the baby."

Usually signs of distrust are more subtle. For example, during a dinner conversation among three sisters and their mother, the sisters were discussing what their toddlers like to eat. When one said that her two-year-old liked fish, their mother cautioned, "Watch the bones." How easy it would be to take offense (though there was no indication this woman did): "You think I'm such an incompetent mother that I'm going to let my child swallow fish bones?" Yet the grandmother's comment was her way of making a contribution to the conversation—one that exercises her lifelong responsibility of protecting children.

It is easy to scoff at the mother-in-law who did not want to leave her son and his wife alone with their own baby. But consider the predicament of parents who become grandparents and see (or believe they see) their beloved grandchildren treated in ways they feel are hurtful. One woman told me that she loves being a grandmother—but the hardest part is having to bite her tongue when her daughter-in-law treats her child in a way the grandmother feels is misguided, unfair, or even harmful. "You see your children doing things you think aren't right," she commented, "but at least they're adults; they'll suffer the consequences. But a child is so defenseless."

In some cases grandparents really do know best. My parents recall with lingering guilt a time they refused to take a grandparent's advice—and later wished they had. When their first child, my sister Naomi, was born, my parents, like many of their generation, relied on expert advice for guidance in what was best for their child. At the time, the experts counseled that, once bedtime comes, a child who cries should not be picked up. After all, the reasoning went, that would simply encourage the baby to cry rather than go to sleep.

One night when she was about a year old, Naomi was crying after being put to sleep in her crib. My mother's mother, who lived with my parents, wanted to go in and pick her up, but my parents wouldn't let her. "It tore us apart to hear her cry," my father recalls, "but we wanted to do what was best for her." It later turned out that Naomi was crying because she was sick. My parents cringe when they tell this story. "My mother pleaded with us to pick her up," my mother says. "She knew what was right."

## I'm Grown Up Now

Often a parent's criticism is hurtful—or makes us angry—even when we know it is right, maybe especially if we sense it is right. That comes clear in the following example.

Two couples were having dinner together. One husband, Barry, was telling about how he had finally—at the age of forty-five—learned to ignore his mother's criticism. His mother, he said, had commented that he is too invested in wanting the latest computer gizmo, the most up-to-date laptop, regardless of whether he needs it. At that point his wife interrupted. "It's true, you are," she said—and laughed. He laughed, too: "I know it's true." Then he went back to his story and continued, unfazed, about how in the past he would have been hurt by his mother's comment and would have tried to justify himself to her, but this time he just let it pass. How easily Barry acknowledged the validity of his mother's criticism—when it was his wife making it. Yet acknowledging that the criticism was valid didn't change his view of his mother's comment one whit: He still thought she was wrong to criticize him.

When we grow up we feel we should be free from our parents' judgment (even though we still want their approval). Ironically, there is often extra urgency in parents' tendency to judge children's behavior when children are adults, because parents have a lot riding on how their children turn out. If the results are good, everything they did as parents gets a seal of approval. My father, for example, recalls that as a young married man he visited an older cousin, a woman he did not know well. After a short time the cousin remarked, "Your mother did a good job." Apparently, my father had favorably impressed her, but instead of complimenting him, she credited his mother.

By the same token, if their adult children have problems—if they seem irresponsible or make wrong decisions—parents feel their life's work of child rearing has been a failure, and those around them feel that way, too. This gives extra intensity to parents' desire to set their children straight. But it also can blind them to the impact of their corrections and suggestions, just as those in power often underestimate the power they wield.

When adult children move into their own homes, the lid is lifted off the pressure cooker of family interaction, though the pot may still be simmering on the range. If they move far away—as more and more do—visits turn into intense interactions during which the pressure cooker lid is clicked back in place and the steam builds up once again. Many adult children feel like they're kids again when they stay with their parents. And parents often feel the same way: that their adult children are acting like kids. Visits become immersion courses in return-to-family.

Parents with children living at home have the ultimate power—asking their children to move out. But visiting adult children have a new power of their own: They can threaten not to return, or to stay somewhere else. Margaret was thrilled that her daughter Amanda, who lives in Oregon, would be coming home for a visit to the family farm in Minnesota. It had been nearly a year since Margaret had seen her grandchildren, and she was eager to get reacquainted with them. But near the end of the visit, there was a flare-up. Margaret questioned whether Amanda's children should be allowed to run outside barefoot. Margaret thought it was dangerous; Amanda thought it was harmless. And Amanda unsheathed her sword: "This isn't working," she said. "Next time I won't stay at the farm. I'll find somewhere else to stay." Because Margaret wants connection—time with her daughter and grandchildren—the ability to dole out that connection gives her daughter power that used to be in Margaret's hands.

## The Paradox of Family

When I was a child I walked to elementary school along Coney Island Avenue in Brooklyn, praying that if a war came I'd be home with my family when it happened. During my childhood in the 1950s my teachers periodically surprised the class by calling out, "Take cover!" At that cry we all ducked under our desks and curled up in the way we had been taught: elbows and knees tucked in, heads down, hands clasped over our necks. With the possibility of a nuclear attack made vivid by these exercises, I walked to school in dread—not of war but of the possibility that it might strike when I was away from my family.

But there is another side to family, the one I have been exploring in this chapter. My nephew Joshua Marx, at thirteen, pointed out this paradox: "If you live with someone for too long, you notice things about them," he said. "That's the reason you don't like your parents, your brother. There's a kid I know who said about his friend, 'Wouldn't it be cool if we were brothers?' and I said, 'Then you'd hate him.' "

We look to communication as a way through the minefield of this paradox. And often talking helps. But communication itself is a minefield because of the complex workings of message and metamessage. Distinguishing messages from metamessages, and taking into account the underlying needs for connection and control, provides a basis for metacommunicating. With these insights as foundation, we can delve further into the intricacies of family talk. Given our shared and individual histories of talk in relationships, and the enormous promise of love, understanding, and listening that family holds out, it's worth the struggle to continue juggling—and talking.

# Two

# "Who Do You Love Best?"

## Family Secrets, Family Gossip: Taking Sides

FAMILY REUNION. THE words alone hum with emotion, suggesting lines of connection and acceptance that create everyone's dream of belonging that is family. And actual family reunions can be joyous occasions where people gather from distant homes, exchange memories and stories, and laugh together. But few family reunions are without painful moments: An older brother asks a question that makes his younger brother feel stupid, just as he did when they were children. A woman sees her mother and sister whispering conspiratorially, and feels a flash of pain at being left out, just as she did when she was small. One moment everyone laughs together, as gloriously in sync as a chorus line all kicking at the same time. Then at another moment everyone laughs but one person doesn't get the joke—and feels bereft, suddenly cast out of the magic circle.

One way to understand both the wonderful feeling of connection and the painful feeling of rejection that family entails is what I call *alignment*. Talk binds individuals into a family by creating alignments that link family members to each other like dots connected in a children's drawing book. When two people align themselves to each other through talk, it is like straight, bold lines connecting the dots. But whenever talk brings two people into alignment, another person may end up connected by dotted lines, crooked lines, or maybe no lines at all—left out. Like metamessages, alignments can be stealth weapons: They wound, but the source of damage is hard to locate because their meaning resides not in the words spoken but in the impact of those words. As with metamessages, alignments yield heart meaning rather than word meaning.

Families are kaleidoscopes of shifting alignments, as members make connections, have arguments, confide in each other, do things together, become estranged, and (sometimes) reconcile. It's like a square dance in which dancers are always changing partners—sometimes to "sashay home" to their steady partners but sometimes caught in an unending series of steps with other dancers in the square. Being part of a family does not automatically make you feel like a full-fledged member. Many of us feel, in one way or another, at one time or another, like square dancers who somehow got left out when the caller said, "All join hands and circle round."

## The Family Fortress

"Our family is a fortress," says Cicily Wilson, older daughter of the family that was featured in the public television series *An American Love Story.* "A fortress" captures the sense in which a family is a bulwark against the world—a protective barrier that no one can penetrate to harm you. The fortress walls are built when family members align with each other against the world, often through talk.

Sitting around the dinner table exchanging stories reinforces the fortress walls. A woman tells how a mechanic wouldn't make good on a car repair gone wrong. A man tells of a friend who refused to help him out, even after he had helped that friend in a similar jam. A child feels that a teacher punished a classmate more harshly than she should have. As family members talk about events and the (mis)behavior of those outside the family, they agree in their assessments of outsiders' actions—and align themselves with each other, reinforcing the walls that ring them in and leave others out.

But fortress walls do not ensure harmony within. Look inside any enclosed community and you'll find anger and hurt as well as love. Even if family members align to face the outside world as a team, within the family—as within any team—there are dissensions, struggles, and friendly-fire wounds that cause pain—sometimes fleeting but sometimes lasting a lifetime. Alignments are key to both the gift of family and the pain that family members cause each other. Understanding how talk creates alignments provides a basis for metacommunicating about why you were hurt by what someone said, and for creating new alignments with new ways of talking.

## Breaching the Fortress Walls: Revealing Secrets

Family relations are a web of alliances drawn and redrawn by talk, as information is shared, repeated, kept secret, or revealed.

When Katherine Russell Rich was diagnosed with breast cancer at the age of thirty-two, she didn't want anyone to know; she told only her mother, trusting that the terrible news would remain secret. Rich learned that the walls had been breached when she received an unexpected telephone call. As she describes in her memoir, *The Red Devil*, "It was my cousin Cia in Denver: 'I just want you to know,' she said, 'I have my church group praying for you.' " Furious, Rich calls her mother and accuses, "You told Cia!" This is how Rich reports the conversation that ensued:

> "No, I didn't," my mother said.
>
> "Yes, you did! She just called! She knows!"
>
> "No, I told your sister. *She* must have told Cia," she said, trying to exempt herself on a technicality.

This brief episode reveals a series of alignments and realignments created by words exchanged. When she called to tell Katherine that her church group was praying for her, Cia was trying to align herself with Katherine, expressing connection: She was letting her cousin know that she cared and was doing what she could to help. Disastrously, from Katherine's point of view, Cia's way of helping involved spreading Katherine's secret to Cia's entire church group. To Katherine, who wanted to keep her cancer private, the phone call was an intrusion into the family fortress—a violation of her desire to control information about what she was going through.

By repeating the information—revealing the secret—Katherine's mother had no doubt been expressing connection to her other daughter, Katherine's sister. But at the same time she redrew the lines of alignment: from Katherine to her mother, fine; from her mother to her sister, maybe. From her sister to a cousin—*tilt!* A cousin, an outsider (from Katherine's, though not her sister's, point of view), was allowed into the family circle when Katherine wanted to feel safe inside.

## Everybody Says So, All Our Friends: Taking Secrets Outside

Hurtful realignments can result not only when information is leaked from inside the family to outside. Sometimes a realignment results when information goes the other way: dragged from outside the family to inside, like tracking in mud without wiping your shoes. And the information need not be cataclysmic; it can be a small observation, even a truly inconsequential comment. The realignment created by whom information is repeated to can in itself seem like betrayal.

Eve was upset about something her husband, Tom, had said. She repeated his remark to her friends, each in turn, to see whether they thought she was overreacting. They supported her view, and she used their support as evidence in making her case to him: "I don't think that was a very nice thing you said to me," she told him. Then she added, "And all my friends agree."

Hearing the last comment Tom was confronted not only with his wife's complaint but also with the vision of his wife and her friends conspiring, huddling like football players to plot strategy against him. This vision created an alignment in which her loyalty was to her friends rather than to him. It was especially distressing because he couldn't explain himself to those friends since they did not speak directly to him. So he was left with the feeling that they would now have an unfairly negative view of him, and there was nothing he could do about it.

This scenario is very common—and very tricky. Many women discuss with friends what's troubling them, because talking about personal problems is one of the fundamental ways that women create friendship. But when a woman's problems involve family members—which they often do—discussing personal problems means taking inside information about family members outside the family. Men, in particular, often perceive this as a betrayal, because they don't understand the purpose: Men's friendships are typically built not on telling secrets but rather on sharing activities—doing things together. From Tom's point of view, Eve's talking to her friends about him was breaching the walls of the family fortress.

There is no easy solution to this conflict. Tom would be happy if Eve never told her friends about their quarrels, but that would clip the wings of her friendships and cut off one of her main sources of comfort. Eve can't really understand why Tom objects, since discussing problems is, in her view, one of the main reasons people have friends. She wishes Tom would talk to his friends more. Seeing the exchange of information in terms of alignments can help each understand the other's reactions. To Tom, Eve's talking about him to her friends redraws her alignment from him to her friends. But from Eve's point of view, talking to friends about Tom reinforces her alignment to him: It says to her friends that her relationship with Tom is central in her life. Knowing this, Tom might try to accept, in a general way, that Eve will talk to her friends about him. For her part, Eve should take her friends' advice into account, be bolstered by it, but speak only for herself when talking to Tom.

## "And Your Sister Thinks So, Too": Spreading Gossip Within

Any family member can sow discord by repeating comments made by another family member to a third. For example, Kristin's mother was upset to learn that Kristin had bought a new car when she was struggling to manage the credit card debt she already had. "I told your sister and brother about your new car," her mother said to Kristin. "They agreed that it was a big mistake. Can you still get out of the contract?" Though Kristin knew she had a problem with debt, and knew that her mother disapproved, hearing that her siblings spoke this way about her really hurt. It gave Kristin the feeling that she was the outsider, her sister and brother aligned with her mother against her.

When adult children talk to each other about their parents—whether to reminisce, consult about their care, or exchange complaints—they are solidifying connections among themselves, aligning as a team. When one or more children talk with a parent about another sibling, the alignment goes another way: parent-child, with the talked-about sibling on the outside. This may or may not be destructive, depending upon the comments (are they criticism, praise, or just news?). But whenever criticism originally spoken in someone's absence is repeated in that person's presence, the meaning of the words spoken is fundamentally changed. The message may be the same, but the metamessage is completely different—and often destructive. The concept of alignment captures how. Kristin can never look at her siblings the same way once she has seen them as aligned with her mother against her.

Kristin's mother's comment was a blend of connection and control. From Kristin's point of view, it was about control—interfering with her decision to buy a new car. Her mother probably focused on connection—protecting Kristin from digging herself deeper into debt. Her mother likely felt that adding the weight of Kristin's siblings' opinion would strengthen her case and increase the chances that Kristin would change her mind. I doubt she wanted to hurt her daughter (though it's possible that, if she was angry, she did), and I don't know if she sensed that speaking this way would disrupt the alignment among Kristin and her siblings. This is the power of alignments: They work indirectly to strengthen ties among family members. But they can also strengthen ties among some members, leaving others out.

Our conversations depend on a network of trust: If I tell you something, I trust you to know whom it's okay to repeat it to, and who should not hear it. We all talk about others in ways we would not talk about them if they were present. That's not evil; it's human. We have made the decision *not* to hurt their feelings when we refrain from making the hurtful remarks directly to them, and we are trusting the people we are talking *to* not to repeat what we said to the people we're talking *about*. But we are handing a weapon to those we are talking to—a weapon they can use to injure the people in question, if they want to. And sometimes they want to.

Of course there are times when people intentionally put forth information—rumors—in order to damage others. In those cases the people who repeat the rumors are accessories to that crime, especially if the rumors are false. There are times, however, when it is an act of friendship to tell others what people are saying about them. A woman who had turned a blind eye to her husband's infidelities, which were many and obvious to everyone but her, was at first humiliated when her brother sat her down and told her the truth. But eventually she was grateful to her brother and disappointed in all the others who had held their tongues. Someone who really wishes you well tells you things that you'd rather not hear, that you need to know. But someone who does not wish you well tells you things you'd rather not hear that make you feel bad, and that you don't need to know. The complex challenge is figuring out what a person really needs to know—and what your reasons are for wanting to tell.

Often, when a person repeats something that someone else said, it is the repeater who provoked the someone else to say it. This is easy to do, because there is pressure, in a conversation, to support what another person says by seeming to agree or at least to assent. Later that agreement can be repeated as if it had been volunteered. So a father might comment to a daughter, "Your brother always asks me to pick him up at the airport. He can afford a taxi now. I'm getting the feeling he's becoming a tightwad." To avoid contradicting her father, the daughter might agree. "Yeah, you've got a point." With this agreement in hand, the father can go to the son and say, "I'm afraid you're becoming a tightwad. Your sister noticed it, too." Or he can leave himself out and just say, "Your sister noticed you're becoming a tightwad."

The ability to repeat what other family members have said is one of the most dangerous weapons lying around the house. In one instance it led to the most extreme form of family conflict—a cutoff. A cutoff occurs when, for a long period of time or a short one, a grown child refuses to talk to a parent or sibling, or a parent, in spite or despair, refuses to communicate with an adult child. I learned of this instance when I asked a woman who had severed all contact with her parents why she'd decided to do so. "I told them not to speak about me in a certain way," she said, "and they did it." I asked how she knew they had spoken of her that way. "My sister told me," she said. The plot thickened. I don't know whether or not her sister foresaw the drastic effect of repeating their parents' words. Nor do I know whether, in the end, severing contact was necessary and beneficial or avoidable and regrettable. What I do know is that, in this case, the cutoff resulted not from a single axis of alignment, between this woman and her parents, but rather from a complex realignment touched off by information her sister passed on.

## "I Stood Up for You"

Repeating what another family member said is always risky, even when your purpose is to support rather than to criticize.

There was a time when my mother was obsessed with my unmarried state. Hardly a conversation took place between us during which she did not express this obsession. If she told me on the phone that she had enjoyed a visit to my home, she'd end by saying how bad she felt when she and my father drove away and left me standing in front of my house, alone. When she heard I was planning to take a trip with my best friend, she would try to convince me to go instead to Club Med, where she was sure I stood a better chance of finding a husband. If I introduced her to a male friend who was not a love interest, she would invariably ask, "Why isn't he interested in you? Is he gay?" (It never occurred to her that *I* might not be interested in *him* that way.) Time and again I'd forbid her to raise this issue, and she'd try to comply, but before long she'd break down, I'd get angry, she'd complain that

I was too touchy, and the cycle would start again. Finally we reached a point where she was managing to restrain her remarks most of the time. But there was a fly in the ointment. My sister.

My oldest sister liked to tell me that my mother had complained about how worried she was that I was unmarried and was spending all my time working rather than husband shopping. My sister would then tell me how she had defended me, explaining to our mother that I was happy with my life, had gobs of friends, loved my work, and so on. She would also tell me how she had explained that my chances of getting married were not wrecked because I refused to go to Club Med—that I was more likely to meet my life partner at one of the many academic meetings I took part in than on the beach in Tahiti. (This turned out to be prophetic.)

Alignment explains both why my sister spoke this way and why it caused me pain. She told me about her conversations with our mother in order to align herself with me. She was letting me know that she had stuck up for me, that she appreciated and understood my situation (which she did). I believe she thought this knowledge would make me feel better. But it made me feel worse. When my mother didn't mention my singleness for a while, I'd forget that she worried about me, maybe even kid myself that she had stopped worrying about it. But when my sister mentioned it, the sinking feeling that my mother disapproved of the way I managed my life came flooding back. Worst of all, when my sister reported to me exchanges she had with our mother about me, a scene took form in my mind: my mother and sister having an intense telephone conversation about me. In this scene my sister was aligned with my mother, and I was relegated to the margins—an outsider, a problem to be talked about. This alignment was more vivid to me than the one my sister had in mind when she said she had defended me.

## Look Who's Talking—About Whom

Any family with siblings abounds in opportunities for a sister or brother to align with one or both parents to the exclusion of another. Such alignments can be temporary and superficial, or they can run deep and persist over a lifetime.

I once asked a single woman in her mid-twenties, Gwen, about her family. I expected her to answer in terms of her parents: what she valued in their relationship, what irritated her. Instead she answered, "I was just talking to my mother on the phone and told her that I managed to spend a whole week with my sister in California—and we only had one big blowup." This took me by surprise. I saw then that the solid line of alignment is drawn in this family from that sister to the parent.

I asked what the blowup was about. "Oh, my sister is a fanatic about cleanliness," Gwen said. "You can't take a step in her house without breaking one of her rules. I tried really hard this time. I didn't cook in her kitchen; I didn't take any glasses or cups outside the dining room; and I always took my shoes off at the door." I asked what caused the blowup. "It was incredible," she said. "I was so careful. But one morning I got up and I didn't see her, so I figured she wasn't up yet. I stepped out on the porch to get the paper. In my slippers. It turned out she was right behind me—and she told me I should put my shoes on to go outside. It was the *porch,* for goodness' sake. And I only took maybe two steps. And anyway, she keeps the porch so clean, it might as well be inside. I'm afraid I lost it."

Just in case I might think the fault really was hers, not her sister's, Gwen said, "My mother told me something even worse that happened when *she* visited. She sat down on the couch to show my sister some pictures she'd brought, and my sister refused to sit next to her. It turned out my sister had this thing about not sitting on the couch because her jeans weren't clean enough. In the end, she went and got a big sheet of plastic—you know, one of those bags that come from the dry cleaner's over your clothes—and spread that on the couch before she would sit on it. Can you believe it?"

Listening to these experiences, I sympathized with Gwen and her mother having to deal with an overly fastidious family member. But what struck me was how the lines of alignment glowed as if they had been painted with fluorescent paint. The mother and Gwen are a team, exchanging stories about how unreasonable the younger sister is.

A mother and child can become a unit so tight that all others in the family are locked out. I once observed two women walking down the street holding hands. They whispered and giggled, hubbubbed and tittered, as they pointed out items in shop windows and leaned toward each other, tipping their heads together till they met in a tender tap. For a moment I thought I was catching a glimpse of two women falling in love. But as I passed them and glanced back, I saw there was a generation of age between them and remembered it was parents' weekend in this college town.

The couple I had been watching were a visiting mother and her college-student daughter. The reactions I caught in myself were mixed: first, envy at the relationship this young woman had with her mother, poignant to me because my relationship with my own mother did not have that intimate character. Second was an irrational, fleeting resentment, as if I were her sister, forever barred from that circle of love. Both reactions were to the fierce, firm lines of alignment between this mother and daughter.

## Family Secrets

Nothing draws and redraws alignments in a family as surely as information—who has it, who doesn't, and who tells it to whom. Secrets kept within the family reinforce the fortress walls, aligning family members with each other. Learning a secret about your family that was kept from you can make you feel like an outsider within.

Sometimes the information is not shocking in itself; it's the fact that it was hidden that gives it power. For example, Sandra had always known, growing up, that her mother was ten years younger than her father. Based on this bit of information, she had developed a romantic image of her parents' courtship in which her mother had been swept off her feet by a dashing older man. But the night before her own wedding, Sandra's mother told her that she was, in fact, one year older than her father. One year older, no big deal. Had Sandra known this fact about her parents all her life, she would have thought little of it. But learning the truth as she did, she felt as if the ground on which she stood had been struck by lightning. She had to reconceive her parents' courtship, their relationship, and consequently her family. Realizing that she had been so misled made her feel thrust out of the family. Learning the truth on the eve of her wedding may have reinforced the brand-new alignment she was forging.

Family secrets that parents keep from their children often lay the groundwork for later heartbreak. Such a revelation occurred when the author J. D. Salinger and his sister Doris learned that their mother, Miriam, was not Jewish, as they had always believed—and had not always been Miriam. A Christian farmgirl named Marie, their mother had assumed the name Miriam—and the Jewish identity that name implied—at the age of seventeen, when she married their father. According to a memoir written by Salinger's daughter, Margaret, her aunt Doris described the revelation as "traumatic." The trauma, I'd wager, derived not from their mother's Christianity but from the deception: learning that your mother is not who you thought she was. (In this case the knowledge also changed the children's identities, since, according to Jewish law, children are Jewish only if their mother is Jewish.)

Siblings, too, create alignments by the information they reveal or keep secret. In another family the father was not the genetic father of the older son, who had been born to their mother before she married their father. The son himself knew this, as did the next son, whom he had told sometime during their childhood. But a sister was born when her brothers were eight and ten, and the family agreed to keep this information from her to protect her. When she learned the truth as a young adult, she was furious that she had not been told: It was one more way her brothers were a team, leaving her out.

The sister felt her brothers had betrayed her by keeping something so important from her. Yet they were honoring their mother's wish to keep her secret. People often ask one family member to keep information from another, sometimes to protect the other, sometimes to protect themselves from the other's reaction. For example, a woman whose son was arrested for drunk driving told one of her sisters but asked her to keep it secret from the other, because she felt that this sister was already too critical of her troubled son. Inevitably, the information came out, and the third sister was angry, accusing her sisters of teaming up against her.

Withholding or revealing information is one of the surest ways to draw lines of alignments in a family. Keeping some information secret while revealing other information is unavoidable. But in deciding what to tell—and what to hear—it's important to keep in mind the power of information to create alignments. On the one hand, you could make clear when you don't want information repeated. On the other, you might want to avoid hearing privileged information, as you would refuse to accept stolen goods. If you sense someone is about to tell you something that should not be repeated to a particular friend or family member, you might want to hold up a metaphorical stop sign: "Better not tell me, because I don't want to be in the position of keeping secrets from her."

## Two Parents as One

In families where there are two parents at home, the alignment between them is in itself a secret that children gradually perceive. The short story writer Eudora Welty captures this in her autobiographical essay *One Writer's Beginnings.*

Welty explains that, when she was six or seven, an illness confined her to bed rest for several months. During this time she spent her days in her parents' double bed. In the evening they allowed her to fall asleep there as they sat together in rocking chairs and talked. She writes:

> As long as I could make myself keep awake, I was free to listen to every word my parents said between them.
>
> I don't remember that any secrets were revealed to me, nor do I remember any avid curiosity on my part to learn something I wasn't supposed to—perhaps I was too young to know what to listen for. But I was present in the room with the chief secret there was—the two of them, father and mother, sitting there as one.

Though she does not use this word, the secret Eudora sensed as a child was the alignment her parents created between them through their talk.

The child Eudora did not feel excluded by the alignment her parents created; she felt included, listening to "the murmur of their voices, the back and forth." Indeed, the perception of her parents' tight alignment provided a feeling of safety, a family circle within which she was embraced. Sometimes, however, parents' alignment with each other can cause a child to feel locked out.

## "I Couldn't Go Against Your Mother"

It is generally regarded as a truism that parents should present a united front to children. When parents disagree, presenting a united front means that one or the other must conceal opinions from the child—and this concealment draws the alignment between the parents in a way that pitches the child out. That, at least, is how it can come across to the child. In one case that's how it came across to me.

Shortly after graduating from college, I applied to enter the Peace Corps and was accepted, assigned to teach English in Thailand. I had a starting date and a ticket to Hawaii, where the training would take place. I had said good-bye to my friends, shopped for the requisite items, gotten my passport and inoculations. But as the date neared my mother's distress at seeing me go sent her into a tailspin. Whenever I arrived home she'd greet me with eyes red from crying. She cajoled, pleaded, and threatened. Thailand was so near Vietnam, I was sure to be killed by a stray bullet from the Vietnam War. When I returned from the Peace Corps I'd be twenty-three, and all the eligible men would have gotten married while I was away.

Though I questioned each of her arguments, my mother's panic seeped in, and her desperation wore me down. The night before I was supposed to leave, I talked first to one friend and then to another into the early morning hours, and made the decision not to go. When the Peace Corps offices opened the next morning, I called and told them I would not be joining the group, announced the news to my overjoyed mother, then went to sleep, exhausted. I began to regret my decision the moment I woke up.

For years—for decades—any mention of the Peace Corps sent

through me a searing flash of regret. But it was not until many years later that I thought to ask my father his opinion. "I never understood why your mother reacted the way she did," he said simply. "I thought it was a good idea for you to go." My heart stopped for a second. Where had my father been when this was going on? When I look back on that painful time, I see my mother and me like boxers circling each other in a ring. My father is nowhere in my memories at all, as if my mother and I were enclosed in a bubble of intense involvement, like the experimental biosphere where people live in an isolated, self-contained environment.

"Why didn't you tell me?" I asked my father. "Why didn't you give me even a tiny hint that you felt that way?" If I had had any inkling that my father thought I should go, that he didn't think my joining the Peace Corps would be a step toward certain death, I would have found the strength to withstand my mother's onslaught.

"I couldn't," he answered. "I couldn't go against your mother. If I had encouraged you to go, she would never have forgiven me. If anything had happened to you, I would never have forgiven myself."

On first hearing this I felt betrayed: How could my father have kept his opinion to himself, leaving me stranded? In retrospect, I can see why aligning with his wife seemed his first obligation.

A husband makes a similar decision in John Osborne's play *Look Back in Anger.* Alison, an upper-class British woman, was rejected by her family for marrying Jimmy, a working-class man. When Alison decides, late in the play, to leave Jimmy, she calls her parents, and her father comes to take her home. As they prepare to leave together, he tells her that although he did not approve of her marrying Jimmy, neither did he approve of the lengths to which his wife went to prevent the marriage. "I have never said anything—there was no point afterwards—but I have always believed that she went too far over Jimmy," her father says. "All those inquiries, the private detectives—the accusations. I hated every moment of it." He adds, "It would have been better, for all concerned, if we had never attempted to interfere." At the time, however, he didn't want to oppose his wife. And his alignment with his wife left his daughter more completely isolated by her decision to marry a man her parents disapproved of.

## Parent and Child United

If children can feel excluded by their parents' alignment, a parent can also be hurt when that bedrock alignment, "father and mother, sitting there as one," is threatened by a child falling into alignment with one parent to the exclusion of the other. Christine recalls that when she was small she was very close to her mother, but as she reached her teenage years she became closer to her father. Their rapport pivoted on lengthy conversations about politics, religion, and all the weighty topics she and her friends were beginning to think about. Often these conversations took place while the family rode in the car.

As an adult, Christine was surprised to learn that her mother had felt excluded and rejected by this closeness. "You and your father would sit in the front seat, having your intellectual discussions," her mother recalled, the memory still rankling, "and completely shut me out." At the time Christine wasn't thinking of her mother at all; she was focused on her conversations with her father. And this focus helped create the alignment that made her mother feel excluded. It must have seemed a double rejection to the mother: Not only had the alignment shifted from mother-daughter to father-daughter, but she had been physically displaced by her daughter, who sat beside her father in the front seat while the mother found herself where children normally sit: the backseat. Because alignments are stealthy, Christine's mother had not foreseen this result when she herself suggested giving her daughter the front seat to make it easier for father and daughter to talk while the father drove.

Any parent-child combination can create a straight-line alignment that excludes other family members. In her memoir, *Dream Catcher,* Margaret Salinger (called Peggy) writes that her father, J. D. Salinger, had that kind of relationship with his own mother—at least according to his sister, Doris. Referring to her brother by his childhood nickname, Doris recalls, "It was always Sonny and

Mother, Mother and Sonny. Daddy got the short end of the stick always."

In her own family, according to Margaret Salinger, her father created an alignment with her that excluded her mother (as well as her brother). For example, she describes letters her father sent when he was away in New York on business and seven-year-old Peggy, her mother, and her younger brother were vacationing in Barbados:

> What I took as my due, but now strikes me as not exactly *normal,* is that all the lavish expressions of affection in my father's letters to us as a family were directed, almost without exception, solely to me. The last letter we received before returning home from Barbados began Dear Fambly, but ended in boldface type that he was convinced more than ever that Peggy Salingers don't grow on trees. It was signed with about a million XXXs.

Looking back as an adult on the letters her father wrote when she was a child, Margaret Salinger sees that the exclusive alignment created by her father's disproportionate attention was damaging to her as well as to her mother; for one thing, it resulted in a "serrated edge" to the punishments her mother meted out to her when she was a child.

In another memoir, *Phoenix,* it is a sibling—the author J. D. Dolan—who is left out of the alignment created between his much-older brother, John, and his father by their mutual interest and expertise in fixing cars. Dolan recalls as a young boy seeing his father's and brother's legs sticking out from under a car they were working on. Crawling under the car to hand them a wrench, Dolan was transfixed by the wordless attunement of their coordinated activity: "I had no idea what they were doing, no idea what they were saying, no idea how one knew when to take hold and the other knew to let go."

Dolan's father and brother also shared a tendency toward silence—or, when words were needed, taciturnity. Having completed their work, they drank lemonade without speaking, until first one, then the other, heard a sound that made his ears perk up:

> Dad set his empty glass on the workbench, turned to John, and said, "Ford." John, concentrating hard, seemed to agree. Then he said, "With a bad lifter." Just then a car drove past our house. It was a Ford, and a faint ticking was coming from its engine.

With these few words, father and son created an alignment between them that the younger brother knew he would never share (just as he knows, looking at "the muscles in their grease-smeared arms," that "my arms would never look like that").

Although, as these examples show, alignments between two family members can exclude a third, they needn't have that effect. A parent can use the power of aligning with a child rather than a spouse to positive effect. A woman told me of a small encounter in which she aligned with her daughter—to her daughter's delight. "We were driving in the car," she told me, "and my husband was hounding our daughter about something. She was digging in her heels, and he was repeating himself. Suddenly he turned to me and said, 'Why don't you support me in this?' I told him, 'I supported you the first six times you said it, but now you're going too far. I think you made your point and should let it drop.' My daughter loved that," she said. "She loves it when I take her side."

This mother—this wife—had managed to balance two alignments at once. By agreeing with her husband on the substance of his complaint but siding with her daughter in regard to his insistence and repetition, she was able to display the dual allegiance that being in a family so often requires.

## A Spy in the House

Few crimes are as reviled as spying. By revealing information, a citizen of one country aligns with an enemy nation. Yet spies are caught constantly, because the temptation to exchange information for monetary or other rewards is ubiquitous. In families, too, spying is a common betrayal, though the reward is not money but love. And in families, as between nations, the exchange of information draws and redraws alignments.

In a memoir entitled *Falling Leaves: The Memoir of an Un-*

*wanted Chinese Daughter,* Adeline Yen Mah describes how her sister Lydia became the family spy. Lydia was the oldest, and Adeline the youngest, of five siblings who grew up with their father and his second wife. The stepmother also had two children with Adeline's father, and she showed egregiously blatant favoritism toward them. She coddled the two children she bore and tormented the five stepchildren who came with the marriage. The stepchildren lived on a different floor, received inadequate food, and were forced to beg for bus fare or walk several miles to school. Her own children lived on a floor with her, were fed generous portions of delicacies, and were chauffeured to school by a driver.

One day the stepmother overheard her five stepchildren, led by Lydia, talking about how they might overcome their mistreatment. Mah recalls the strategies they considered: "Hunger strike? Rebellion? An interview with Father alone?" Rather than confronting and punishing the children, their stepmother realigned them: She offered Lydia her own room on the privileged first floor, with luxuries like her own desk and matching bedspread and curtains. With one foot in each family, Lydia reported to her stepmother on the doings of her siblings, for which they would be punished, and "was rewarded with special favours: candies, treats, pocket money, new clothes, outings with her friends." In other words, their stepmother converted Lydia from leader of the opposition to spy.

Most instances of repeated information are less powerful, less pernicious, but they are the currency with which family alignments are bought and traded. In Charles Randolph-Wright's play *Blue,* for example, a boy whose father and older brother run a funeral parlor is caught between fearsome figures. His brother tells him that he is using the hearse to take out a girl—and threatens to lock the boy in a coffin if he tells. But their mother, whom the boy adores, soon demands that he tell her where his older brother went. The boy is torn between the two alignments: He is eager to keep his word to his older brother but also eager to obey and please his mother. In this case the pull of his mother is stronger; he tells. And this tells a lot about the alignment in this family.

Realigning by revealing information can be a deliberate betrayal. Two brothers in their thirties, reminiscing about their childhood, recalled such an incident. Here, too, it was the younger who "tattled"—that child version of spying for the reward of aligning with adults.

Jeff asked his younger brother, "Do you remember the time that I threw a hot dog over the fence?"

"I remember that *really* well," Tim replied. "Then you had to wash it off. And you had to eat it."

This small recalled incident reveals how information can be bartered in a family to reinforce and shift alignments. Tim didn't just happen to see his older brother throw the hot dog. Much as the older brother in *Blue* announced to his little brother that he was taking the hearse as he left for his date, Jeff made a point of showing Tim that he was going to throw a hot dog over the fence. Having an audience makes it more delicious to do something daring.

But having witnessed the action gives the younger brother power—a power that Tim, like the little brother in *Blue,* decided to exercise. Tim told their mother what Jeff had done. Retribution was swift. Their mother marched Jeff to the spot where the hot dog landed, had him dig it out of the bushes, and made him eat it. Knowing that he had betrayed his brother by "tattling," Tim recalled, "I spent the whole night trying to make it up to you. I gave you a poster I think." Tim knew he had to do something significant to restore his alliance with his brother.

Sometimes a child—especially a young one—reveals compromising information inadvertently. Twelve-year-old Mickey told me that his seven-year-old brother causes trouble for him by releasing information "when you don't want somebody to hear." For example, his younger brother once helpfully explained to their parents, "You know why Mickey is in a bad mood? Because he got an F." Mickey had depended on his brother to keep his failing grade secret. By revealing it the brother betrayed this fraternal trust and aligned himself with their parents, who directed their displeasure at Mickey. Perhaps the seven-year-old really didn't realize this damaging information was supposed to be kept secret. Or maybe he sensed he could use the information to temporarily shift alignments and take, for a moment, the coveted position of nearest-to-parents that his older brother occupied by seniority.

Learning what information can safely be repeated is a big part of growing up. Sometimes children reveal information that redraws alignments because they haven't yet grasped what information is to be kept secret. Hank Ketcham used this as a frequent source of humor in his Dennis the Menace cartoons—for example, when the innocent little Dennis watches a guest drink from a glass and remarks, "I don't think he drinks like a fish." It's funny not only because Dennis took an idiom literally but also because he repeated in front of the family friend a comment his parents had made behind his back—confident it would stay inside the family walls. A real-life analogue is a story that became legend in one family: When the youngest child was four, during a visit to his grandparents, he announced with insouciance, "My parents make fun of you!" With this the fortress walls were permeated: Information meant to be kept within was carried outside.

## Fido, Family Member

"You love the puppy more than you love me!" a little girl protested to her mother. She was one of those children who always want to be held and cuddled; her mother, a physical person herself, thought she obliged as often as her daughter required. But the new puppy had to be lifted and held and taken from room to room all day long or he would have been stuck in one place on his own. Seeing the small, helpless creature cradled in her mother's arms triggered the child's longing.

Her mother's arms around the puppy created an alignment that this little girl felt left her out. Pets are often lightning rods for a family's conflicting alignments. I have seen families in which a child stands forlorn while a parent showers physical affection and baby-talk endearments on the dog, who responds with wet kisses. In some cases a parent who snuggles the dog would have liked to snuggle the son or daughter instead, but the child has reached the age when many children recoil from any such attempt with groans of protest.

In her novel *The Dangerous Husband,* Jane Shapiro creates a scene in which a dog becomes the object of affection, providing a counterpoint to human alignments. The narrator is a woman recently married to a man, Dennis, who seems perfect at first but gradually begins showing a destructive streak. The emerging risk in his affection for her is set in contrast to the unbridled adoration he heaps on his dog, Raleigh:

> Laying eyes on Raleigh, Dennis looked as though he might weep. "Oh, Raleigh, Raleigh boy! Raleigh boy! Raleigh boy! Raleigh boy! Raleigh Raleigh Raleigh, Raleigh boy, my Raleigh boy, my nice nice doggy boy!" and he hugged the dog's thick middle while the dog tried to whip around and nip him, and they struggled together for a long time, embracing on a stoop slick with drool.

The repetition of the dog's name shows Dennis's total, uncomplicated commitment to his pet. The words he speaks don't matter much; "doggy boy, Raleigh boy" is something to say while giving himself over completely to his dog. It is an all-embracing alignment—the kind we yearn for from those we love. That is why watching family members with pets can set in relief failures of alignment with ourselves.

A woman who was showing more affection to her dog than to her daughter had it called to her attention by the daughter. The incident is recounted by Mary Catherine Bateson, who quotes the woman directly in her book *Full Circles, Overlapping Lives:*

> "I did not recognize that I was just damn depressed until my daughter said to me, 'I want my mommy back.' I said, 'What are you talking about?' and she said, 'You are just . . . just relating to the *dog*.' "

Sometimes it is easier to show attention and affection to a dog, who asks no questions, does not argue, and never objects to being patted, petted, or hugged. The woman in this example didn't realize she was depressed until her daughter pointed out that she had shifted her alignment from her daughter to her dog.

Often it's children who pour their hearts out to the pet, who is completely understanding—unlike parents, who rain down affection, yes, but also judgment and disapproval. And parents can take advantage of this alignment, pressing a pet into family service. In a conversation taped by a volunteer in my research, a mother told of having discovered that the family dog provided a way to get her sluggish teenage daughter out of bed. "In the morning I put her on Tammy's bed," the mother explained, "and she wakes Tammy up. She gives her a nudge and licks her. With me, it's 'No, I don't want to get up!' With the dog, she's fine." Like the woman who didn't know she was depressed, the teenage daughter found kisses easier to take from the dog than from her mother, probably because her mother's kisses came along with expectations and judgments she might not want to face first thing in the morning.

Knowing how easily her daughter aligned with the dog, this mother was able to use the dog to communicate with her daughter. Because pets are such easy objects of affection, people often use them to establish, reinforce, or negotiate alignments with others. If you want to approach a stranger on the street, you need a pretty good reason, like asking directions or the time. But a person walking a dog is open to approach from strangers who want to comment on the dog—or use the dog as an excuse to start a conversation with its owner. Talking about the dog can keep the conversation going long after a person asking directions or the time would be expected to walk away.

People talk not only *to* their pets but also *through* them. Family members sometime use dogs or cats to put into words thoughts or emotions that might otherwise be left unsaid. In other words, they ventriloquize their pets, and the speech thus created becomes a line of dialogue in a drama between adults.

A couple invited another couple to their home for dinner. At one point the guest wife addressed the hosts' cat sitting on the windowsill: "What are you thinking when you look out there, kitty?" she asked, while stroking the cat's fur. The host husband replied by speaking for the cat in a high-pitched, childlike voice: "She says, 'I'm just figuring out how I can get out there.' " Soon after the dinner party the host wife learned that her husband and the guest wife were having an affair. In hindsight she could see their intimacy in the interchange over the cat. With the cat as cover, her husband had addressed his lover with the tenderness of baby talk, aligning himself with her rather than with his wife. Alignment explains why that interchange made her uncomfortable at the time—but also why she had been unable to put her finger on the reason. In retrospect, she felt that, by speaking through the cat, her husband had expressed his own desire to "get out there."

## "Give Us a Break, Daddy": Speaking Through Others

Children too young to say much can also provide alter egos through which family members can voice thoughts they might be reluctant to say in so many words—and thereby reinforce or rearrange alignments. In this example (which was captured on tape), the mother, Andrea, had spent the day with their eighteen-month-old daughter, Ginny, when the father, Fred, arrived home from work.

The segment begins—and the scene is set—as the time of Fred's return from work approaches. Andrea prepares Ginny for a joyous reunion with her daddy by talking about him with excitement: "Daddy's going to be home in a minute." "Are you going to give Daddy a fruit pop?" "Are you going to tell Daddy to take his shoes off?"

But when Daddy actually arrives, he is tired and hungry, as many of us are at the end of a long day. He doesn't know—he can't know—how his wife has been trumpeting his homecoming. When Ginny wants to climb on him, he has a moment of pique: "I'm eating!" he snaps, then adds, more plaintively, "Daddy eats."

Ginny begins to cry, and Andrea explains the child's reaction by speaking in a child's voice, as if for Ginny: "She got her feelings hurt." Then Andrea addresses Ginny directly: "You were missing Daddy, weren't you? Can you say, 'I was just missing you, Daddy, that was all'?"

Ginny answers, through her tears, "No," which is an honest answer—she can't say that because she does not yet put words into sentences that long. Andrea knows this, so she obviously intends the explanation for her husband more than for her daughter. By ventriloquizing Ginny, she is suggesting how Fred should reframe his reaction to his daughter: Take her climbing on you as a sign of love, not pestering.

A few minutes later Andrea asks Fred, "Why are you so edgy?"

"Because I haven't finished eating yet," he replies.

She suggests, "Why didn't you get a snack on the way home or something? Save your family a little stress." Then she expresses her daughter's point of view: "Give us a break, Daddy. We just miss you. We try to get your attention, and then you come home and you go *row row row row.*"

Ginny echoes the growling sound: "Row! Row!"

Ventriloquizing helps Andrea balance alignments with her husband and daughter. She aligns herself with Ginny, speaking for her to help her understand her own feelings. At the same time, she is explaining to Fred his part in making Ginny cry, and why his reaction is unfair from the child's point of view. By speaking through Ginny she avoids taking a position in direct opposition to Fred, and this may have helped avoid an adult argument. An indirect result, however, also resides more in the alignments than in the words. Andrea could have aligned with Fred by telling Ginny, "Daddy's tired and hungry. We have to let him eat something before we climb on him." By speaking as she did, Andrea aligned with Ginny as a team. Fred might have felt temporarily bumped outside the family circle.

Whenever one parent has been with a child or children and another returns—whether at the end of a workday, following an excursion, or after spending time in an activity at home—a realignment has to take place so the new family member can be integrated. Clearly this is what Andrea is trying to accomplish. The need for Fred to get back into the family circle is communicated as much through the alignments created as by what is said.

## Taking Sides

Alignments in families can shift subtly, moment by moment, many times in a single conversation. An example from sociologist Sam Vuchinich's study of how arguments end during dinner-table conversation shows such small-scale realignments. It's a mundane interchange, one of those myriad conversations that go by without anyone paying much attention but that establish and rearrange alignments within a family.

The trouble starts when ten-year-old Ann criticizes her mother's cooking: "The meat is dry."

Her mother defends it: "No. I think it's delicious."

The exchange could have ended there, or Ann and her mother could have continued to negotiate about whether the meat was dry or delicious. What happens is that twelve-year-old Joyce steps into the circle and comes to their mother's defense: "It's not dry," says Joyce. "It's just . . ."

"Put some mushroom sauce on it," their mother suggests.

Ann soon backtracks: "It's not dry, it's just hard."

And Joyce reinforces her support for the meat: "It's good, though."

Joyce takes the role of peacemaker by defending her mother's cooking: "It's not dry." Yet she also aligns with Ann by continuing, "It's just . . . ," allowing that something is wrong with the meat. This gives Ann the opening to agree with Joyce and revise her judgment ("It's not dry") but also stick to her claim that the meat has a problem ("it's just hard"). The mother, for her part, indirectly concedes there might be a problem because she suggests a solution ("Put some mushroom sauce on it"). Joyce wraps the whole thing up with a vote of confidence for their mother's cooking: "It's good, though." What a delicate balancing act, what an affable ending.

In any conversation family members create and shift alignments to balance and rebalance the teams. Linguist Shari Kendall, also studying dinner-table conversations, found shifting alliances in a family of three: Elaine, Mark, and their ten-year-old daughter, Beth. Kendall's analysis shows how casual comments and jokes play a role in creating and undercutting alliances.

Mark and Beth frequently engaged in humorous bantering. You can see this happening in one of the excerpts of their conversation that Kendall analyzed. Mark offers Beth food (which Elaine prepared), and Elaine chastises her for the way she refuses the offer.

"You want another bowl?" Mark offers.

"Ew," Beth responds, sounding very much like the ten-year-old she is.

When Elaine questions Beth's response ("Mm?"), Beth elaborates, "No, they're disgusting."

At this Elaine challenges, "Excuse me!"

And Beth, chastened, says, "Sorry!"

"Just say, 'No thanks,' " her mother instructs, and Beth complies: "No thanks!"

By correcting Beth's way of declining food, Elaine teaches her a lesson in politeness. Beth shows she's learned the lesson by repeating the more courteous "No thanks." In doing so she aligns with her mother and reinforces Elaine's authority.

But a few seconds later Mark makes light of the situation by echoing the expression for which Elaine castigated Beth. He repeats the word *disgusting* under his breath in a humorous way, like a conspiring sibling whispering behind their mother's back. Beth responds by giggling, showing appreciation of Mark's remark.

By whispering a single word in a particular way, Mark aligns with Beth, at the same time lightening the mood through humor. (He also, Kendall points out, may be undercutting Elaine's authority.) In just this way, innumerable times each day, family members create, shift, and readjust alignments in daily conversation.

## "Let Me In!"

All family members struggle with the conflicting needs to be safe in the family's protection and free from the family's control—to get a center seat in the family pew and to avoid being left out. And these struggles are reflected in our conversations and in our conflicts.

My father likes to tell about the mother who had a dozen children. "I wouldn't give you a penny for another child," the woman says, "but I wouldn't take a million dollars for any of the ones I've got." Parents treasure every one of their children, the anecdote says. Yet there is hardly a family in which there isn't a child who feels that another child was favored, got advantages, had it easy, or was spared indignities and deprivations that he or she suffered.

The most fundamental rivalry, it seems, is the sibling kind. And siblings seem always to have their antennae rolled out to pick up any signal indicating their parents are favoring a brother or sister. There are few parents who would admit to favoring one child over another but also few adults who cannot tell you which sibling they think was favored by *their* mother or father.

Nothing brings out the conviction of favoritism—or fears and resentments about it—as dramatically as the death of a parent. Battles over inheritance are as ancient as the Bible story of Jacob and Esau—a stage on which siblings strive to realign themselves with respect to parents. Jacob, the less favored son, tricks their blind father into bestowing his blessing on himself, thus stealing his brother's birthright by stealing their father's love and approval. In this spirit, adult children often find themselves in bitter disputes about inheritance. On one level the dispute is about money: a chance to get sometimes significant amounts. But these tragic eruptions are as common when there is little of financial value at stake. As one man put it, describing a battle that broke out among his brothers when their mother died, "It is your last chance to claim the love for yourself."

Adeline Yen Mah's memoir, *Falling Leaves,* recounts a family drama played out on this stage. Mah describes how she was persecuted as the least-favored child, and how she tried as an adult to repair this alignment by becoming successful and helping members of her family. She sees how futile these efforts were when she learns she was cut out of her stepmother's will—and, by implication, deprived of her father's legacy, since he had died first. Her negotiations with her siblings around this devastating news in turn reinforce the alignments established in their childhoods.

The youngest of the five stepchildren, Adeline was persecuted not only by her stepmother but also by her two oldest siblings: Lydia (the one who passed information on to their stepmother) and Edgar, the oldest of three brothers. The brother closest in age to Adeline, named James, was her secret ally (though he did not dare defend her publicly).

When she grew up Adeline attended university in London, became a physician, established a successful career in the United

States, and married happily. Yet, driven by a desire to change the family dynamic, she ended up reinforcing it. As the child who was most victimized, most rejected, she was the one who most wanted to restore the family so she could be accepted into it. Lydia had been caught in mainland China when the rest of the family moved to Hong Kong and had managed to alienate her parents and siblings, so when she got back in touch with the family after years of estrangement, her brothers and stepmother resisted resuming contact. But Adeline pressed her stepmother, with whom she had achieved a fragile reconciliation following her father's death, to reconcile with Lydia.

As a result of Adeline's efforts to bring her back into the family circle, Lydia repeated the pattern from their childhood: She turned their stepmother against Adeline, with the result that Adeline was cut out of the stepmother's will. The brothers then took their places in the constellation. When James (the only one who did not torment Adeline as a child) suggested that the other siblings give Adeline her rightful share of their inheritance, Edgar and Lydia, who had been cruelest to her as a child, refused. It is as if the family had been handed a script that could not be changed. Even in death her stepmother had drawn the lines of alignment in a way that excluded the youngest sister.

## Rivalry by Proxy

Inheritance is a last chance because the parents are gone, but before that there is another battleground. Adult children who have their own children can find that those new family members, extensions of themselves, can become rivals by proxy for parents' approval. In one grown family the younger of two daughters was the first to give her parents a grandchild by marrying a man who had a son by a previous marriage. She basked in the attention her parents showered on this little boy, especially since she had always felt her sister had gotten more of their parents' approval than she did. So when her older sister became pregnant, she could not share her parents' unalloyed joy. She feared that her sister's grandchild by birth would supplant her grandchild by marriage in their parents' affections. Underneath, she feared that, once again, her sister would win the contest for favored child. Whatever ground she claimed, it seemed, her sister would come along to bump her off it and raise her own flag higher.

It isn't only siblings who fear losing a share of love to another family member. In a *Newsweek* essay, Diana Friedman, mother of two children, writes of the resentment she initially felt when her father married a second wife who was only eleven years older than she. The first loss was of her childhood home, and with it the emotional "home" of being first in her father's affections: "Within a few years the house in which we had grown up was sold, and I found that I could no longer assume that my father was automatically available to me." Friedman discovered that becoming a mother herself didn't transform her, like a pumpkin becoming a carriage at the touch of a magic wand. "I found myself weeping incessantly," she recalls, "when he adopted a seven-year-old girl two weeks before I had my own daughter. I felt that whatever thrill the birth of his first grandchild might have brought us was tempered by the fact that at 61, my dad once again became a new father."

Friedman's tale has a happy ending: Her children and her stepmother's children became close and brought their mothers together. But in many families these fault lines continue to shift under pressure, even as children become adults and have their own children.

## Turning the Tables

Alignments set in childhood persist long after children grow up. But sometimes alignments change, and the redrawn lines can be difficult for sisters or brothers who thought they had a lifetime appointment as chief child.

In one family, for example, Walt, an older brother, was a real estate agent who received citations and awards for his civic activities; his picture was taken beside the mayor and in a group with his congressman. Walt passed these photos on to his parents, who displayed them, framed, throughout their house. Meanwhile, Walt's younger brother, Arnie, was writing short stories and working as a waiter. Walt aided his brother's efforts to become a writer, offering financial as well as psychological support.

But things slowly began to shift. Arnie published first stories and then a novel. Then his second novel was a big success and was made into a movie. Walt was surprised to find that his joy at his brother's success was not unalloyed. When Walt called his parents to chat, they now spent less time asking what was new with him and more time telling him of Arnie's latest triumphs. And when he visited them, he couldn't help noticing that his framed citations and photos had been pushed aside to make room for photographs of Arnie with this or that famous person. Although he was genuinely proud of his brother and pleased at his success, Walt also felt unseated in the one area where he had been safe in his superior rank—the family.

In a similar constellation, Brad, a law student, was oddly unnerved when his younger sister married a stockbroker who had a daughter by a previous marriage. In one fell swoop the tables had turned: She and her husband bought a house, whereas Brad still lived in a student apartment; they bought stylish furniture while he was still living with yard-sale bargains; and, most upsetting of all, she presented their parents with a ready-made family, while Brad was still laying the foundations for the family he planned one day to begin. When such milestones are reached first by an older sibling, they provide a model that younger siblings may either aspire to or decide to eschew. But when they are reached by a younger sibling first, the older one can feel displaced, knocked off track by an unexpected and seemingly unjust realignment.

## The Big Switch: As Parents Get Older

Perhaps the biggest realignment of all takes place in those families who are lucky enough to have parents live to old age. When growing older shades into growing old, adult children begin to take on responsibilities in caring for their parents, and the roles of helper and helped, at one time safely apportioned by age, are gradually reversed.

I witnessed a scene in an airport where a grandmother was treated like a child. Because her son's family was united in their way of treating her, she seemed as helpless to escape as if she had been a prisoner in a cell with her son's family a team of keepers. The scene had special resonance for me because I was waiting to check in for a flight to visit my own parents in Fort Lauderdale.

I was getting nervous—and so was the woman who was in front of me in line. She looked to be in her early seventies, and the young woman accompanying her, clearly a granddaughter, looked to be about twenty. It was five minutes to twelve, and the Fort Lauderdale flight was scheduled to leave at twelve-twenty, but the long line hardly seemed to be moving. Another flight, headed for a different destination and not scheduled to leave until one-ten, was posted right next to the Fort Lauderdale flight, and customers checking in for both flights were jumbled together in line.

The grandmother in front of me had the same idea I did and acted on it just as I was contemplating a similar move. Maybe there should be two lines. Surely those checking in for the earlier flight should be given priority. She stepped out of line and approached the counter, trying to get the attention of the agent to pose these logical questions. But before she could address the agent, her son, a man in his fifties who had been standing to the side with his wife and another daughter, swooped down on his mother. "Just get back in line!" he chastised her loudly as he coaxed her back to her place in line. "Do you want to start an uprising?"

The grandmother tried to explain why she had stepped out of line, but her voice was drowned out as the entire family laughed at and built on his joke. "You want to make your life more exciting!" her granddaughter quipped, sparking more laughter from her mother and sister when she repeated it for them: "She wants to make her life more exciting!"

The laughter was good-natured, not cackling or mean, but it had unmistakable overtones of condescension. The grandmother stayed in her place in line. Soon a second small drama ensued. "They'll need your ID again," her granddaughter told her, and she began fishing in her grandmother's purse as it hung from her shoulder. Finding it awkward to locate what she sought from that angle, she pulled the purse toward her, pressing it against her own body as she searched inside. I saw a flash of confusion (I'd even say desperation) on the older woman's face as she saw her purse flying away from her and into someone else's hands, but she did not object.

The grandmother never really protested any of this treatment; maybe she figured she'd be on the plane and on her own soon enough. Maybe she appreciated the attention and show of caring. Having a whole family take you to the airport is surely a sign of devotion. But the scene made me worry about all I did to try to help my own parents. How do you show you care and help them out without making them smaller and more helpless in the process?

The granddaughter in the airport handled her grandmother's property without asking permission, in the way an adult might take an object from the hands of a child. But even if she hadn't done that, the very act of helping sends metamessages of competence (the helper's) and potential condescension (toward the helped). These metamessages reside in the alignment established by helping.

## Back Home, You're Still a Kid

Another grandmother—a character in Joe DiPietro's play *Over the River and Through the Woods*—puts the metamessage of helping into words: "You want to help them. So much. Like you did when they were little. It doesn't matter how old they get. You just always want to help them." In the play this grandmother does get to help her grandson, Nick, a twenty-nine-year-old man who is visiting his Italian grandparents in Hoboken, New Jersey, as he has done every Sunday of his life.

Nick has recently broken the news that he will move to Seattle to accept an important promotion. His grandparents—all four of them—have tried to convince him to pass up the promotion and stay near them. Nick wants to do what's best for his own life but does not want to leave the grandparents he is so close to. Act One ends in a crescendo of his confusion and mixed feelings: He shouts at his grandparents that he now understands why his sister and parents moved away: " 'Cause they wanted to live without constant interference! And judgment! And criticism!"

Nick continues in this vein until he works himself up to fever pitch, screaming, "Guess what—and this will be news to you all—but I am an adult! Yes! There is a fully functioning, grown-up man standing before you who is perfectly capable of taking care of himself—taking care of him—" He is unable to complete his declaration of adulthood because he collapses, clutching his chest and gasping for breath.

As the next scene opens Nick is installed on his grandparents' couch, where they have been taking care of him after his asthma attack. Even as he wailed his protest that he was an adult, his behavior was testimony that he was acting like a child. His collapse was evidence that he was not quite capable of taking care of himself.

Alignments are key to why this scene is funny: Though growing up changes alignments so that adults no longer are taken care of by their grandparents, when adults return to their grandparents' (or parents') homes, they often find themselves right back in the position they were in when they lived there—dependent, childlike. Thus, Adeline Yen Mah writes, when she returned to Hong Kong after completing university, medical school, and a medical residency, "Though I had been in England for eleven years and was now a physician, at that moment I felt no different from the schoolgirl who left in 1952." Or, as the author J. D. Dolan puts it, describing a return to his childhood home: "Back here, I was a little kid again. Back here, I was terrified by monsters, terrified of the dark."

## Shifting and Reshifting Alignments

Years ago, when I taught writing to college students, I used an exercise to demonstrate how ideas could be organized into essays. I asked everyone in the class to form a circle and put an object—any object in their possession—on the floor in the center of the circle. A typical collection might include pens, pencils, a wallet, keys, a notebook, a tube of lipstick, eyeliner, a compact, and so on. Then I'd ask for volunteers to organize the objects in a logical way.

One person might organize the objects by shape, pushing cylindrical pens, pencils, eyeliner, and lipstick into one group, rectangular notebook and wallet into another, perhaps leaving an odd-shaped object, like a whistle, alone. Then someone would organize by function, gathering the pens, pencils, and notebook together in one group, the lipstick, eyeliner, and compact in another. A third person might reorganize by color, putting a blue-covered notebook with a blue compact, a black-covered notebook with a black-enameled tube of lipstick. Just when everyone thought that every possible organizing principle had been exhausted, someone would come up with another, such as materials: plastics in one group, paper products in another, metals in a third. Each new organizing principle made us look at the objects in a new way.

Families are like that exercise; the different organizing principles are like shifting alignments. Lines of connection—or lines of control—are drawn between family members by the ways we speak to each other; the topics we speak about; the information we reveal or conceal; the myriad shared interests, perspectives, and experiences that a life together affords. But each alignment between two or more people potentially excludes one or more others. This helps explain the ever-emerging comfort and pain of life in a family. Once you understand how alignments work, you can talk about them—explain to family members why you reacted as you did. You can also try talking differently, in order to alter alignments so you, or someone you love, will sit more comfortably in relation to the others in your family.

## A Brief Interlude I

# "Go Ahead, Treat Me Like a Stranger"

My mother often complains that my father does not confide in her. For example, she might notice that he has been lying down frequently and eventually pry out of him that his back is hurting.

"How long has it been hurting?" she asks.

"Oh, just a couple of weeks," he says.

And she replies, with wounded irony, "Go ahead, treat me like a stranger."

"Like a stranger" here means "You don't tell me anything." It means "You are pushing me away." To my mother, not telling when something hurts him is a violation of connection. And that hurts her.

At the end of Art Spiegelman's autobiographical book *Maus,* the son, Art, finally walks away from his father, who has become overwhelming in his authoritarianism. The last word of the book is the father's devastating word to his son: "Stranger!"

This is the worst thing the father could say. Yet if he really regarded his son as a stranger, the father would not care if Art walked away. The rejection is devastating precisely because Art and his father are family—and the proof is their continuing power to hurt each other deeply.

One of the most heartbreaking experiences imaginable occurs when a family member really regards another as a stranger, and this is one of the most calamitous results of Alzheimer's disease. Just this experience is described by a woman named Sally, who is taking part in a support group for those giving care to family members suffering from Alzheimer's. Quoted in an article by Jaber Gubrium and James Holstein, Sally tells her group that her husband, Al, "turned around . . . just like that . . . and asked me, 'Who are you? What are you doing in here?' It was like I was a stranger in the house or something. God, that set me back." Sally was able to calm herself by recalling another group member's similar experience: "I remember how Cora reacted when her mother yelled at her about not wanting a stranger running around in the bedroom," she says. "I felt like that." And she reminds herself that it was not her husband but his disease that caused his confusion.

In both Sally's and Cora's recollections, the word *stranger* reflects the sense of intrusion that the people with Alzheimer's expressed when they were not able to recognize their caregivers as family members. Sally's husband asked what she was doing *"in here."* Cora's mother didn't want a stranger *"in the bedroom."* A stranger is someone who belongs outside the family fortress. Only family members belong *in*side. If *family* suggests belonging, then the opposite is *stranger.*

Many conflicts arise from differing senses of the rights and obligations of family—as distinguished from strangers. A woman in her sixties recalls that from the time she married and moved into her own home, her parents refused to ring the bell when they arrived for a visit. Bells, they felt, were for strangers. Family just walks in. When their children were small, the woman and her husband bought a house that had several entrances: the front door, a side door, a back door, and a way in through the garage. When her parents came to visit and found the front door locked, they walked around the house trying all the doors in hopes of finding one unlocked so they could enter as they should—like family.

This image of parents walking around the house searching for an unlocked door is a metaphor for family: You want to find your way in and be treated as if you belong there. When your children become adults, the quest takes on urgency because, in a way, you *don't* really belong there—not completely, not unquestioningly. Not in the way you belonged in their lives when they were small.

The same goes for children who have moved out of their parents' home. They object when their old bedrooms are turned into offices or dens, when their parents ask them to take their stored cartons out of the attic. Even though they have moved out of their parents' home, they want to keep their rightful place inside the family.

All of us feel, at some time, that we are like strangers in our own families. My mother recalls, her voice shaky and lowered to a whisper because even now it makes her feel rejected, that when I was seven I said I didn't think she was my real mother: I must have been adopted. I have learned, since, how common this is. Many children, especially around that age, feel, "I don't belong in this family. I must be adopted." *Adopted* is a way of expressing that you don't fit in, you feel you're not cut from the same cloth. Children who are, in fact, adopted have a concrete circumstance to point to when they feel this way. Others borrow this circumstance to capture how they feel.

The idea of alignment shows the role that talk plays in creating and dispelling the feeling of not quite belonging in your own family. The idea of strangers—the counterpoint that gives meaning to the idea of family—shows why it matters so much.

THREE

# Fighting for Love

## Connection and Control in Family Arguments

"THOSE WHO LOVE each other fight with each other," says a Ukrainian proverb. Many couples can tell you not only about their first kiss but also about their first argument. (In my case it was about linguistics.) In a way a relationship moves to a deeper level of intimacy when a conflict arises—and is resolved. Nowhere is this truer than in families, where "I only say this because I love you" often means that what I say makes you mad.

Small-scale arguments or large-scale verbal fights break out at one time or another in all families. Many people try heroically to "communicate"—to solve problems by talking about them. But sometimes ways of talking aggravate disputes rather than solve them, and trying to work things out through talk either escalates into a bigger fight or gets you completely off track until you're arguing about how to argue. In this chapter I'll look at arguments that actually took place in families in order to show how people used words to express their frustrations and get their way, how the ways they argued at times worked well and made things better, but at other times made things worse—and how, in those instances, they could have talked differently with a better result.

First let's look more closely at the dynamics that often underlie conflicts—dynamics that both drive and complicate everything said in a family.

## The Connection-Control Grid

Every relationship, every conversation, is a blend between the desires for connection and for control that I wrote about in Chapter 1. But it's even more complicated, because neither connection nor control is a one-dimensional dynamic. If we think of each as a continuum between two poles, we can see more subtly what is at stake in family conversations, and how ways of talking fulfill or undermine these simultaneous, and sometimes conflicting, needs.

Let's start with the drive toward control. We can think of any utterance—or any relationship—placed somewhere on a continuum between hierarchy at one end and equality at the other. At the hierarchy end every relationship is a power struggle: Someone is one-up, and someone is one-down. The one-up person gets to tell the one-down person what to do. In this sense the one-up person keeps control. That's why I call this the *control continuum.*

Age is one factor determining who's up—and families almost always include people of different ages. Parents (or other adult caretakers) are one-up, children one-down. Older siblings are one-up as well, and younger siblings are one-down. (These constellations can be reversed—or at least complicated—when children become adults, and parents need more help from their children than the children do from their parents.)

On the equality end of the control continuum, no one is dominant and no one subordinate, so neither gets to tell the other what to do. But this is an ideal that is rarely achieved. In a family one person's wishes or needs always impinge on others' actions, curtailing freedom. Even for parents, or two adults living in the household, equality is a goal continually negotiated through talk as well as actions. One adult may have more say in some matters, another in others. A parent may have more say than a stepparent, but not always: A parent who is afraid that a stepparent will be driven away by difficult stepchildren may pressure those children to walk on eggshells around the stepparent.

It's important to emphasize that hierarchy is not inherently bad; it is not all about either getting your way or being pushed around. And equality is not inherently good. A hierarchical relationship entails *mutual* obligations. Yes, children have to listen to their caretakers and do what they're told, but parents (or other adult caretakers) have obligations, too: to protect, support, and help the children in their care. There is safety in being lower on the hierarchy, and responsibility in being higher. Being one-down entails privileges as well as humiliations.

You might think that the goal is for adults to move as close as possible to the equality end of the control continuum, but this is not necessarily the case. For the person who is one-down, moving more toward equality entails a loss of protection and help. For the person who is one-up, moving toward equality means a loss of the connection that comes from feeling responsible for someone else. These trade-offs are in the spotlight when children become adolescents, edging toward adulthood. Surely they account for some of the sadness, as well as the relief, that parents feel as children grow older, become more independent, and move out to live on their own (if they do).

Family talk is a matter of finding just the right blend of responsibility, caring, and independence—the right footing, in other words, on a continuum between hierarchy and equality.

At the same time, though, there is another continuum along which all conversations—and relationships—move. The desire for connection is really a matter of finding the right footing on a continuum between closeness and distance. Here the questions are How close do I want to be to the other person? Would I rather—or would he or she rather—put more distance between us? You can move too far in either direction: If you move too far toward the closeness end, you risk feeling suffocated, invaded, or overwhelmed. If you move too far toward the distance end, you risk feeling abandoned, left out, cut off. I call this the *connection continuum*.

The control continuum and the connection continuum are not separate; they are inextricably intertwined, just as the dynamics of control and connection overlap, intertwine, and entail each other. For example, a danger in moving too far toward the closeness end of the connection continuum is feeling engulfed by another person—and hence out of control. Similarly, it might seem that being in a hierarchical relationship with someone means you're distant, like a boss and an employee. But in a family greater hierarchy often means greater closeness, as with a parent and infant or a grandparent and grandchild.

Think, too, of the devotion—the idolization—that a younger sibling typically feels toward an older one, or the equally passionate devotion felt by an older sibling given responsibility for taking care of a younger sister or brother. The poet Delmore Schwartz wrote, "In dreams begin responsibilities." We might change that a bit and say, "In responsibilities begins love." In a family being one-up means being responsible for and taking care of someone—and the act of caring creates mutual affection.

Family relationships are fundamentally hierarchical as well as deeply connected. The two continua—between hierarchy and equality on the one hand and between closeness and distance on the other—are in play, and interplay, at every moment. In Chapter 1, I showed that anything said in the spirit of one dynamic can be taken in the spirit of the other. So if your mother (or brother or sister) says, "You need to dress better. I only say this because I love you," you can focus on connection (the caring) or control (telling you how to dress). But now we can go further. To the extent that saying you need to dress better implies criticism, it puts you down (on the control continuum, you're closer to hierarchy) but it also creates distance (pushing you toward that end of the connection continuum).

You can think of the relationship between these two continua as a grid with intersecting axes:

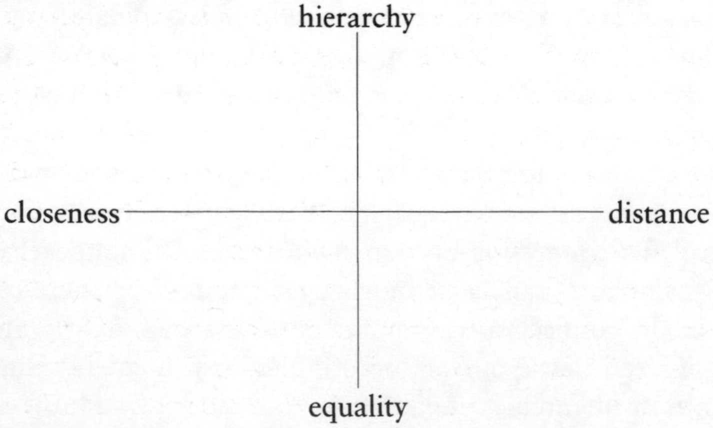

In any family relationship you have to find the right place on the grid—that is, the right position between hierarchy and equality as well as between closeness and distance. Finding that place drives family conversations.

Arguments often result when you feel yourself, or someone else, moving around the grid in ways that make you uncomfortable: too much closeness and too much hierarchy, for example, or too much equality and too much distance.

## What's the Good of Arguing?

Before we listen in on arguments between family members to see how they can be avoided or better managed, we need to consider that arguing has a positive side: Sometimes it can improve relationships in a family.

We think of arguments as driving people apart—pushing them toward the distance end of the connection continuum. But arguing can also bring people together. Expressing anger can bring a relationship to a new level of closeness when it exposes disagreements that have simmered below the surface. For Danzy Senna, daughter of a black father and a white mother, an angry argument led to a breakthrough in her relationship with her Irish Protestant grandmother.

A college student on a holiday visit, Senna overheard her grandmother yelling at her housekeeper, a Greek woman named Mary, who had accidentally broken a vase. "Idiot! You damn fool!" Senna's grandmother shouted. "You stupid stupid woman! How in bloody hell could you have done something so stupid!" When Senna appeared, Mary scurried away with the shards of broken vase, and her grandmother turned to Senna, all sweetness and consideration. But Senna was enraged. She writes: " 'Don't you ever talk to her that way,' I shouted. 'Where do you think you are? Slavery was abolished long ago.' "

Perhaps it was Senna's reference to slavery, or just her grandmother's abiding awareness of her mixed-race background, but her grandmother said, "It's about race, isn't it?" Incredulous,

Senna replied, "Race? Mary's white. This is about respect—treating other human beings with respect." And then her grandmother delivered the verdict: "The tragedy about you is that you are mixed." Senna struck back: "Your tragedy is that you are old and ignorant. You don't know the first thing about me."

It is easy to imagine a scenario in which this is the end of the relationship. You can hear Senna telling this story as the explanation for why she stopped speaking to her grandmother: the truth of the old woman's racism came out. But as Senna tells it, this was not the end. It was the beginning:

> I left her apartment trembling yet feeling exhilarated by what I had done. But my elation soon turned to shame. I had taken on an old lady. And for what? Her intolerance was, at her age, deeply entrenched. My rebuttals couldn't change her.
>
> Yet that fight marked the beginning of our relationship. I've since decided that when you cease to express anger toward those who have hurt you, you are essentially giving up on them. They are dead to you. But when you express anger, it is a sign that they still matter, that they are worth the fight.
>
> After that argument, my grandmother and I began a conversation. She seemed to see me clearly for the first time. . . . And I no longer felt she was a relic. She was a living, breathing human being who deserved to be spoken to as an equal.
>
> I began visiting her more. . . . In her presence, I was proudly black and young and political, and she was who she was: subtly racist, terribly elitist and awfully funny.

The angry confrontation allowed Senna and her grandmother to become closer because once they were talking honestly to each other, they could have a relationship as two individuals related by family. Danzy wanted her grandmother to see her for who she was—and, after their argument, her grandmother began to do that. At the same time, Danzy came to understand who her grandmother was, given her own life before Danzy came into the world.

## SORE SPOTS

No one comes to a relationship as a blank slate. We all bring with us long histories of life experience that have left us bruised in different ways—and each lingering bruise is a sensitive spot that family members can inadvertently (or intentionally) bump into, causing pain. Many older brothers and sisters quickly learn their younger siblings' sore spots (a brother is chubby, a sister wears glasses) and deliberately kick them there when they get the chance. But adult partners sometimes bump into each other's sore spots inadvertently, upsetting the balance on the control-connection grid.

The radio talk show host Diane Rehm recounted on the air an argument she had with her husband of forty years. "The other night my husband and I were in a meeting with two other people," she said, "and one of the other people suggested something. And John immediately looked at me and said, 'Write that down.'

"I had an intake of breath and I smiled and said, 'Don't forget, I'm not your secretary. Of course I'll make a note of it.' And when we left the office I said to him, 'You know it did feel as though you were talking to me as though I were a secretary.' " This had special resonance for Diane because when she and John met, she was a secretary at the State Department, where he was an attorney.

Realizing this, John replied, "I think you're overly sensitive about that."

Diane agreed: "You're right. I *am* overly sensitive, and so I would appreciate your taking note of that. If you had simply said to me, 'Would you be good enough to write that down?' or, 'Do you have a pencil? I'll write it down,' it would have been a totally different reaction."

This exchange holds several truths that apply to any relationship. First, areas of sensitivity must be taken into account, whether they come from shared history or an individual's personal history. They are part of who we are, and we need to feel that we can trust loved ones not to step on a sore toe, not to squeeze a sore hand. In that sense (from Diane's point of view), John's comment showed a failure of connection. He should know her well enough to know what her sensitive spots are.

At the same time, Diane's reaction focused on the wording her husband chose, which sounded peremptory to her. That's what created the impression that he felt it was her job to take notes at the meeting. In this sense John's comment invoked hierarchy, implying (from Diane's point of view) that he was one-up, giving orders, and she one-down, taking them. Here is an example of where the grid comes in: To many people hierarchy is distancing and closeness implies equality.

Yet the way John asked Diane to "write that down" could be seen as a *sign* of closeness rather than a violation of it. For many people, being close means you don't have to stand on ceremony. So you can say to a family member, "Give me that pen," whereas you would say to someone you don't know well, "Would you mind handing me that pen, please?" John could easily have felt that speaking to Diane as he would to a stranger would be a failure of closeness.

The sources of these different reactions are all the cultural and personal influences that affect conversational style. Diane's preference for a more "polite" request might be influenced by where she grew up (Washington, D.C., when it was southern in atmosphere) or her ethnic background (her parents had been raised in an Eastern Orthodox community in the Middle East). Gender differences could also be playing a role here: Diane's expectation that a request be made in a "polite" way reflects styles more common among women.

Context is important, too. Diane might not have reacted as she did if John had spoken to her that way in private rather than in a meeting. Perhaps it was the alignments suggested by the setting—a man and woman come to a meeting with others; he tells her to take notes—that gave the fleeting impression that he was talking to her as if she were his secretary.

Diane's story continued. "Later on that same evening," she said, "I got up from the dinner table—just the two of us—and I said, 'Well, I'm finished.' And he said, 'You know that's exactly like my saying to you, "Would you write that down?" ' He said, 'I am sensitive to the fact that I wasn't finished with my dinner.' " John, too, in other words, was asking for a level of consideration that would automatically be granted to a guest: not getting up and leaving the table while someone is still eating. By unilaterally standing up and announcing she was done, Diane was probably following the "rule of breaking rules" that applies in many families: We don't stand on ceremony when talking to family members because we are close. But her gesture could also be perceived as distancing (insensitivity to his feelings shows a failure of caring) or condescending (a person who is one-up does not have to wait while an underling finishes). I doubt either of these dynamics was operating in Diane's intentions, any more than they were in John's when he spoke earlier. But one or the other dynamic—or both—could underlie their reactions.

Diane Rehm's anecdote had a happy ending: Because she and her husband were able to talk about what had happened and listen to each other's explanations, they both felt they had learned from the experience and would walk more carefully in the future to avoid bumping into those sore spots.

Another lesson that comes from this example is a universal danger in the lives of families. It can be easy to take family members for granted and neglect to offer those you love a level of courtesy and consideration that you would offer automatically to someone you know less well. Following the rule of breaking rules entails a risk; it is wise not to carry that conviction so far that loved ones feel slighted when a small gesture of consideration would make them feel cherished.

## What's the Point? When What You're Arguing About Is Not the Issue

The initial disagreement between Diane and John Rehm was about ways of talking; Diane had no objection to taking notes at the meeting. Some arguments, though, are about true differences of opinion or desires. And sometimes arguments seem to have no point at all, or, if they have a point, it never comes out. The issue in dispute isn't really the issue. An example from my own experience comes to mind.

I married at twenty-three and separated at twenty-nine. One of the biggest shocks to me was my first husband's temper. He was never violent, but he would explode suddenly in anger. This upset me, but it also struck me as morally wrong. I had never heard my father raise his voice, and my father was my model: People should be, above all, rational.

One outburst sticks in my mind: My husband exploded in anger because I had put the toilet paper roll into its holder with the paper unfolding from below rather than from above. I still recall my disbelief and outrage: He had never told me that he preferred the toilet paper installed that way. If he wanted the toilet paper to unfurl from the top, all he had to do was say so. (It didn't occur to me, back then, to suggest he could install the toilet paper himself.) I was incredulous that he would be so unreasonable.

Looking back, I am incredulous at my naïveté. I really thought my husband's anger was about toilet paper. What a silly idea. In retrospect, I surmise that the reason he never told me, calmly, how he preferred the toilet paper roll to unfurl is that he didn't care that much—when he was calm. He was upset about something—maybe something at work, maybe something personal—and his emotional outburst took aim at the first minor frustration he encountered. How foolish it was of me to assume he meant it literally. I should have caught my breath, taken a step back, and either tried to find out what was really bothering him or just ignored it until it passed. It would have been pointless to seek a constructive way to settle our differences about how to install toilet paper; that simply wasn't the real issue.

We do, however, need to find ways of using talk to settle substantive disputes, whether large or small. Many disagreements in families are about truly conflicting opinions or preferences, such as major purchases. No amount of talking can erase the differences, yet talking is the best way to address them. (The alternative is silence, which has its uses but also its limits.) In some cases talking things out resolves differences. In others it simply makes things worse, as the disagreement escalates into an argument and eventually into a fight. With this in mind, let's look at a series of arguments that occurred in families to see how ways of talking made things worse and how talking differently could have made them better.

## "I Ain't Arguing": How Sarcasm, Yelling, and "Cussing" Get in the Way

One dispute was captured on tape by Sam Vuchinich in his study of how conflicts end during family dinner-table conversations. Listening in on this argument is an object lesson in how talking things over can fail in working things out. The husband and wife have a fundamental difference of opinion about what house they should buy, but their chances of resolving this difference go way down because they never confront the issues underlying their dispute. Let's examine how they argue to see the way elements like tone of voice, exaggeration, or the words they choose get in the way of resolving the dispute.

The first sign that an argument is brewing shows up when the wife slips into a common linguistic mode: sarcasm. Apparently, husband and wife agree that they need a new house, but they disagree about which house to buy. She wants to have a house built on a lot they have located, but he wants to buy a house that is already built. In arguing for his point of view, he says, "Why go out there and pay twenty-two dollars a square foot to build one when I can buy it for less than eighteen already built and not have that trouble?" She counters, "Cause it ain't big enough is what." Then she adds, "What am I supposed to do, give away my furniture?"

Ouch. Because the idea of giving away her furniture is obviously absurd to her, it dramatizes the wife's point. But sarcasm is risky; it raises the emotional temperature of an interchange by introducing an insulting tone. Rather than address her husband's claim directly, sarcasm ridicules it. And it does so by its tone as much as by its words, which makes it harder to respond to in a constructive way.

The husband disputes his wife's objection with an exaggeration of his own. "That house is almost as big as this house right here," he says. She responds, "JOHN IT DON'T GOT NO DEN IN IT and a dining room neither." Once again it is the wife who turns the heat up, this time by raising her voice, as Vuchinich shows by printing the line in capital letters. But what drives her to raise her voice is probably his exaggeration—dismissing "no den and no dining room" as "almost as big."

The husband tacitly accepts this correction by offering to solve the problem of size. He says it would be "no trouble to put up" new rooms. His wife counters, "That's a lot of trouble to me." He disagrees, saying, "It ain't no damn trouble to you cause you ain't gonna drive no nail in it." Her response to this is silence. He then lowers the emotional volume: "Now, how can it be trouble for you? It'll be there when you move in." Again she is silent. When she finally speaks she simply explains why she won't answer: "If that's the only way you can talk to me is cussing then I don't even want to talk about it."

Refusing to continue a discussion that has turned into an argument can be a very good thing to do, especially if you can tackle the problem at another time, when your tempers are cooler. But if you never confront the issues, it's not necessarily good. In this example the wife never explains how building an addition would be trouble to her, though one can guess. Because she does not lay out her misgivings, the husband does not have to explain how he would overcome them. From his perspective the issue seems to be money: He doesn't want to pay more for a house than he thinks is absolutely necessary.

Bringing some of these issues to the surface would have improved this couple's chances of finding a solution. What made the conflict harder to resolve were the little linguistic cues guaranteed to irritate without clarifying anything: sarcasm (hers), exaggeration (his), yelling (hers), and cursing (his). It's useful to keep these cues in mind as what *not* to do if you want to settle differences rather than argue about them.

If the person you're talking to uses one of these tactics, you can try metacommunicating rather than upping the ante by using nasty tactics of your own. You could say, "Don't be sarcastic," "That's an exaggeration," "Please don't raise your voice," and so on. Although this won't always halt an argument, sometimes it will. Other times you might decide to put off discussing the topic until you both feel calmer.

## How Not to Resolve an Argument: It's All in the Timing

Not saying what's on your mind can cause trouble, but saying what's on your mind can cause trouble, too, if you do it at the wrong time. Sometimes arguments flare up because of bad timing.

Kay was upset with Frank. She had driven him to the train station that morning as usual. As he was getting out of the car, just before they exchanged kisses, she said, "I think you should call your therapist for an appointment. You've been under stress lately. Our friends have noticed it, too." Kay expected Frank to take this like any other suggestion she might make as he was leaving for work, such as "Don't forget to call the plumber" or "Call your mother; it's her birthday." But Frank didn't react that way. He became angry and left the car in a huff, which made her angry. She thought his reaction was unreasonable because what she said was true and obviously meant to help.

Kay was probably right about Frank being under stress, and this, no doubt, contributed to his reaction. But it was all the more reason for her to be more mindful of when to bring the matter up. Like doctors who bemoan "doorknob complaints"—patients who mention their most serious ailment just as the visit is coming to an end—many of us balk when emotionally laden topics are broached at a moment we're not expecting them, or when we don't have time to address them. From this point of view, it would have been better for Kay to make the suggestion at home, during or after dinner or on a weekend afternoon.

In addition to poor timing, the alignment created by Kay's comment was hurtful. As I discussed in Chapter 2, adding "Our friends have noticed it, too" creates an image of his wife talking to their friends about Frank in a way that (in his view) reduces him to a topic of conversation. It is tempting to call upon the testimony of others to support a point, but in most cases it is best to resist that temptation: doing so is more likely to anger the people you're talking to than to convince them. Though getting others' opinions may be reassuring to you, when it comes to presenting your case, it is fairer and safer to speak only for yourself. As in a courtroom, hearsay evidence is better disallowed.

## Other No-Fair Tactics: Socrates at Home

There are other tactics that can make a situation worse rather than better. It's common for family arguments to get derailed when one party (or both) calls the other "silly," "stupid," or worse. For example, in an actual argument between a married couple, the husband objected to something his wife said this way: "Well then, that's—that's stupid!" and added, "I don't know what that's supposed to mean." You will not be surprised, I'm sure, to learn that the wife did not tell him what she meant. Instead, she responded, "You don't need to call it stupid!"

Let's look at the conversation this exchange comes from, which took place during a therapy session recorded and analyzed by communications experts Frank Millar, L. Edna Rogers, and Janet Beavin Bavelas. The argument is, on the surface, about whether the husband enjoys "alone time," but the ways both husband and wife argue sidetrack them. Chief among those ways is the wife's using a homegrown variety of the Socratic method.

The Socratic method, according to philosopher Janice Moulton, is frequently (though not accurately) identified as "a method of discussion designed to lead the other person into admitting that her/his views were wrong, to get them to feel what is sometimes translated as 'shame' and sometimes as 'humility.' " I use the term *Socratic method* to refer to a style of arguing in which you try to get others to admit they were wrong—and to agree to your conclusion—by getting them to agree to one after another step along the way, much as the Greek philosopher Socrates (as we see in Plato's dialogues) posed a series of questions, the answers to which exposed others' ignorance or uncovered contradictions in their beliefs.

In this example the problem begins when the wife asks, "Do you enjoy alone time?" It is not clear—to us or (as far as I can tell) to her husband—why she asked it. Using the Socratic method, she tries to get him to answer one question and then another so she can lead him to a conclusion that will support her point of view. It is very frustrating to argue with someone who does this, because you don't know where your answers are going to land you; it feels like being led down an alley blindfolded. So it's not surprising that many people resist answering the questions, as this husband does. Instead, he reacts with sarcasm, ridicule, and insults—tactics as unlikely to have positive results as the Socratic method itself.

The argument, as Millar, Rogers, and Bavelas present it, begins when the wife asks, "Do you enjoy alone time?"

"Oh yes, yeah," the husband replies. "I think I could live my life out alone. If I never ran into another person the rest of my time, I'd be happy. I think I would get—"

The wife does not accept this answer. She asks, "What if you couldn't go to the races or figure with your calculator?"

Apparently intending to show how ridiculous her question is, the husband responds, "Well, you mean just sit in a jail cell or something?"

As usual, sarcasm turns up the emotional heat. The wife then repeats her question. "No, no, no," she says. "What if there were no races you could go to and your calculator was broken?" The authors describe her tone here as "challenging."

The husband still doesn't answer her question. First he ridicules it again ("Well, am I allowed to sit there with a pencil and write any . . ."); then he asks a legitimate question: "I mean, why am I limited that way?" This question sounds to me like an objection to the Socratic method. He wants to know where his wife is taking him with her questions.

The wife replies, "I'm just curious"—a clearly disingenuous answer. The couple is in a therapy session, not a context for tossing out questions inspired by idle curiosity.

At this point it would have been good for the husband to insist that she explain what she's getting at, or state directly that he doesn't want to answer. Instead, he continues ridiculing her question by proposing an equally unlikely situation to her. "Well, is alone time good for you if you are not allowed to read a book?" he asks. Then he adds the line we saw before: "Well then, that's—that's stupid!"

The husband's and wife's tactics—her using the Socratic method, and his using sarcasm and ridicule—have gotten them off track. They are now arguing not about whatever the wife had in mind when she asked her husband whether he enjoys alone time but about the logic of her question. Though the husband's frustration is understandable, he would have accomplished more had he metacommunicated, by asking directly, "What are you trying to get at by asking that question?" Instead, he, too, asked a question he did not really want to know the answer to ("Well, is alone time good for you if you are not allowed to read a book?") and, without waiting for an answer, resorted to an insult ("That's stupid").

Now that an insult has been introduced, the argument heats up and, not surprisingly, focuses on the insult.

"You don't need to call it stupid!" the wife retorts.

Laughing, the husband replies, "Well, yeah, . . . well, I'm just trying to get you upset."

"Oh, you did that a long time ago," she responds.

"What?"

"I've been upset a lot tonight."

"No, no," the husband objects.

"Yes I have."

"No you haven't been. You're just playing out a role."

At this point each of them seems to be opposing every statement the other makes, like fencers trying to block each other's every move. They sound as if they were exchanging childlike taunts: "Yes I am!" "No you're not!" "Yes I am!" "No you're not!"

We never find out—because the couple never confronted (in this conversation)—what the wife had in mind when she asked her husband if he likes alone time. The Socratic method got her nowhere. Perhaps if she had said outright the end point she was aiming for they would have been more successful.

I can guess one thing that might have been in her mind when she introduced the hypothetical situation. It has to do with a metamessage that threatens the wife's footing on the continuum between closeness and distance. When the husband said he could happily live his life out alone, his wife probably heard this as a rejection: He was saying he would be perfectly happy without her. This is a shocking thing to say to a spouse. It's an ultimate threat to closeness, a deafening metamessage of a failure of love. When she asked whether he would enjoy being alone if he couldn't go to the races or figure on his calculator, I would guess that she was trying to lead him to recognize that although he is happy alone when he can do certain things he enjoys, he cannot spend every waking moment doing such things; a time would come when he would run out of things to do, and then he would miss her.

These issues were never confronted because the conversation remained on the level of refuting each other's statements rather than trying to understand each other's point of view. It's an object lesson in how not to argue: Avoid the Socratic method. In other words, don't ask questions that are designed simply to show others that they are wrong—to induce a feeling of shame. That tactic leads the discussion onto sidetracks that take you away from the point of the argument.

At the same time, when others use the Socratic method in arguing with you, don't respond with ridicule, insults, or sarcasm. Instead, metacommunicate: Insist that they state their points directly.

## What's the *Real* Point?

The previous example was recorded during a family therapy session where a man and woman were grappling with significant problems in their marriage. With so many marriages ending in divorce, conflicts this serious are certainly common. But arguments, large and small, erupt in even the strongest relationships, as people struggle to find just the right footing between hierarchy and equality and between closeness and distance. One source of conflict that can erupt at some point in almost every family is when a person promises to do something and then doesn't do it.

No matter how hard we try, we all sometimes forget to do things. You have a letter to mail but it stays in your pocket or on the seat of the car. You know you have to make a phone call at a certain time, but you get caught up in what you're doing, and the hour comes and goes without your making the call. Even if you are the only one who suffers the consequences, it's frustrating. But a family is like a complex business, with each person's fate wrapped up in the others' actions. When one person trips, everyone stumbles. If you told your spouse, parent, or child that you would mail the letter or make the telephone call, then the oversight takes on more meaning. There's meaning on the message level: With everyone running double time to keep the life-support system going, a slipup by one person puts pressure on another. But there is also meaning on the metamessage level: What does your negligence say about the relationship?

Again, Sam Vuchinich's recordings of family conflicts at dinner captured just such a scenario. It's a relatively minor altercation—too brief to call a fight, or even an argument—but it's about a topic that causes tension in just about every family: Someone did not do what she promised to do. In this case the wife did not put pepper on the corn plants to keep animals from eating them.

The brief interchange begins when the husband asks, "Did you put that there uh pepper on the corn?"

"Nope," his wife responds. "I didn't have time since I got home."

"Didn't have time," he says. "I didn't think you would."

*Tilt.* Two linguistic elements up the emotional ante here. One is that now familiar tactic, sarcasm. Presumably, if the husband really didn't think his wife would have time, he would have made other arrangements. So the implication is, "I suspected you would not fulfill your obligations because you have failed to do so in the past."

The husband's other linguistic tactic is more subtle. Repeating others' words can be a sign of closeness: It shows you heard what they said, and the repetition can be a kind of ratification. But repeating can also be used for mockery—and this seems to be the spirit in which this husband repeats his wife's words ("Didn't have time"). The mockery is particularly caustic because a sign of closeness (repetition) is turned into a sign of hierarchy (repeating to sneer).

The wife meets this challenge with a counterchallenge. She says, "Well when did you expect me to have time?" to which he replies, "Well hell you could've done it last evening." The wife then says, "I'd've been up 'til about midnight." That was the end of the argument; they let it drop.

Like the couple in the therapy session, this couple never gets to the heart of their dispute—at least not in this conversation. Apparently, she feels overburdened with responsibilities, and he seems oblivious of the burdens she bears. This mismatch probably lies at the heart of many family conflicts. The conflict over putting pepper on the corn plants could have presented an opportunity to address this deeper dispute.

I heard a newspaper editor in a radio interview comment that sometimes it is necessary to change the lead story at the last minute: It means the staff has to work late, he said, and they're not happy about that, but it can't be helped. I thought what a meager description that was—"they're not happy about that"—to describe the mayhem that might break out in a family when someone expected at a certain time arrives late. The argument that might result from the editor's decision to change the lead story at the last minute would be a very real one: "You promised to be home by six; I have a meeting; now I'll miss it." Or it might be disappointment: "This evening was to be our first time alone together in weeks."

Given that the lives of family members are intertwined, one necessity for resolving disputes is finding a way to explain—and making an effort to understand—the daily pressures that each family member faces.

## A Tug-of-War—You're the Rope

Most of the examples I've given so far are of arguments between spouses. But fights can break out between any two (or more) family members. Here's one that erupted between a woman and her son-in-law. It also illustrates the challenge of finding the right position on the connection-control grid.

A family visit was coming to an end. Nathan and Joan were taking their leave of Joan's parents. Holding the hand of her three-year-old daughter, Joan wobbled under the weight of a pregnancy nearing its term. As everyone uttered good-byes, Joan's mother, Nora, said, "I'll see you when you give birth. I can't wait to get that call when you go into labor!" This remark caused both Joan and Nathan to stiffen.

"We're not going to call you when she goes into labor," Nathan said firmly. "I'll call to tell you when the baby is born."

Nathan's words were like a red flag waved before a bull, and Nora charged. She protested vehemently that he had no right to keep such crucial knowledge from her. He belted out that he was keeping control this time, that the birth was going to be quiet and private. Nora insisted that she would not intrude if they did not want her, but she had a right to know what was happening to her own daughter. Nathan countered that if he told her when Joan went into labor and it was a weekend, she would come even if they asked her not to—just as she had when their first child was born.

Nora defended herself: It had not been her idea to come ahead in that case; it had been her husband's. (Seeing how nervous she had been while sitting by the phone, he had suggested they might as well be driving to the town where Nathan and Joan lived, so they'd be closer when they got the go-ahead to come to the hospital.) Nora promised to abide by any rules they set, but not telling her when her daughter went into labor was too cruel an exclusion.

This did not pacify Nathan; it made him angrier. When their first child was born, he said, everyone was calling—not only Nora but all their friends and relatives. The phone even rang in the birthing room. Sounding increasingly panicked, Nora said, "You don't have to give me the phone number in the birthing room. I'll give you my word I won't call, so long as you promise to call me." To explain why it was so important to her to be kept informed, she described a scenario: If it turned out to be a difficult birth and went on at length, then she would want him to call her and say, "This is what's happening. . . ."

This scenario didn't prove Nora's point to Nathan; it reinforced his. It was just the unlikely situation that he would want to avoid: If his wife were having a hard time in labor, he wanted to be completely absorbed in it and in her. The last thing he would want is to have to go out and call someone to give a report and listen to her concern. "You're being selfish," she charged, and he pleaded guilty: "That's right. I am."

There is something archetypal about this family argument. It is a struggle for closeness and control, with Joan the rope in the tug-of-war. Marriage creates overlapping families: Joan is both wife and daughter. To Nora, being excluded from her daughter's life at the crucial time of giving birth was the unkindest cut. Simply keeping her informed seemed like the smallest courtesy; denying her even this connection seemed spiteful and malevolent. But to Nathan, the birth of their child was a moment that he and his wife should experience themselves, with no intrusions.

Nathan and Nora were both struggling to find their footing on the connection-control grid. He was feeling an assault on his sense of control of his family (a power struggle, reflecting hierarchy), and she was feeling an assault on her sense of connection (distanced, cut off from her daughter). But Nora was also feeling a loss of control—she'd feel like her hands were tied at a crucial moment—and Nathan was also feeling a loss of connection—with his wife.

Neither view is right or wrong. Family style and individual personality influence how we react in situations like this. Some readers will think, My goodness, of course I would want to be alone with my partner at this intense time. Everyone else should wait until it's over to hear the outcome. Others will think, My goodness, of course I would keep my mother/mother-in-law (or sister or father or best friend) informed moment to moment; that's part of the excitement. One who clearly would react that way is the author Winston Groom, who, in describing his daughter's birth, mentions that while he and his mother-in-law donned gowns to enter the delivery room, "twenty or thirty of our friends anxiously occupied the waiting room as well as our room on the obstetric ward and also spilled out into the hall." It seems safe to say that Nathan would not have been comfortable with this situation, though Groom thought it was great.

Nathan and Nora reacted to the impending birth in their own ways. But in expressing those reactions they both said things they shouldn't have. She should not have painted a scary scenario, and he should not have taunted her by telling her he would not call when Joan went into labor. Moreover, he should not have spoken to his mother-in-law in so harsh a manner. Their relative positions with respect to hierarchy were not clear-cut. He held the real power because he would be there and she would not. Joan lived with him, not with her mother. But the hierarchy of family rank was also in play: Nora deserved a certain level of respect as Joan's mother.

In arguments we all say things we shouldn't say. That's why they're arguments. Just as Nora reacted to the feeling of being locked out of her daughter's life at a crucial moment, Nathan reacted to the threat of intrusion from a relationship that predated his and Joan's—and that he may have sensed was too powerful (and too close) to subvert. Yet they both could have achieved what they wanted by other means. Nathan could have said, courteously, that he understood Nora's desire to be involved, but he wished to keep the birth private and would call her as soon as the baby was born.

For her part, Nora could have tried to argue her case in a calmer setting—by letter, or by laying out how she felt and what she would be willing to promise. It probably would have helped to say she was sorry she had come uninvited the first time, rather than trying to evade responsibility by saying—albeit accurately—that it had been her husband's idea, not hers. Admitting having done something wrong in the past provides reassurance for the future.

I doubt it was a coincidence that this fight broke out when everyone was saying good-bye. Just as fights often erupt in the evening, when people are tired, moments of separation can be like kindling to a fire. It was probably because they were saying good-bye that Nora felt the need for connection—to reaffirm when she would see her daughter next. At times people who are saying good-bye seem to get angry almost on purpose, as if it is easier to take leave of someone you are angry at.

## Fighting About Fighting

The disagreement between Nathan and Nora hinged on a real difference that needed to be worked out. But sometimes the most frustrating family arguments are those that spin out of control when the conflict that caused them was so minor that afterward you can't believe you ended up fighting about it. In these cases often what causes the fight to spiral is ways of arguing.

Peg and Manny had an argument that started small, ballooned into intense anger, then disappeared during the night like a fog that burned off. Manny had to leave home earlier than Peg the next morning, and he was going to be tied up in meetings all day, so he asked her to make an airplane reservation for him, and Peg gladly complied. She made the call from her own office, but when she completed the transaction, she realized she did not know which credit card he wanted it charged to. The travel agent made a reservation that would be held for twenty-four hours. Since Peg would be returning home late that night, she left a message on their answering machine telling Manny to call the travel agent when he got home and leave the correct credit card number on the agent's voice mail. When she got home she asked Manny casually if he had made the call, and he said he hadn't.

Slightly annoyed, Peg said, "If it was important enough to ask me to do it for you, why wasn't it important enough to take twenty seconds and leave your credit card number?" Manny explained why he hadn't made the call, beginning with how busy he was and how demanding his job was.

"We're talking about a twenty-second phone call!" she reminded him, exasperated.

"I didn't hear the part of the message where you said I just had to leave the number," he said. Then he added, "Anyway, I didn't have the number because the message got erased."

Peg zeroed in on this last excuse: "What do you mean, the message got erased? Did you erase it by mistake?"

Manny refused to put it that way. It got erased.

When Peg pushed for an explanation, Manny said there was something wrong with the answering machine. Finally, Peg figured it out: On their answering machine the button you pushed to erase one message was the same button you pushed to erase them all. If you wanted to erase the message you were listening to, you tapped the button briefly. To wipe out all the messages, you held the button down. So Manny had held the button too long, intending to erase another message, and inadvertently wiped out the one that held the travel agent's number.

Now Peg was no longer annoyed. She was furious—not because Manny didn't leave a message for the travel agent but because he insisted on explaining what happened in a way that avoided saying he had done anything wrong, which made his explanations roundabout and mystifying, as if he were throwing up clouds of smoke to confuse her. Peg ended up really angry, and Manny ended up really defensive, feeling unjustly attacked.

This argument had a happy ending. The next morning Peg apologized for overreacting and Manny apologized for "digging in my heels." He offered to make the call, and she said that was okay, she would make it, which she did. Yet this argument provides a road map to the pathways by which small annoyances can mushroom into arguments. Manny felt he was being accused of something so minor that if he admitted fault it would be like pleading guilty to a felony when he had committed only a misdemeanor.

For her part, Peg was annoyed by Manny's oversight but infuriated by his excuses. The sheer number of excuses—he didn't have time, he hadn't heard the message, the number had gotten erased—only reinforced her impression that he was grasping at straws to avoid saying he had goofed. The last straw he grabbed—last straw for her, that is—was blaming the machine for his mistake.

Peg felt Manny was going to absurd lengths to avoid admitting fault; he felt she was going to absurd lengths to pin blame on him. And here's where the control-connection grid comes in: Making excuses, from Peg's point of view, is distancing, because it shows Manny as more focused on saving face for himself than on making amends. Insisting that he admit fault, from Manny's point of view, is trying to control him, and to put him in a one-down position.

Either of them could have headed off the fight: Manny could have ended the argument by admitting some responsibility, no matter how small. And Peg could have ended it by giving up her insistence that he admit fault. With both intensifying their determination and neither willing to back off, they ended in an argument about arguing.

## Fighting to Get Close

One more aspect of verbal fighting is like an overlay enveloping every argument: how the speakers feel about arguing.

"Family is fighting," an Israeli man said to me, and many would agree. But many—including his American wife, who was sitting right beside him—would not. "We've been together more than twenty-five years," she said. "He still feels something is missing because I won't fight." For some, arguing means there is something wrong with the relationship. But for others, arguing means you are involved, and the end of anger means the end of involvement.

In other words, the fact of fighting can send very different metamessages to different people. When Sarah finds herself arguing with Roy, she is quickly overcome with despair: "Here I am arguing with my husband," she feels. "We have a terrible relationship, and I'm stuck in it and can't escape." Roy is genuinely baffled by her response: "All couples argue at some time," he tells her. "It's just human." Imagine if Roy not only tolerated arguments but actively sought them.

A Japanese woman married to a Frenchman cried her way through their first two years together because she kept finding herself in the middle of arguments. Everything in her upbringing had taught her that arguing is destructive, to be avoided at all costs. But he had learned, growing up, the opposite lesson: that being able to engage in spirited disagreement is a sign of a good relationship. It's evidence of mutual interest and mutual respect for each other's intelligence. He kept trying to instigate arguments, which she found so upsetting that she did her best to agree and be conciliatory. This only led him to become more adamant or seek another topic to argue about. Finally, she lost her self-control and began to yell back. Rather than being angry, he was overjoyed. "Now I feel really close to you," he said.

Like this Frenchman, many people place positive value on fighting. Others, like his wife, would be happier if they could avoid fighting at all. One way or the other, living together as a family—or being in a family, whether or not you live together—means there will be conflicts of interest, varying desires, and clashing styles that will cause arguments at some point.

## Fighting Fair

In discussing the examples in this chapter, I have tried to show how some of the ways that people argue get them off track, preventing rather than providing resolutions to the differences that sparked the conflict. Here are the principles that emerge from the examples.

First, all family members should understand what arguing means to them and to everyone else: Are its metamessages comforting or frightening? As a result, do they seek or avoid arguments? Both approaches carry risks. Those who seek arguments can cause unnecessary anguish to those who wish to avoid them at all costs. And those who will do anything to avoid arguments may allow dissatisfactions to fester that could be resolved if they were brought out into the open, even at the cost of arguments.

When a remark seems like a power maneuver—an attempt to control you or put you down—consider that it might also be a connection maneuver. Seeing it that way may make it easier to figure out why others speak (or act) in ways that seem unreasonable, and how their concerns could be addressed.

Ignore sidetracks; stick to the main road. It's easy to seize on an arguable point and run with that, even if you know it's not the main point. Resist the temptation. Let small points go; stay focused on what's really at issue.

Don't play Socrates. Don't try to lure others into traps by insisting they answer questions or concede points that you think will get them to admit they were wrong and you were right. No one wants to walk down a path blindfolded. Be explicit about the end point you are heading for.

Don't sling insults; don't resort to name-calling. These tactics raise the heat without shedding light.

Avoid sarcasm. It's the tone that's insulting, and this metamessage tends to overshadow the message of your words. Sarcasm generally provokes anger and matching—or escalating—insults. It does *not* inspire a sincere response to the message your comment conveys.

Don't exaggerate or describe absurd scenarios to dramatize a point. Both are more likely to make the other person angry than to make your point. Exaggerations or absurdities also provide tempting decoys to argue against, sidetracking the conversation from the real issue.

Treasure apologies. Use them if you can. But don't get so wedded to demanding an apology that the demand becomes a battering ram.

Metacommunicate. Avoid getting bogged down in pointless squabbling about the message if it's the metamessage that's really the point.

All these strategies will be impossible to enforce when you're angry. But expressing anger may be necessary at times. It lets others know how much you care about what you are saying, how deeply their actions or words affect you.

Finding solutions to problems is often easier if you are *making* an argument rather than *having* one. Making an argument means putting ideas together in a logical way to persuade someone of your point of view. Having an argument entails all the confusions that the examples in this chapter showed. When you are *having* an argument, you are not trying to understand what the other person is saying. You just want to win the argument. You listen like a cat peering inside a mouse hole—not to understand mouse behavior but just waiting for something to pop out that you can pounce on. When you are having an argument, the chances of really working things out go way down.

Once each person knows how strongly the other feels about an issue, it is sometimes useful to put the argument aside until you're calmer. At that time you might also metacommunicate about ways of arguing. There may be a particular aspect of your style—such as sarcasm, or demanding an apology, or denying the obvious to escape blame—that especially sets off others in your family. Knowing this, you might try to avoid or temper those tactics next time around.

There are few families that avoid fights altogether, in part because of the interplay of connection and control. Anything you say can set off alarms by giving the impression that you're telling the others what to do—controlling their actions. At the same time, along the other continuum, anything you say can give the impression that you don't care enough—a failure of love.

Fighting is often preferable to ignoring real differences and dissatisfactions. It can also make opponents feel closer: Being locked in battle is a powerful kind of involvement. And sometimes the emotions stirred up by anger can be converted into affection.

(Think of the stock scene in movies where a couple begin by play-fighting then end up kissing, as their harmless blows are gradually reframed as gestures of affection.)

Understanding how ways of speaking place you on the connection-control grid can help sort out confused or conflicting reactions to chance comments or lengthy arguments. There's power in realizing that the same words can be interpreted differently if looked at both from the perspective of the connection continuum (where does it place you with respect to closeness versus distance?) and from the perspective of the control continuum (where does it place you in terms of relative hierarchy or equality?).

Insight into the forces that drive our arguments—as well as caution in using the verbal tactics that fly into our mouths when we're angry—can help prevent small sparks of disagreement from bursting into major conflagrations. With this insight and this restraint, we can better manage even the major conflicts that every family grapples with at one time or another.

FOUR

# "I'm Sorry, I'm Not Apologizing"

## Why Women Apologize More Than Men, and Why It Matters

A THREE-AND-A-HALF-YEAR-OLD told his mother that he did not like the holiday Yom Kippur—the Day of Atonement, when Jews take stock of the past year and are required to ask forgiveness of anyone they have hurt. His mother was surprised; she had never heard him say he didn't like a holiday. She asked why and was astonished by his reply: "Because you have to say you're sorry."

At this so-young age, her little boy was already sharing a dislike with his father—a dislike that irritated his mother no end. When she confronted her husband with a complaint, he too typically avoided saying he was sorry; instead, he went on the offensive with a countercomplaint. She discussed Yom Kippur with her son further, explaining to him the logic of the holiday and the advantages of apologies. In the end he decided that he would apologize only to family members, because they were the ones he could hurt the most.

How right this child was. Our ability to hurt each other is enormous, but nowhere is it more powerful than in families, so nowhere are apologies more frequently needed—and resisted. Apologizing—that small linguistic act—is often a pressure point, especially when one person demands an apology and another refuses to deliver. But it can be a pressure point in a positive sense, too. As with acupressure (a kind of pressure-point acupuncture), sometimes applying an apology magically quells anger and dispels pain.

## Love Means Always Having to Say You're Sorry

"I'm sorry I hurt your feelings," my husband says to me.

I know he's really trying. He has learned, through our years together, that apologies are important to me. I can forgive almost anything if he says he made a mistake and he's sorry. But he resists saying these words. It sometimes seems to me that he thinks the earth will open up and swallow him if he admits fault. So I know that by saying "I'm sorry I hurt your feelings," he has made a major advance (advance in my terms, retreat perhaps in his). Yet it doesn't do it for me, because his phrasing leaves open the possibility—indeed, strongly suggests—that he regrets not what he did but how I reacted, my "hurt feelings."

My husband doesn't see why hearing an apology means so much to me. As a matter of fact, neither do I. Sometimes I know he is sorry, and I tell myself this should be enough. But it's not. Being sorry doesn't seem to count unless he says it. Like the words "I love you" (which, I am happy to report, he says easily and often), the words "I'm sorry" seem to take on magical power.

I know some people will think that insisting a person admit fault is like wanting him to grovel, to humiliate himself. This is a valid view, to the extent that demanding an apology is a power maneuver. If you see it that way, resisting the demand for an apology makes sense. But an apology can also be a connection maneuver: a way of acknowledging the impact of one person's actions or words on another. If you see it that way—as I do—it's easy to admit a mistake and apologize. I do it all the time; it's no big deal. The problem is, it becomes a big deal when he won't.

I'm not unique. Mara, who lives in a rural area, told me of a similar reaction. One day she gave her husband, Ryan, something to mail for her since he was venturing forth that day and she was not. She stressed that it was extremely important for the letter to be mailed that day, and he assured her he would take care of it.

The next day they left the house together, and she found her unmailed letter on the car seat. He said, "Oh, I forgot to mail your letter yesterday." Just like that. No explanation. No apology. She was furious—not because he had forgotten (though that certainly irked her) but because he didn't apologize. "If I had done that," she told me, "I would have fallen all over myself saying how sorry I was. And if he had said he was sorry, I would have been upset about the letter, but I would have forgiven him."

Ryan's offense, from Mara's point of view, was a failure of connection: He didn't seem to care that he had let her down. If he didn't care about the inconvenience he had caused her, how could she depend on him in the future? Evidence that he felt bad about it would have provided assurance he would not do the same thing again. This explains, in part, why apologies are so important: Repentance restores trust. But in Ryan's view apologizing is pointless: It wouldn't change the fact that Mara's letter wasn't mailed. To him, making a show of regret would seem hypocritical, as if he thought he could undo an action with mere words.

## The Power of Apologies

The good an apology can do (if it seems sincere) is to dissipate anger, to calm roiling waters.

I saw this in action while I was visiting friends—a married couple—when they had an argument in front of me. The wife, Cathy, and I had been preparing dinner in their kitchen; the husband, Peter, had just returned from an errand that had kept him out all afternoon. Cathy was angry that Peter had stayed away so long, since he had agreed in advance to help with the dinner preparations. He saw her point but explained that he had figured he was not needed because I was there to help. To Cathy, the point was not getting the work done—yes, my help had been sufficient for that—but that she had looked forward to doing it with Peter, and he had unilaterally made the decision to exempt himself rather than check with her whether this change in plans would be okay. He saw her point; she saw his; yet she was still angry.

Peter and Cathy seemed to have reached an impasse. Peter said aloud, "I don't know what to say."

In a gesture of mock secrecy, I raised my hand to hide my lips from Cathy as I mouthed to him, "Apologize."

"What?" he said.

I added a whisper: "Apologize."

Still uncomprehending, Peter walked over to me, and I stated in a voice loud enough for both to hear: *"Apologize."*

He laughed out loud. "That never occurred to me," he said.

And Cathy said, "Yes, if you'd apologize, I'd forget it." So he did, and so she did. And so did I observe once more the power of that small conversational act to restore peace.

What is it about apologies? Why are they so disarming, so palliative? And why do women and men have such different ideas about them?

## Why Women Love Apologies

"Don't apologize. It's not your fault," women are often told. And women themselves have asked me, "What's wrong with me? Why am I always apologizing?" It's true that women, on average, tend to say "I'm sorry" more frequently than men do. And because they do, others often conclude that they lack self-confidence or are putting themselves down. I don't take this view. I see apologies as a conversational ritual that is an automatic feature of many women's conversational styles. By the same token, I see the avoidance of apologies as a common feature of many men's conversational styles. And these different perspectives reflect the different ways women and men tend to find their place on the connection-control grid.

On the connection dimension, apologies are one of many conversational rituals by which women take the other person's experience into account. "I'm sorry," in this spirit, does not always mean "I apologize." Sometimes it means, "I'm sorry that happened," much as someone might say "I'm sorry" at a funeral. This use of *sorry* is focused outward, taking into account the experience of the person you're talking to.

Regarding "I'm sorry" as evidence of a lack of self-confidence misinterprets this other-focused strategy as if it revealed the speaker's inner state. For example, let's say a son asks his mother whether his favorite shirt has come back from the cleaner's, and she replies, "Oh, I'm sorry. I went to get it, but it wasn't ready yet." She knows it isn't her fault that the shirt wasn't ready; she did her part by going to pick it up. By saying "I'm sorry" she is acknowledging that he will be disappointed.

Even when "I'm sorry" is an apology, it isn't always a very significant one. Women often say "I'm sorry" as an automatic courtesy, like a verbal tipping of a hat. This is the "sorry" that you might say when you accidentally bump into another person—or a parking meter. It's the one you say when you drop something you were handing someone—or the other person drops it. You're not fussing here about who is at fault; you're just taking into account that there has been a slipup.

Apologies work their magic in myriad ways. Among the most surprising: Offering an apology can be a way to get someone else to admit fault. For many of us (more women than men), apologies come in pairs and constitute a ritual exchange: I apologize for *x*, then you apologize for *y*, and we both consider the matter closed. The apologies are a verbal equivalent of a handshake that marks the settling of a dispute. So if I think you are at fault, one way I can get you to apologize is to utter the first apology myself; this should compel you to do your part and utter the second. For example, if I say, "I'm sorry I blew my stack when you broke that glass; it's only a glass, I overreacted," I expect you to say something like, "That's okay; I'm sorry I broke the glass. I'll try to be more careful."

If, however, you simply accept my apology—if you say, for example, "Yes, you often overreact. It's really annoying"—I feel like a child on a seesaw who trusted another child to stay put on the opposite end. If the other child jumps off unexpectedly, the first goes plopping to the ground. That is often the result when conversational rituals are not shared, and consequently the other person doesn't say what you expected. If a person who values apologies and expects one apology to beget another hears one from a family member, it's evidence that the ritual is shared.

Any time conversational rituals are shared, the result is reassuring on several levels. Not only is the immediate conflict resolved but resolving the conflict—the very fact that you shared the ritual—in itself sends a comforting metamessage that you are on the same wavelength, that you are both doing things right, that all's well in your family world.

We all draw conclusions about what others mean and feel according to what we would mean or feel if we said the same thing in the same situation. We compare what they say with what we expected them to say, which is typically based on what we would say. So men tend to overinterpret women's apologies as evidence that they lack self-confidence, because most men don't recognize the ritual nature of women's apologies and don't expect people to apologize when they don't have to.

By the same token, women tend to overinterpret men's *not* apologizing. The very suggestion that an apology is missing—that the man *resisted* apologizing—reflects the woman's view. She sees a lack because she expects an apology; he sees nothing missing because he does not expect apologies to pepper conversations.

## Why Men Handle Apologies with Care

In the examples I've given so far, it's been women who yearn to hear the words "I'm sorry" and men who resist uttering them. And this has been the pattern in most of the cases I've encountered. It's also the case for a professional apologizer.

Several years ago the Washington, D.C., National Public Radio station WAMU reported on a service called the Apology Line. For a basic fee of ten dollars, the creator, Willette Coleman, would make a telephone call offering an apology on behalf of her customer. (Sending flowers or a gift incurred an additional charge.) Coleman found that "men are our largest client because men truly seem to not feel comfortable apologizing to another person face-to-face." A man who used her service explained, with a laugh, that this was "a good way to kind of say I'm sorry . . . and not have to say it." For many men apologies are simply not in the repertoire.

A woman who purchased an iMac computer was ready to return it. Whenever something went wrong a built-in voice would intone, "It's not my fault," before explaining how to fix the problem. This woman had always found refuge in her work when frustrations with her family threatened to get the best of her. Now the computer was sounding just like her husband and teenage sons! With two sons and two daughters, she was struck that, whenever she registered a complaint, both her sons—but neither of her daughters—would shower her with a barrage of excuses in place of apologies.

One reason many men resist apologizing is that it seems superficial, too easy. Any cad can try to get himself off the hook by saying the right words. What really matters is actions. This perspective is verbalized in Gonen Glaser's *"It Will End Up in Tears . . . ,"* a documentary film about an Israeli family. In one scene, the parents are discussing how the father can make amends: His daughter had called him to come and help when her car broke down, but when he arrived and discovered that her lesbian partner was with her, he left without helping. The mother now tells him he should apologize. "It wouldn't mean anything," the father says glumly. "It would mean something to her," says his wife.

Another reason many men resist apologizing is that they are more inclined to avoid talking in a way that puts them in a one-down position. Viewed this way, apologizing implies weakness, which others could exploit in the future. Just how such weakness can be exploited is dramatized in another movie, *The Kid.* A man (played by the actor Bruce Willis) gets to go back to a scene from his childhood and change it for the better. Watching his eight-year-old self get beaten up by the class bully, he recalls what resulted: He was pushed around for the next eight years. To change this fate, the adult man encourages his child self to fight back and knock the bully down. Sitting astride his vanquished foe, the child victor orders his nemesis to admit defeat: "Apologize!" When the formerly tough boy utters the words "I'm sorry," his humiliation is sealed. The words were a verbal equivalent of raising the white flag of surrender—a ritual sign of submission.

## TWO MEANINGS OF *WRONG*

I have long pondered the contrasting ways that women and men tend to view apologies. The following anecdote gave me a new perspective on one potential source of the difference.

A man was upset because his adult daughter was angry at him, and he was at a loss how to repair the rift. His daughter, who lived in a distant city, had been visiting her parents in the town in which she'd grown up. She had mentioned one day that she was curious about what had become of Justin, her high school boyfriend, who had broken her heart when they were in their teens. The father said maybe she should call him up; she said she would rather write him a letter; he said he could find the young man's address; she said, "Okay." So he was sure his daughter would be pleased when he telephoned her with the news, "I got Justin's phone number from his father. Then I called Justin and got his address. He said he'd be happy to hear from you."

Instead of being pleased, his daughter hit the roof. "How could you?" she erupted. "How dare you call him up and tell him I was thinking of him?"

"But I told you I was going to get his address," the father protested. "You didn't tell me not to."

"I never thought you'd *call* him," she retorted.

Their phone call ended in anger, and the father continued to feel bad about it for days. His wife suggested he call their daughter and apologize, but he objected: "I told her I was going to get his address. I didn't do anything wrong."

Did he or didn't he do anything wrong? From the point of view of his action, no. He was trying to help his daughter reach a goal she herself had mentioned. He did not know—from his point of view, had no way of knowing—that she would object to the method he used. But if you focus on the *effect* of his action rather than on the intention, then it *was* wrong. It was the wrong thing to do because it upset his daughter.

If he defines *wrong* as a judgment of his behavior, the father understandably would be reluctant to apologize, because he feels his behavior was justified. But if he defines *wrong* as a judgment of the outcome, then he could acknowledge his daughter's distress without feeling he was pleading guilty to a crime he did not commit. It is likely that his daughter would appreciate his apology as a sign that he regrets having caused her pain. In the absence of an apology, she is left with the impression that he doesn't care what effect his action had on her; he is only concerned with justifying himself. This is sad for them both, because he *did* feel bad about having upset her—and, from the start, he only wanted to help her out. Reframing his understanding of *wrong* is a way out of the impasse, which one man described this way: "We feel bad but we don't want to *be* bad."

## The Mutually Aggravating Spiral

When one person is bent on receiving an apology and the other is determined to avoid offering one, the result can be a mutually aggravating spiral by which each person's response drives the other to more extreme forms of the opposing behavior. A term I like to use for this ever-widening gyre was coined by the anthropologist Gregory Bateson: *complementary schismogenesis*. A schism is a split, and genesis is creation, so this term refers to the creation of a split in a complementary, or mutually aggravating, way. Although Bateson used the term in a very different context, I find that it captures what happens in conversation when each person's ways of talking drive the other to ever-exaggerated forms of the opposing behavior.

Here's a simple example: Suppose one person tends to speak slightly more loudly than another. The softer speaker may speak even more softly to encourage the other to follow suit, while the louder speaker speaks even more loudly to encourage the whisperer to speak up. Each time one adjusts the volume to set a good example, the other intensifies the opposing behavior, until one is whispering and the other is shouting, both exaggerating their characteristic styles.

Just such a mutually aggravating spiral can result when one person seeks an apology and the other resists offering it. You can see this happening, step by step, in an argument that was captured on videotape by anthropologist Elinor Ochs and her students Carolyn Taylor, Dina Rudolph, and Ruth Smith at the University of California, Los Angeles, as part of a study in which they recorded families having dinner at home. The wife let her husband know that he let her down; he avoided admitting fault; she intensified her efforts to explain why she blamed him, and he intensified his efforts to escape blame, until the minor offense ballooned and he was as angry at her for blaming him as she was for his original offense. Let's see how it went.

The argument centered on the sort of daily occurrence that constitutes family life. Apparently, the family had been intending to make copies of particular photographs ("the pony pictures") for a friend named Susan. Susan had been visiting, so Mom sent their six-year-old daughter, Janie, to ask her dad, Jon, where the negatives were, and Dad told Janie he didn't have time to look for them. That evening, as the family is sitting around the dinner table, Mom turns to Dad and asks, "Jon, do you have those negatives? From the pony pictures?" Dad says, "Yeah. They were all in your cabinet." At that Mom shows annoyance. "I wish you would've told Janie 'cause that's why I sent her down, is Susan wanted them when she came so she could go if she took my roll of film." It's a small complaint, but a clear one: Dad was wrong not to tell Janie where the negatives were.

Dad offers a perfunctory apology—"Sorry"—but quickly moves on to justify himself: "Janie didn't ask me that," he says. "What Janie asked me was, can I get the negative for Susan's picture." In other words, *he* was not wrong, because Janie didn't ask where the negatives were—something he could easily have answered—but instead asked him to *find* the negative, which would have required him to stop what he was doing and taken a lot of time.

From there things escalate into what the researchers call a "complaint-countercomplaint" match, as each partner tries to pin the blame on the other. Mom asks, "Are they all together? Could I have gone through it?" and Dad answers, "Sure."

Score one for Mom (from her point of view): All Dad had to do was tell her where they were. She could have found the right negatives herself. In a way Mom is using the Socratic method of arguing to lead Dad to that conclusion. (From Dad's point of view, this question and its answer have no bearing, since Janie did not ask where the negatives were.)

Mom then asks, "Did you know Susan was here?" Continuing with the Socratic method, she will score another point if Dad answers "Yes," because then he should have figured out both that Susan would want the negatives and that Mom could not leave her guest to ask him where they were. That was why she sent Janie.

Dad doesn't miss these implications. He says, "I didn't know anybody was here." The transcript shows that now Dad and Mom speak at once. He asks, "Now are you trying to find blame?" at the same time that she is asking her next question, "Are they separately packaged?" Dad answers, "Each one's in a separate package" and "You need to look at the negative till you find the person's—" So Mom never has to respond to the question about finding blame. And Dad is building his case, that *finding* the negative would have taken too much time, so it was reasonable for him to say no to what Janie asked.

At this point Mom turns to three-and-a-half-year-old Evan, who is crying. When Evan is quieted, Dad shows how the problem can be solved: "If you want to look at them now, you can look at them now. Bring them over to her or something, I don't know." But this is irritating rather than reassuring to Mom, who says, "Well that's what I'd *have* to do because I wasn't able to give them to her this afternoon."

Now let's think about this for a moment from Mom's point of view. She has four young children to take care of (in addition to Janie and Evan, there is eight-year-old Dick and a year-and-a-half-old baby) and a business to run (she maintains a day-care center out of her home). So having to make a special trip to give Susan negatives is no small thing.

## How to Say You're Sorry—Without Apologizing

At this point Dad apologizes. Yet there is something unsatisfying about his apology. He says, "I'm sorry. Okay?" Though the word *sorry* is there, Dad doesn't really sound apologetic. Following an apology with "Okay?" somehow cancels out the apology. It seems to say, "Are you satisfied now?"

Dad further undercuts his apology when he continues to explain his behavior and deny that he did anything wrong. Beginning with the line used by the iMac computer, Dad says, "It's not my fault." As if he is stiffening himself against criticism, Dad's diction gets very formal. Sounding like a witness on the stand, he says "the information that I was given" instead of "what Janie said"; "I did not know" instead of "I didn't know"; and "the location of the film" instead of "where the negatives are." Here's how it sounds:

DAD: I did the best I could with the information that I was given. I did not know that you needed to know the location of the film. If Janie had come out and said to me, "Dad? Can you tell Mommy where the films are from the pictures?" I would have said, "Yes, Janie."

The authors point out that Dad also seems to be placing blame on the six-year-old, Janie, who did not convey the message properly.

Mom responds by defending Janie and implying that Dad is wrong to expect such precision from a six-year-old: "Well when she's about eight or nine I bet she'll be able to do that." And Dad responds, "*You* are over eight or nine are you not?"

Ouch. Here Dad turns up the heat of the argument not only by using formal diction ("are you not" rather than "aren't you?") but also by using sarcasm and by posing a rhetorical question, the answer to which is obvious—and incriminating.

Though she does not respond to the sarcasm, Mom continues to insist on her innocence: "Yes and that's exactly what I told her to say, to find out where the negatives were so I could give them to Susan." Still in his formal voice, Dad says, "I see. Well, she didn't give me your message in the form you asked."

Not ready to concede, Mom returns again to the question "But did you know Susan was here?" Since Dad has already answered this question in the negative, Mom seems to believe that he did know.

Dad, however, reaffirms his ignorance and hence his innocence: "*No,*" he emphasizes. "I didn't know who was here, Marie. I didn't know what was going on. I was busy with plumbing. Is it really extremely important to you to prove that I did something wrong? Is that important enough to carry it to this extreme?"

Mom replies, "Not extremely important, no."

The argument comes to an end here, when the eight-year-old son whispers to his father, "Daddy, we're being filmed."

Reading the transcript of this argument, I was especially intrigued by Dad's last turn. These few sentences are doing so much. For the first time Dad addresses Mom by her name, Marie. This is one of those ironies by which using someone's name, which should show closeness, actually shows annoyance; it even hints of hierarchy, as it is reminiscent of parents using their children's full names rather than nicknames when chastising them. More significant, by saying he was "busy with plumbing," Dad implies that he was doing something more important by far than finding the negatives of the pony pictures to give Susan. Therefore, it is unreasonable to fault him.

Furthermore, Dad has turned the tables of accusation. His wife's complaint against him becomes in itself the basis of a complaint against her: She is causing the fight by insisting on proving he did something wrong, and she is carrying her determination to prove him wrong to an "extreme."

It is easy to read this transcript from that point of view: Why was Mom so intent on proving Dad wrong? Her questions sound like cross-examination. But from another point of view, why was Dad so intent on proving he was blameless? If he had responded differently to the complaint, the conversation might have gone like this:

MOM: I wish you would've told Janie 'cause that's why I sent her down, is Susan wanted them when she came so she could go if she took my roll of film.

DAD: Oh, I'm sorry. I misunderstood. I thought you wanted me to *find* the negatives. If I'd known you only wanted to know where they were, of course I would have told her.

This is, after all, the essence of Dad's argument. But this way of getting to it is very different. First, it begins with an apology that sounds sincere, not a perfunctory "sorry" that is a prelude to self-defense or counterattack. Second, it takes *some* responsibility, even if only the small fault of having misunderstood. What happened instead was complementary schismogenesis—a mutually aggravating spiral: Mom did seem relentless in her determination to blame Dad. But what provoked her to go to these extremes was his dogged determination not to accept any blame at all.

## Like Father, Like Microsoft: The Risk of Admit-No-Fault

Public events often mirror private ones. Both the appeal and the risk of refusing to admit fault emerged in the U.S. government's antitrust case against the Microsoft Corporation. Microsoft executive Steve Ballmer stated the company's approach in a *Newsweek* interview: "When you believe in the propriety, integrity and righteousness of what you've done, I don't think the thing to do is have a mea culpa. The thing to do . . . is to argue your position, your innocence." (This is what Dad did in the pony pictures example.) But when Judge Thomas Penfield Jackson issued a ruling very damaging to Microsoft (that the company be broken into two separate corporations) he "left little doubt," according to *Newsweek,* "why he went for the ax, as opposed to milder restrictions." First among his reasons was that "the company consistently maintained that it has done nothing wrong." As a business school professor put it, "They had a very detailed presentation in which essentially they denied everything, and said everything they did was right." In particular, *Newsweek* noted, the judge was angered by a videotaped interview in which Microsoft's founder and CEO, Bill Gates, "denied the obvious."

In other words, the admit-no-fault tactic may have contributed to Microsoft's success in business, but it did not serve the company well in court. Discussing the debacle, one Microsoft insider commented, "We shouldn't have pissed off the judge." The same lesson could be applied to family arguments: Don't risk angering your partner by denying everything and insisting everything you did was right. Refusing to admit any fault at all will provoke anger and set the wheels of complementary schismogenesis in motion—driving the offended person to greater extremes in demanding you admit fault, which in turn renews your resolve to avoid blame.

At the same time, the wife in the pony pictures example—or other wives in similar arguments—might ask herself why it was so important for her to hear words of apology. One approach might be to accept that her husband has a hard time saying he's sorry and try to get along without those words. After all, what's really important is the future: making sure he does not do the same thing again. A more constructive way to end the argument might have been to find what they could agree on: from her side, "Next time I'll try to go myself instead of sending Janie," or "Next time I'll give Janie a note rather than a verbal message"; or, from his side, "Next time Janie asks me to do something for you, I'll make sure I got the message right before I say no."

## What Makes a Good Apology?

In ruling against Microsoft, Judge Thomas Penfield Jackson said, "If they don't admit they did wrong before, how do we know they won't keep doing it?" This statement encapsulates why admitting fault seems so important in family conversations. Dad, in the pony pictures example, did say "Sorry," yet he didn't seem to have apologized because he didn't acknowledge having done anything wrong. A key—perhaps *the* key—to an effective apology is the admission of fault. That's why "I'm sorry I hurt your feelings" falls short. It masquerades as an apology without taking blame, like crossing your fingers behind your back. In addition, there has to be some promise of action to make amends.

Another reason Dad in the pony pictures example didn't seem to have apologized is that he didn't seem apologetic—in other words, contrite. That's why saying you're sorry isn't enough. You have to say it as if you mean it; you have to appear sorry: your face should look dejected, your voice should be, well, apologetic. And the depth of regret evidenced should be commensurate with the significance of the offense. An offhand "sorry about that" might suffice for an insignificant error, such as dropping the piece of paper you were handing someone. But if you spill a glass of red wine on someone's brand-new white suit, a perfunctory "sorry about that" is not going to suffice.

What about Dad's explanations for why he didn't tell Janie where the negatives were? An explanation is a possible but not an essential element of a good apology. Explaining why something happened, why you did what you did, can be helpful—so long as you don't imply that you are therefore off the hook. That's the difference between an explanation and an excuse. An excuse is an explanation that implies you didn't do anything wrong: because you had a good reason, it wasn't your fault, or someone else made you do it. But an explanation that does not evade responsibility can be an effective element of a good apology.

## Apologies in Action

If you tend to avoid apologizing because you think that apologies weaken your position, it may be hard to imagine how they could help. Let's look at a real-life example where apologies work well to make amends for an oversight. It is instructive to see how they are woven into the fabric of a couple's continuing conversation. The dialogue shows apologies in action, as taped by the couple themselves.

"So, nine-thirty?" says Faye, as she and Kenny are finishing a hurried breakfast and preparing to meet their day.

"Nine-thirty?" asks Kenny, puzzled.

"Doctor's appointment," Faye clarifies.

"Is that today?" Kenny asks, then exclaims, "Oh, shoot." His day is already overbooked. He was wondering how he was going to finish the report he had promised his boss. And now this.

Faye is incredulous: "You forgot our doctor's appointment?" Faye is pregnant, expecting soon, and the joint visit to the obstetrician has been on their calendar for more than a month.

Kenny takes their daughter to school, as usual, and makes it to the doctor's office in time for the appointment, but this means he'll be late for work, and his brain is racing to calculate how he can still meet the deadline for the report. To make matters worse, the doctor keeps them waiting. And waiting. And waiting. Finally, Faye tells Kenny that if he has to get to work, she'll understand, and he takes her up on that. But she still feels let down that he had forgotten the appointment. And she feels even more let down when he has to stay late at work to make up for the time he lost in the morning.

Kenny's and Faye's conflicting pressures have to do with time and external demands as much as with their individual choices, but they try to work their way out of the maze of frustrations through talk. Listen to how the conversation went—and how apologies, offered by both husband and wife, helped pave the way.

That evening Kenny says, "Well, I—I'm sorry I didn't remember about this morning, but I did go. And I'm sorry—"

Faye acknowledges, "You did go," but she reminds him that he seemed impatient while waiting for the doctor: "Then you sat there like this the whole time: 'Whoa, I've got to get out of here, ugh ugh.' "

"You were making more noise about it than I was," Kenny reminds her.

Faye does not dispute that she, too, was frustrated when the doctor made them wait. But she points out, "Yeah, but you left, didn't you? I don't get that luxury. I don't get to leave. I have to stay there." In fact, Faye was late for a meeting at her job as a result.

Faye also explains her disappointment when Kenny came home later than planned: "I just don't do well with sudden changes. I had this nice little fantasy in my head of us having a nice dinner and walking and all of this stuff and y'know then when it just didn't seem like that was going to happen it just really bummed me out."

At this it would have been easy for Kenny to justify himself. It certainly was not his fault that he had a report due at work, and that he had to stay late to finish it. But he still says the magic words: "I'm sorry, dear. Believe me, it's not my first choice either." This "I'm sorry" does not mean "I apologize," but rather "I regret." And that captures the connection—the caring—about the effect of what happened, without implying he was at fault.

Faye then focuses on the future: "But I do want you to promise that you'll be aware of the appointments, too."

Here Kenny admits that he was at fault. "Yeah, I really am sorry about that, honey," he says. "I had written it down and everything and I don't have—as I said, I just don't have any excuse why I didn't remember that."

In other words, Kenny accepts responsibility for having forgotten the appointment but declines responsibility for having come home late, though he uses the word *sorry* in both cases. Though Faye does not hide her disappointment and frustration, neither does she intensify her recriminations and efforts to blame, because Kenny does not deny any responsibility.

In other conversations both Faye and Kenny apologize, acknowledge responsibility, and look forward to improvement. While waiting in the doctor's office, Kenny says that forgetting things is his Achilles' heel; he knows that he must get in the habit of keeping a closer eye on what's in his appointment book. Over the weekend, as they are driving somewhere, Faye says, "I'm sorry if I'm not as flexible as I might be," and Kenny says, "I understand what's going on. You've got a lot of things going on right now, and I do understand that and— We just need to take it one day at a time." He also lets her know that he is likely to be late certain days during the next week, because of looming deadlines. If she's prepared, she will be less likely to get "bummed out."

How moving it is to listen to this brave young couple keeping their tempers and showing their love as they face the challenge of coordinating their overcommitted family and work lives. And it is instructive to see the role that apologies play in accomplishing this task.

## Acknowledgment as Apology

One of the most important elements of apologies is acknowledging another's experience of the world. Adults who feel their parents mistreated them when they were children are deeply comforted to hear their parents, years later, acknowledge that they had let their children down. If the parents offer an apology, it can provide a kind of closure. But even an acknowledgment alone can work like an implied apology.

Sometimes adults are lucky enough to get that kind of closure from their parents, but sometimes they are not. When Bonnie was a child, her mother had criticized every move she made and told her daily that she would come to no good. When Bonnie grew up and achieved a great deal of success in her career, she longed for her mother to acknowledge both pride in her daughter's success and her own error in predicting her daughter's failure. As her mother aged and became ill, Bonnie realized that her chances of hearing either were slipping away. She took a leave from work at a difficult time in order to spend several weeks caring for her mother. Underneath, she hoped to hear some acknowledgment of the discrepancy between what her mother had predicted and what Bonnie had achieved. When the day came that Bonnie had to return to her home city, she said good-bye to her mother, who indirectly reinforced rather than directly acknowledged how she had misjudged her daughter. She said, "I never dreamed you could be so helpful." These parting words remained a painful testament to the missing apology and acknowledgment.

Even when offenses are so egregious that apologies would seem meaningless, children can yearn to hear them—or their stand-ins, acknowledgments—in order to come to terms with the past. Sue Silverman's memoir *Because I Remember Terror, Father, I Remember You* is a heartbreaking account of incest: Her father sexually molested and raped her throughout her childhood, and her mother withdrew rather than confront her husband to protect her daughter. Silverman writes of the vigil she kept beside her father as he lay dying:

> This visit he can barely speak, and I can barely understand him. He sleeps more. But every time he opens his eyes I tell him I love him. He nods his head and mouths, "I love you, too." I want more. I say these words insistently, as if now, even at this late moment, he can be redeemed, as if something can be said or done, if not to erase the past, then to diminish it. If he would ask forgiveness. If he would tell me he'd made a terrible, terrible mistake. If he would even just acknowledge it. . . . Still, like a stub-

> born, willful, yet loving child, I sit by him in his room, waiting for some acknowledgment before he dies.

So deep is her longing for acknowledgment that Silverman waits to hear her father utter the precious words even after he is physically unable to speak.

## Apology as Degradation Ritual

Many family conflicts founder, and run aground, on the rocks of apologies: One person demands an apology, the other refuses to provide one, and they stop speaking to each other—for a brief or sometimes an extended period of time. As a result, the apology swells in importance until a whole relationship—and consequently the entire family's unity—rides on it. Such a struggle can become a false front that covers more significant family dynamics. That was the case with Pam and Betty, who have a third sister, Kate. Betty and Pam's impasse over an apology is the tip of an iceberg composed of a struggle over their alignments—the inherent instability of three.

A successful businesswoman, Pam can afford expensive vacations. Since she is single and does not like to travel alone, she often invites a sister to come along. Most often she invites Kate, whose company she prefers. This upsets Betty, who accuses, "You like Katie better than you like me."

To avoid hurting her, Pam and Kate try to keep their trips secret from Betty, but Betty usually finds out in the end, and then the secrecy compounds the offense. When Betty is hurt she becomes belligerent: "You two shut me out," she accuses. "How dare you keep me in the dark!" Just such a conversation had taken place shortly before Christmas, and it was left unresolved. Pam had promised to take Betty on a trip sometime, though she didn't really see how she could, and Betty wasn't really assured she would. In any case, that wasn't the point. The point was that Betty knew Pam preferred to take Kate, and promising Betty a booby-prize trip didn't change that.

Then came the holidays. Betty invited Pam as well as her husband's sister for Christmas dinner. Though everyone drank wine with dinner, Betty drank more; by the time dinner was over, she was telling raunchy jokes and laughing too raucously at them. Pam saw an opportunity to explain—and justify—her own behavior. After a particularly embarrassing joke, in response to which only Betty's own laughter was ringing out, Pam said, "That's why I don't like to take you with me on trips. You can't control yourself when you drink too much." This remark sent Betty over the edge; she began yelling at Pam—and has refused to see her again until she apologizes. Pam insists she will not apologize because what she said is true and Betty was the one who misbehaved by making a scene.

The first thing to be said about this dilemma is that the truth of Pam's statement is beside the point. Many things are true, but this does not mean we can say them to anyone, anytime. (For example, it's true that Pam likes Kate better than she likes Betty, but she doesn't say that to Betty.) Betty had a right to be hurt when Pam put her drinking problem on the table for all to see—displayed with the turkey and roast ham. To make matters worse, Pam had also put on the table the fact that Pam prefers to take her other sister with her on vacations. This adds public humiliation to Betty's private pain of feeling excluded by her sisters. Worst of all, Pam did this in front of Betty's sister-in-law as well as her husband and son, so the humiliation was doubly public.

In this context, an apology becomes a kind of degradation ritual. Because Pam humiliated Betty, Betty wants Pam to humiliate herself to make amends. But Pam dug in her heels and refused to apologize, even under pressure from Kate (and their parents), who wanted family unity restored.

What way out could there be? For one thing, demanding an apology might not be the best way to get one. It reinforces the degradation-ceremony aspect of apologies, framing the apologizer as subservient (doing as she's told) and the apologized-to as superior (making a demand). Betty would have been more likely to get an apology if she had said something like "I felt humiliated when you said that in front of my family, especially my sister-in-law." Expressing hurt is more likely to result in Pam saying, "I'm sorry I made you feel that way. I guess my timing was bad." In making a case based on truth, Pam ignored Betty's feelings. So anything that acknowledged Betty's feelings would be a step in the right direction.

Another reason Pam did not want to apologize was that she felt Betty had verbally abused her in response to her remark. But Pam could acknowledge Betty's feelings without approving her way of showing them. She might, for example, say, "I'm sorry I said that in front of others; I shouldn't have. But I also was very hurt when you yelled at me like that in front of everyone."

In other words, there can be something between a direct demand for an apology and an absolute refusal to supply one. Some form of apology can be negotiated while abject submission is avoided.

## Pass the Apologies, Please

When a family's unity is threatened by a struggle over an apology, you know that apologies are potent. And this power can be harnessed. A husband who tried saying those magic words almost as an experiment was amazed at how quickly his wife backed off and their arguments ended. A lawyer, he felt he had discovered a kind of alternative dispute resolution for family relations—parallel to mediation as an increasingly popular alternative to protracted and expensive litigation in settling conflicts in the public sphere.

The way mediation worked in a medical dispute sheds light on how apologies can function in family relations. Health care mediators Leonard Marcus and Barry Dorn give the example of a mother who filed a complaint against a medical practice because her three-year-old child, running around the waiting room, had grabbed something off a supply cart and been stuck by a used hypodermic needle. Though the child was not permanently harmed (she was not infected by HIV or hepatitis), the negligence of leaving a used hypodermic needle exposed seemed, to the mother, unforgivable. The reaction of the office receptionist, however, had focused on what she saw as the mother's negligence: "Don't you know how to control your own child?"

In mediation the mother told her physician what had happened and the effect it had on her, the child, and the family. Her doctor listened. When she finished, Marcus and Dorn explain, the doctor "apologized for what happened and for the pain it caused them. He then described changes instituted in the office" to make sure it could not happen to anyone else. The mother was satisfied and dropped the complaint. This physician could easily have spoken as the office receptionist had done, reversing blame: The mother should not have let her child run around the waiting room. But that would have further infuriated her. Instead, he apologized, including the elements required to make the apology effective: He acknowledged her feelings, took responsibility for what had happened, and assured her it would not happen again.

In contrast, by substituting litigation for the simple human gesture of apology, many people end up more frustrated rather than less. A caller to a talk show on which I was a guest put her finger on this when she commented on my observations about the power of apologies to restore peace between people: "I'm a lawyer," she said, "and I couldn't agree more. I was recently involved in a legal dispute with a neighbor. We've been paid money, but I still feel unresolved because what I really wanted was an apology."

## Hold the Apologies, Please

I have been saying that family conflict can be avoided or mollified if men come to understand why apologies are important to women and recognize how powerful they can be to end conflict. But the other side of that learning process is for women to understand and accept why the men in their lives might avoid apologizing. With this understanding, women might try to put aside the unwavering conviction that apologies are always necessary.

Women often miss the implied meaning of a man's indirect apology, just as men often miss the implied meaning of a woman's indirect request. In making requests many women don't want to come across as overbearing, so they indicate preferences by phrasing them as questions. An example I often give is the woman who, while riding in a car, asks, "Are you thirsty? Would you like to stop for a drink?" because she is thirsty and is hoping to initiate a conversation in which she can express this preference and learn the other's disposition rather than make a unilateral demand. By the same token, many men find indirect ways to express contrition without uttering what they would perceive as a demeaning apology.

One man, for example, had inadvertently sent his college-age daughter on a wild goose chase. She had been struggling with a project for which she needed a certain kind of paper. He remembered a store that sold all kinds of paper products and told her where it was. But when she got there she discovered it had closed several years before. When she returned frustrated, her father said, with chagrin, "I guess I wasn't much help." Though this was not, strictly speaking, an apology, it seemed intended to function as one because he acknowledged that he had let her down.

Another father found a way to apologize without speaking any words at all. Linguist Robin Lakoff, in an academic essay about apologies, gives an example from her own life. Once when her father had offended her, he sent her a copy of a book entitled *The Portable Curmudgeon.* She took this as an indirect apology ("I'm just an old curmudgeon; what can I do?") and forgave him.

Often, though, women don't accept indirect hints of contrition any more than men accept indirect requests. One man, having heard me explain why a woman might make her preference known without coming out and asking someone to do something, commented that he recognizes this pattern in his wife—and sometimes he knows quite well what she wants, but he won't do it because it seems to him that she hasn't asked properly. This is just what's going on when a woman is dissatisfied until she hears a man apologize directly even though she senses that he is trying to make amends without speaking the words.

Of course there are exceptions to any pattern; there are men who apologize frequently and directly, and there are women who prefer to apologize indirectly. One couple who taped their conversations in connection with my research reversed the typical gendered pattern: The husband apologized more often than the wife did. On one occasion when the wife apologized, she did so indirectly. She said, very softly and affectionately, "Hey, hey." She then repeated this and added, "Don't we love each other a little bit?"

Her husband seemed to accept this as an apology when he replied, also with affection, "Yes, a little bit."

Exceptions like this notwithstanding, more men than women tend to avoid apologizing directly. With this in mind, women might try to give up their insistence on the words "I'm sorry" and become more attuned to their husbands', brothers', or sons' actions: Are they showing contrition in other ways? Have they made efforts to change their behavior?

Ironically, the more a woman demands an apology, the more a man may resist complying, because the demand in itself makes apologizing seem more like a degradation ritual. In other words, complementary schismogenesis is set in motion. One woman found a way of breaking that cycle: She discovered that if she held her tongue, her husband was more likely to loosen his.

Julia saw the pattern in their relationship as unbalanced. If her husband, Matt, told her he was upset with something she'd done, she'd begin apologizing even before he finished lodging his complaint. But if she told him that something he did had hurt or upset her, he had armsful of talk he'd unload: excuses, counterattacks, deflecting the blame—anything but admitting he'd made a mistake and was sorry. Then his failure to apologize—from her point of view, to take responsibility for what he'd done and express remorse at having hurt her—would continue to irritate, causing a wound that festered rather than healed.

One time Matt had promised to be home at six o'clock to prepare dinner and watch the kids so she could go out to a late meeting regarding an important new account. He didn't get home until seven—and he walked in without apologizing for being late. Julia dashed out but was still late for the meeting, and in the interim her boss assigned the new account to someone else. When she returned that night and told Matt the news, he took her side, railing against her boss. But he said nothing about his role in making her late. Julia was tempted to remind him of it, but she didn't, because she knew the reason Matt had been late: He was driving around the city trying to find a store that sold just the type of jewelry she really loved, because her birthday was coming up.

Julia could not bring herself to berate him because it seemed too ungrateful given his efforts to get her a birthday present. So she said nothing, nursing her wound in private. To her amazement, two days later he volunteered that he felt bad about having made her late for the meeting. In fact, he mentioned it several times over the next few days. Because she did not assault him (from his point of view) with her complaint, his defensive posture had not been provoked. Because no one was coming at him, his fists did not automatically rise to protect his face. And without his fists obscuring his view, he could see on his own that he had contributed to her losing the new account. By not verbalizing her complaint, she had broken the pattern.

Alternative dispute resolution at home can mean either more apologies or fewer. What works magic is breaking the impasse by which two people dig their heels in deeper, as one demands and the other refuses to provide an apology.

## Apologize, Kiss, and Make Up: One Family's Way

Among the families who participated in my research by tape-recording their daily conversations is a couple who have lived together for over a quarter century. They have raised three children, ranging in age (at the time of taping) from mid-teens to early twenties, all of whom were living at home when they taped their conversations. One aspect of their interactions that struck me was the easy way apologies were exchanged, accepted, and balanced. I'll present one example in some detail because it's a snapshot of a common frustration of conflicting demands—and a glimpse of how a successful family avoids conflict with the help of apologies.

Gregory, the husband, after a long day's work, is about to take Nugget, the family dog, out for his daily run. On his way out he passes his wife, Rachel, and tells her, "I'm going to take him out."

"He's been out once," Rachel informs him. "We had a long walk this morning."

"Oh, I didn't know that," Gregory says.

And Rachel says, "Sorry. I meant to tell you. I kept forgetting to tell—"

At this point Rachel laughs as Gregory asks the dog, "Well why didn't *you* tell us?" And he proposes a compromise, "We'll do a short one then, okay?"

Gregory has reason to be annoyed at Rachel: Since they share responsibility for taking care of their family—including the dog—they should keep each other informed of what they have done in that regard. Gregory could well have turned this into an accusation: "Why didn't you tell me?" Instead he makes a statement about his own ignorance ("Oh, I didn't know that"). For her part, Rachel apologizes, even though Gregory does not blame her ("Sorry. I meant to tell you"), and explains, "I kept forgetting." Notice how Gregory uses humor to avoid blaming Rachel, when he asks *the dog,* "Well why didn't *you* tell us?" Had he addressed this question to Rachel, it would have come across as criticism.

As the conversation continues, Gregory lets Rachel know that he's been inconvenienced. He says, "I would've stayed and worked if I'd known."

"Sorry," Rachel says simply, accepting responsibility without offering an excuse.

"Well I probably should've asked you," Gregory responds, restoring balance by taking part of the responsibility on himself. In this way neither is left holding the bag of guilt for the small breakdown in communication.

Another example from Rachel and Gregory shows how the day-to-day business of organizing a family's life can create inconveniences—and how this couple prevents them from turning into conflicts. With schedules, cars, and comings and goings all in a delicate balance, an unexpected change in one person's schedule forces everyone else to adjust. In this example Rachel and Gregory are planning to take their son Don out for dinner and a movie to celebrate his seventeenth birthday. (The celebration has already been delayed a day because Rachel had a class on the actual birthday.) Gregory has been able to take the day off because he is between the many trips that his work requires. Don will forgo basketball practice for the occasion. And Rachel plans to leave work early. The schedule is to go out to dinner at 5:00 and make an 8:10 movie. At 3:15 Gregory begins trying to call Rachel at work. When he doesn't get through to her, he leaves messages telling her that their daughter Tina needs a car by 4:30 to go to work; he'd rather Tina drive Rachel's car, so would she please call if she can't make it home by 4:30.

Rachel gets home at 6:15. One can imagine a conversation that might start with recriminations like "Why didn't you call and tell me you'd be late?" or exclamations such as "I've been calling you all afternoon! I left messages everywhere!" Instead, the conversation that ensues includes no recriminations, not even a mention of frustration. After both parents affectionately align with the family pets (in addition to the dog, Nugget, there is a cat named Raisin), Rachel's lateness is cursorily handled by an apology, an explanation, and a readjustment. This is how it went:

RACHEL: Hi! Nugget, get out of the way. Raisin wants to come in.
GREGORY: Watch out. Come on, Raisin.
RACHEL: Come on, baby!
GREGORY: Come on what. [*singsong greeting to cat*]
RACHEL: Have they been fed?
GREGORY: What.
RACHEL: Have they been fed?
GREGORY: No.
RACHEL: Hi. [*kiss*]
GREGORY: Hi. [*kiss*]
So, it's going to be a tight squeeze here, getting supper in and a movie and all that sort of stuff.
RACHEL: Sorry, I got sucked into an interview. I'm ready to go now.

Both Rachel and Gregory call attention to each other's lapses without doling out blame. Gregory lets Rachel know that her lateness presents an inconvenience, but the expression "tight squeeze" and the extra words "all that sort of stuff" lend an air of casualness to his complaint. For her part, Rachel could have accused, "Why didn't you feed the animals?" But she didn't. Gregory goes to feed the pets, and the family soon heads out for the birthday celebration.

This family provides an inspiring example of accommodating to shifts in schedules, minor slips, and oversights without letting blame and excuses drag them into conflicts. Using humor is one way they do this. In addition, apologies play a part in this family's style, in which there is little ado about much inconvenience. The ready offer and easy acceptance of apologies go hand in hand with a paucity of accusations. By acknowledging errors and seeking forgiveness, family members can wipe the slate clean and go forward with renewed affection and trust. The logic, in fact, is something akin to the spirit of Yom Kippur, the Day of Atonement.

FIVE

# "She Said," "He Said"

## Gender Patterns in Family Talk

MY PARENTS WERE planning a trip to California. As I sat with them at their dining room table after dinner one evening, my mother introduced a range of options: What date should they leave? Should they fly to Los Angeles and travel up to San Francisco or the reverse? Should they travel by car, bus, or plane between the two California cities? Whom should they visit along the way? My mother and I discussed these variables as my father sat, silent. Suddenly, my mother turned to my father with pique and said, "Eli, we have to make a decision." My father replied, "How can you make a decision if you keep talking?" He then picked up an envelope that was lying on the table, turned it over, and on the back listed the dates of the trip and an itinerary. He slid the envelope over to my mother with satisfaction that he had done his part. After glancing at his handiwork, my mother turned back to me and resumed our discussion.

It was a brief exchange, a small part of a pleasant family evening, yet the form this conversation took reflected inexorably that we were two women and a man.

For my mother the pleasure of the trip began with the planning: Talking about the many options was what I call *rapport-talk,* the verbal give-and-take that makes family what it is: intimate, close, relaxed. You might say that for her the whole decision-making process was one big connection maneuver.

My father's silence evidenced not a lack of interest or willingness to contribute but a different view of the place of talk in family. To him the trip was not an excuse for talk but a decision to be made—one he was happy to help make. You might say he expected what I call *report-talk,* conversation focused on impersonal information. (In another context it could entail holding forth on irrelevant topics.)

Had I been a son rather than a daughter, I might well have been as puzzled as my father was by my mother's desire to go back and forth over every option, seemingly more eager to worry about the decisions than to make them. Instead, I aligned with my mother, happily participating in the rapport-talk. I also understood her frustration with my father: first his silence, and then his single-handed decision making.

What goes on among family members is the result of innumerable forces, like tectonic plates in the earth that move this way and that. One of those forces is the gender patterns of talk and interaction. The drives toward connection and control provide an enduring fault line as well.

## "Why Should I Give Him Advice?" Different Notions of Communication

"My wife and I have good communication," said a taxi driver taking me to the NBC studios in Rockefeller Center, when he heard that I had written a book about communication between women and men. I was favorably impressed. Then he added, "But sometimes when she talks to me, I just don't answer." I was less favorably impressed. I asked why he wouldn't answer, and he replied, "Because what she says just doesn't make any sense." When I asked for an example, he said, "Like the other day we were watching television, and she said, 'What should my brother do?' " Catching my eye in the rearview mirror, he shrugged: "Her brother's thirty-five. Why should I give him advice?"

Here was the kernel of a misunderstanding that wreaks havoc in conversations between women and men, especially those who live together in families. The problem begins with timing: He wanted to watch television; she wanted to talk. For him the comfortable intimacy of marriage was created by doing something together, in this case watching television. So he was feeling fine. But for her, intimacy is created by talk—especially rapport-talk, in which you tell each other everything that is on your mind. So she felt something was missing. To fill that gap she brought up a topic for talk.

But not just any topic. A favorite kind of talk that reflects, reinforces, and re-creates intimacy for many women is troubles talk.

## Trouble with Troubles Talk

Ordinary troubles provide fodder for conversation that helps speakers think about life's challenges—not just to find a solution (though it can certainly do that) but as a kind of philosophical investigation: How do others deal with situations like this? What is the best way to think about them? Most of all, just talking this way creates connection.

A problem does not have to be overwhelming for a woman to bring it up for discussion; any problem can make a good topic by providing an opportunity to reaffirm mutual interest and connection. But many men assume that if someone brings up a problem, it must be serious. One woman complained daily about situations at work; her son said, "If you hate your job so much, why don't you quit?" She was puzzled; she liked her job. He misinterpreted her run-of-the-mill stresses and strains as serious complaints because *he* would not talk about them unless they were major problems he wanted to solve.

Another woman had a similar experience. She brought her husband to an office party, where he met her co-workers for the first time. "They were really nice people!" he exclaimed in the car on the way home, in a tone of surprise.

"Of course they are," she said. "Why did you think they wouldn't be?"

"The way you talked about them," he said, "I got the idea they were awful." He had taken too literally—and blown out of proportion—her rapport-talk complaints.

The taxi driver's wife, having no troubles of her own to bring up, probably mentioned her brother's dilemma as a way to get conversation going. Just to talk about it. Just because it was on her mind. But because conversations like that are not typical for most boys and men, her husband figured she must be bringing it up in order to get him to *do* something: to give her brother advice.

So what could the driver have had in mind when he said he and his wife had good communication? I asked him. He explained that when they had a decision to make, such as where to go on vacation or what car to buy, they sat down together, discussed the pros and cons of all their options, and made a joint decision. To him, communication is goal-focused. In other words, it's not rapport-talk but report-talk.

This difference in assumptions about what constitutes communication explains why "lack of communication" is the most common complaint of women about their marriages, whereas men who are parties to the same marriages do not typically mention communication as a problem. If you don't realize that you're dealing with a kind of cross-cultural communication at home, you can end up blaming your partner, yourself, or the relationship. I describe these patterns—the hurt they cause between couples and how that hurt can be healed—in *You Just Don't Understand.* But gender differences affect everyone in a family; whether you're married or not, straight or gay, family forces you into close relations with people of the other sex—parents, children, siblings, aunts, uncles, and grandparents. Wherever people of different sexes gather, there are bound to be stress fractures along gender lines.

## "Give Us a Feeling Here": For Women, Closeness Means Talk About Personal Relationships

A key type of rapport-talk is exchanging information about personal relationships. One way that many adult sisters maintain their closeness is by keeping tabs on each other's lives. If one or another is unmarried, that often includes keeping each other up-to-date on the status of romantic relationships.

But watch what happens when Celia (in a conversation she

taped) tries to create closeness with her brother Lou by asking about his girlfriend, Kerry.

"So how's things with Kerry?" Celia asks.

"Cool," Lou replies.

"Cool," she repeats, then asks, "Does that mean very good?"

"Yeah," Lou says.

"True love?" Celia presses.

"Pretty much," he says.

"*Pretty* much?" she asks. "When you say *pretty* much, what do you mean?"

"I mean it's all good," he says.

Lou just isn't providing the kind of information Celia is looking for; as she probes for it she starts to sound a bit like an inquisitor. In fact, their conversation sounds rather like a mother talking to a teenage child.

The pain for parents when children enter their teenage years can be severe, but especially painful to mothers is their children's drawing away. Mothers feel shut out, deeply hurt that the children who used to tell them everything now tell them nothing. This reflects the particular meaning of talk and of telling secrets as the key to closeness, which for many women is a measure of a relationship. Mothers' relationships with their children can puzzle fathers, many of whom do not understand why their wives are so upset that their teenage children no longer confide in them.

A glimpse into life with a teenage child is *An American Love Story,* a real-life documentary in which the filmmaker Jennifer Fox filmed a family's daily life for nearly two years, beginning in 1992, and used excerpts in a series that aired on PBS in 1999. The family is composed of the parents, Karen Wilson and Bill Sims, and their two daughters, Chaney and Cicily. In connection with a seminar I taught on family communication, Alla Yeliseyeva identified a conflict that arose between Chaney, who was twelve, and her mother over Chaney's first "date" with a boy. One aspect of this conflict is the mother's attempts to initiate—and the daughter's determination to avoid—conversations about what Chaney is feeling. The interchanges sound very much like the one we just saw between Celia and her brother.

The boy (who was thirteen) failed to appear on the appointed day. After the entire family spent several hours waiting for him, Chaney got a phone call explaining that his grandmother did not permit him to go. At this point Karen tries to get a conversation going with Chaney, who responds minimally.

Karen begins, "That's too bad. Aren't you mad?"

"No," Chaney says, offering little.

"I mean just in general," her mother presses.

"What do you mean?" Chaney asks.

"Not at him, just in general."

"No, not that much."

Karen begins offering specific words, as if giving her daughter a multiple-choice questionnaire. "Disappointed?" she asks.

"No, not that much," Chaney replies.

"Relieved?"

"No," Chaney says, and laughs.

At this point Karen laughs, too, and says what so many mothers must have wished to say so many times to their teenage children: "Give us a feeling here, Chaney!"

Through her questions and comments, Karen is showing her daughter the kind of conversation she expects to have—a conversation about how she *feels* about what happens.

To everyone's surprise the boy turns up unannounced two days later, and Chaney goes for a walk with him. When she returns she finds her parents eagerly awaiting her. Karen asks, "So where did you go?"

Chaney responds minimally ("Just walked around") and heads for her room to call her best friend.

"Come sit and tell us all about it," Karen urges.

"I have to call Nelly," Chaney protests.

Karen insists, "Come, tell us all about it first. I am your first priority here."

Chaney complies by sitting down, but she volunteers nothing. She offers only cryptic and minimally informative answers to Karen's questions. Throughout the conversation Chaney laughs or chuckles.

"Where did you go?" Karen asks.

Chaney replies with an itinerary: "We walked by the botanical garden, up the main street, walked by my school, walked around, and then we sat down in the lobby."

"Did he hold your hand?" her mother asks.

"Yeah," Chaney replies and laughs.

"How did that feel?" Karen asks.

"His hands were cold."

Pressing for more specifics, Karen asks, "Did you kiss?"

"Yeah," comes the minimal reply.

"Where?"

Chaney chuckles and replies with a question: "Where do you think?"

"On the lip?"

"Just a short one."

On hearing this Karen whispers, "Oh my God!" then continues to press for specifics in a normal voice: "At our door?"

"Yeah," Chaney answers.

And now Karen asks about Chaney's reaction: "What did you think?"

"Nothing" is the reply.

"Did you have any feelings about it?" Karen asks.

"Yeah," Chaney says, but she doesn't offer any comment on what those feelings were.

So her mother once again gives choices: "A good one or a bad one, or a stupid one?"

"Good," Chaney says.

Then Karen asks, "When are you going to see him?"

"Probably in June," her daughter replies.

And her mother says, "That's nice and safe."

At this point Chaney laughs and tries to get up. "Bye!" she says.

But the conversation is not over from Karen's point of view. "So are you happy to see him?" she asks.

"Yeah."

"Is he the same you thought he would be?" Karen asks.

"He's just the same."

At this point Chaney makes her getaway. To learn how she really felt about her date, we would have to hear a tape of her conversation with Nelly. And that must be a source of frustration to Karen, as it would be to most mothers of teenagers.

Although Chaney answers her mother's questions, providing a fair amount of information about her date, the interchange feels more like an interrogation than a conversation. Chaney seems to be giving as little information as possible. Since it is the mother who supplies specifics (the boy kissed her "on the lip," "at our door"), we can't be sure if they are accurate. (It is easy just to assent to someone else's assumptions and doesn't feel quite like lying, as it would if you originated false information.)

One way Chaney avoids revealing information is by hiding in a literal interpretation, responding to "How did that feel?" by saying, "His hands were cold." Technically, this is an adequate answer. Most likely, however, Chaney knows that her mother is seeking an emotional—not a temperature—reading.

This interchange is especially resonant of the strains that develop between a mother and a teenage daughter, because it is women who tend to gauge relationships by how close they are, and for whom conversations about relationships—and the feelings associated with them—create and reflect closeness.

## "She Doesn't Tell Me Anything": The View Is Different for Mom and Dad

A standing joke between my parents revolves around a frustration common between men and women. If my father spoke to someone on the phone when my mother was absent, she'll ask, "What did he say?" My father will reply, "He said, 'Hello.' " This uninformative answer is my father's admission of defeat: He knows he will not be able to recall the conversation in the kind of detail that my mother seeks.

I was reminded of that facetious reply by a conversation that took place in another PBS documentary, *An American Family,* aired in 1973. In this conversation the mother and father, Pat and Bill Loud, discuss their teenage daughter, Delilah. Throughout we see that Bill is concerned with Delilah's actions whereas Pat is concerned with Delilah's feelings—and whom she confides them to.

Pat had taken sixteen-year-old Delilah, and one of Delilah's friends, on a trip to New Mexico, but Delilah and her friend returned home early. Upon her own return Pat and Bill are having dinner at a restaurant when Pat asks, "What did Delilah say when she came home?"

Bill replies, "What'd she say? Well, um, she said that she wanted to stay at Nancy's."

This is about as informative as my father's reply that the caller said "Hello." So Pat clarifies, "Well, no, I don't mean that. I mean uh did she say it was horrible? Did— I haven't talked to Delilah yet, and I just want to know."

Bill's response seems geared to reassuring his wife that Delilah's reasons for returning home early were not related to her mother: "She said, 'I never saw our mother try to make us happier in our lives.' " He repeats complaints Delilah made about aspects of the trip that had no relation to Pat: " 'There aren't any boys here, there aren't any girls here.' She said, 'It's dusty and hot,' and then she said, 'I just wanted to get home.' Well, y'know, her only problem is that she is— It's the first time she really really likes her boyfriend."

But Pat is not reassured. When the conversation moves to other topics, she says, "Okay, now let's get back to Delilah."

Pat moves quickly to what is important to her: her frustration that her teenage daughter does not confide in her. "Frankly," she says, "I don't like her to be afraid of me, that she wouldn't feel free to tell me." Bill can't see why this is important, while Pat can't see anything else.

Pat tries to explain further. "Because she needs to confide in her mother," she says, "or in someone who is understanding, and older, and I am. She needs me, she needs me more than she needs uh um—"

"Me?" Bill suggests.

Soon it will come out that this is probably what Pat had in mind: She feels that Delilah confides more in her father than in her. But for this conversation she just concludes, "I do think that she does need to feel some sort of freedom with me, and I'm shocked and surprised that she doesn't feel that way."

As the conversation proceeds Bill continues to focus on action, while Pat continues to focus on whether or not her daughter confides in her. "Honey," he says, "don't worry about that or things like that, because they're just going to happen, and I know you don't like it, but there's nothing you can do about it."

Pat responds that she likes Delilah, she admires her, and, most important, "I really love her." That's why it's hurtful "for her not to be able to come to me, and say, 'Now listen, this is where—what the problem is.' "

This conversation—and Bill's and Pat's different reactions to their children's teenage distancing—is a family version of the importance of rapport-talk in women's relationships. For Pat, seeing that her daughter is more likely to confide in her father than in her is an added blow. Bill tries to minimize the significance of this by saying, "She just knows that I'm weaker—that I'm weaker than you, that's all." Pat does not accept this explanation and is not comforted by it. "She isn't saying these things to you because she thinks you're weaker. She is saying those things to you because she feels closer to you, which is a very healthy thing. I—I understand that. But the only thing I feel is that I—I want her to be able to say those things to me. . . . And she doesn't tell me anything."

Bill's and Pat's differing views are right there: For Pat, the most important thing is being close, and closeness is created by intimate, self-revealing talk.

## "I Love It," "I Hate It": Watching Kids Fly the Coop

Another of my seminar students, Maureen Taylor, examined the conversations of Pat and Bill Loud. Taylor begins by describing the family as an institution that can "enthrall and ensnare, comfort and reject, pacify and enrage." She was interested in the differences between Bill's and Pat's responses to their children growing up and moving out. Pat said, "I hate to see them go like that. I just hate it. I hate it."

Bill said, "I love it."

Taylor points out that the contrast—Pat's sense of desolation and Bill's sense of liberation at their daughter's (and all their children's) growing up—reflects the gender-specific roles they took in the family. During the period of taping, Bill announced to Pat that he wanted a divorce, and the couple separated. Since Pat has devoted her married life to caring for her husband and children, she experiences their departures as abandonment. As she tells her brother and sister-in-law, "All my kids are leaving me. And what have I got left? I haven't got anything left. And that scares the hell out of me."

In contrast, Taylor points out, Bill has spent his life traveling: first in the navy and then in connection with his business. This reinforces the interpretation he gives to his children's growing up: Although Pat sees them leaving her, he sees them gaining freedom for themselves.

Bill's and Pat's reactions also reflect differences in what women and men tend to focus on in relationships. Pat's main concern is losing closeness with her daughter—and that she will no longer be needed. For Bill, closeness, as measured by self-revelation, is not the yardstick by which he judges his relationships with his children, so he does not feel the same sense of loss. Instead, he is focused on their—and consequently his—increasing independence.

Let's look at Bill's response to Pat when she says how bad she feels about her children growing up and growing away. His reassurance is almost poetic, with its soothing rhythms and mesmerizing repetitions. You can see this effect in print when his comments are laid out in breath groups, as if in a poem:

BILL: You want to feel blessed
that they want to get out
and go do their own thing.

And you want to feel blessed
that people aren't hanging on your neck
for the rest of your life.

And you want to feel blessed
you've got a girl like that
who doesn't want to sit around the room,
and she wants to do,
and she knows wh— how the hell she's going to do it.

Don't worry about it, Patty.
You've got your own life
and she'll be back again in about ten years.

But Pat is not reassured. Later in the conversation she comes right back to where she started: her disappointment that her daughter does not confide in her—and that this is evidence of a failure of closeness. "But that's why I am so appalled and amazed," Pat says, "because I always thought that we were extremely close, and that she could tell me uh almost anything she wants to say to me."

Bill goes on to say that he has decided to stop worrying. But from his point of view, that means giving up worrying not about his children's talk (whether or not they confide in him), but about their actions—whether or not they go to work and earn money. Once again, presenting Bill's comments in breath groups captures in print the poetic effect of the spoken words as he goes down the list of their children:

BILL: Kevin doesn't want to pour the cement?
Forget it.
You don't have to pour the cement.
I don't have to support him.
He'd better start supporting himself.

She wants to dance?
She'd better get out there
and earn a couple of bucks,
and do her own dancing.

Michelle doesn't want to go play with the girls?
I'm not going to worry about it.
She can sit in her room
for the rest of her whole living days
as far as I'm concerned.

I'm not going to worry about it.
Life's too short to worry about all that jazz.
That's what I've learned about this vacation.

Bill's description of what *he* won't worry about makes it clear that the burden of family for him has been a financial one: the responsibility for supporting everyone. That is the burden from which his children's growing up liberates him.

It is almost a cliché that teenage daughters and their mothers often lock horns. There are many exceptions to this—many mothers and teenage daughters who get along well and never stop confiding in each other—but there are also many who fit right into the typical pattern. These dueling needs contribute to this constellation. If a mother has defined her relationship with her daughter in terms of closeness, then the daughter's gradual transfer of loyalty to her friends will meet with far more protest from her mother than from her father. He is not losing something as fundamental either to his daily life or to his sense of what makes a good relationship.

## "Look at Me When I Talk to You": Gender Patterns Begin at the Beginning

Genderspeak creates confusion between parents and children of the opposite sex just as surely as it does between parents themselves. For mothers, having sons can be a mystery, just as having daughters can be a mystery for fathers. The seeds of these confusions are planted in the different ways boys and girls relate to their friends while growing up. So adults who were girls and adults who were boys often have greater automatic understanding of the children who were the same kind of children they were.

Some years ago, I conducted a research project in which I asked pairs of best friends, boys and girls, to take chairs into a room and talk. When I show clips from these tapes to audiences, they always laugh at the contrast. In the first clip, two five-year-old girls sit directly facing each other. They lean in toward each other; one reaches out to adjust the other's headband; and both talk intently while keeping their gazes fixed steadily on each other's faces.

Then come the five-year-old boys, who look lost and antsy in their little chairs. Sitting side by side, they never look directly at each other—never turn toward each other at all. They bounce in their seats as they talk about what they'd rather be doing—activities like blowing up the house (but only the upstairs, where I have forced them to sit and talk, not the downstairs, where the Nintendo is). A few moments after this sequence, the boys were up out of their chairs, running around the room. I quickly called a halt to the taping when I saw, from my seat beside the camera operator outside the room, that one of the boys had lifted his small plastic chair above his head and was running with it straight toward the camera.

Then come the ten-year-olds. The girls sit and face each other, talking intently; they never take their eyes off each other's faces. The boys sit side by side, awkwardly shifting and squirming, and their eyes never meet: When one turns his head slightly toward the other, the other is always looking away.

The fifteen-year-olds always spark laughter. The girls sit directly facing each other, their gazes fixed unswervingly on each other's faces as one describes to the other a gift she bought for a friend. Then come the boys, sitting side by side, leaning forward. One boy rests his elbows on his knees and looks at the floor; the other rests his right foot on his left knee as he plays with his shoelace, keeping his eyes firmly fixed on his foot rather than on his friend.

You can observe similar patterns on a sunny day when pairs of women and men are sitting outside having lunch, or just about anywhere friends are lounging in a casual setting: The women sit face-to-face and keep their eyes focused on each other's faces as they talk incessantly; the men sit at angles or side by side and look around them while talking intermittently.

These different patterns often lead to confusion and frustration between women and men: The woman complains, "You're not listening to me," to a man who is not looking at her, and the man feels wrongly accused. He would be uncomfortable if the person he was talking to looked too intently at him. If it's a man, the direct gaze feels like a challenge; if it's a woman, it feels like flirting. But many women perceive the lack of direct gaze as a failure of listening—which to them is the most important gift a person can give. A letter published by *Newsweek* following an article regarding women's sexuality reflected this value: "Now, if only the pharmaceutical companies could develop a drug to increase blood flow to men's ears," wrote Julie Wash, "*that* would be the women's Viagra."

Imagine a scene in a kitchen when the kids come home from school. Mother and daughter sit at the kitchen table facing each other. The mother asks what happened at school, and the daughter tells her. She talks about the teacher, her friends, and the conversations they had. In another kitchen a mother asks the same question of her little boy and gets in reply the equivalent of the 1950s popular book title: "*Where did you go?*" "*Out.*" "*What did you do?*" "*Nothing.*" But there is hope: Instead of expecting their sons to sit opposite them and talk, many mothers find they are more likely to hear information they are interested in while doing something with their sons, like driving in the car or weeding the garden. One mother on hearing me say this exclaimed, "That's true! And my son is only four!"

Many fathers understand this automatically. David Reimer, a man who was raised as a girl following a surgical accident that destroyed his genital organ, tells of the moment when he was nearly fifteen and his parents revealed to him the truth of his birth. The teenager, who up until then knew herself as a girl named Brenda, suspected something was up when her father picked her up and suggested they get some ice cream instead of going straight home. Looking back, David recalls that his first thought was that something dreadful had happened to his parents or his brother: "Usually when there was some kind of disaster in the family, good old dad takes you out in the family car for a cone or something. So I was thinking, 'Is Mother dying? Are you guys getting a divorce? Is everything OK with Brian?' " In other words, the teenager immediately sensed that the father was setting the stage for a momentous revelation—probably involving a family member—by arranging for them to sit side by side, with eyes fixed straight ahead.

## Competition: Playing It Up or Playing It Down

It isn't only physical orientation that differs when boys and girls, women and men, talk to their same-sex friends. Differences in the kind of conversations they have can cause even more confusion. A father who frequently drove his son and the boy's friends in carpools had a new experience when he was driving his son to a chorus rehearsal, and the son's companions were three girls—all fifth graders.

First the father was amazed at how different the girls' conversation was. He was used to hearing his son banter with other boys about sports and their Pokémon cards. The girls were talking about friends and television characters. And his son, apparently as puzzled as his father was, was unusually quiet. At one point the boy tried to join the conversation. "I got a new Pokémon card today," he announced with heartfelt excitement. This remark was greeted with silence, which was broken when the girls returned to their talk about people. It was just the kind of clash that makes office workers feel excluded when they try to join a conversation taking place among co-workers of the other sex—or that makes the women repair to one room and the men to another following a family gathering.

Mothers and fathers can be baffled by remarks made by their own children of the other sex. A training video that I made to improve communication between women and men at work includes clips of children playing at a day-care center in Minnesota. When I show these clips to audiences, many parents tell me they finally can make sense of their other-sex children.

One video clip caught three small boys sitting together and talking about how high they can throw a ball.

"Mine's all the way up to here!" boasts one.

"Mine's up to the sky!" claims the second, to the giggling delight of both.

Not to be topped, the first makes a comeback: "Mine's up to heaven!" Again, the boys exclaim and laugh in appreciation.

And then the little boy who has been quiet until now serenely tops them all: "Mine's all the way up to God."

A woman approached me after seeing this clip and told me of hearing her son and two friends talking in the backseat as she was driving. "When we went to Disneyland we stayed four days," she heard one boy say.

"When we went to Disneyland we stayed *five* days," said another.

And then her own little boy said, "We're gonna *move* to Disneyland!"

The mother was uncertain how to handle this. Should she expose her own child as a liar? ("No, no, Johnny. You know we're not going to move to Disneyland.") I assured her that she needn't worry. The boys, I am sure, knew that her family was not going to move to Disneyland. Trying to top each other was a verbal game. Her son won that round.

In the next clip from my training video, the camera caught two little girls of the same age sitting together at a small table, drawing with Magic Markers.

The clip begins as one little girl stops drawing, looks up, turns to her friend, and announces, "Did you know my baby-sitter, called Amber, has already contacts?" ("Contacts" seems to refer to contact lenses.)

After a slight pause, the second little girl responds enthusiastically, "My *mom* has already contacts and my *dad* does *too*." In this she matches not only the action—wearing contact lenses—but also the peculiar syntax that the first girl used ("has already contacts").

The girls go back to drawing, but then the first little girl raises her head again, lights up like a lightbulb, and exclaims, with evident pleasure, "The *same*?!"

The girls show as much excitement about being the same as the boys did about topping each other. And the girls are exercising their imaginations as well. I would not be surprised if the second girl's parents didn't really wear contact lenses any more than the boys could throw a ball to heaven and to God.

Just as boys' play rituals come as a revelation to many mothers, girls' can be a revelation to fathers. One father told me that he had heard his little girl's best friend say to her, "I have a brother named Benjamin and a brother named Jonathan."

His daughter replied, "I have a brother named Benjamin and a brother named Jonathan too."

But she didn't. And he couldn't imagine why she would say she did. To him, too, I offered reassurance: His daughter's best friend probably knew she didn't have two brothers, let alone brothers with just the same names as her own. What his daughter did was reinforce her solidarity with her friend by making an effort to be the same, and her verbal offering was no doubt appreciated in that spirit. While boys create connections through friendly competition, girls create connections by downplaying competition and focusing on similarities.

Yet another father found that the video clips of girls talking helped him make sense of a conversation that had puzzled him. Attorney Jesse Ruiz is Mexican and Italian; his wife is Japanese. One day he and his wife were discussing ethnicity with their three young children. Suddenly their five-year-old daughter began bawling. When he asked her why, she explained, sobbing, "Mommy's Japanese, and my brothers are Japanese, and I'm Japanese, but you're not!"

"Do you want me to be Japanese?" he asked.

"Yes," she replied through her tears.

"Okay," he said. "I'll be Japanese too."

This declaration stopped her sobs, as she rejoiced: "We're all the same!" Though her father was glad to have found a way to comfort his daughter, he had never quite understood why she reacted as she did.

After I had delivered a lecture at the Wharton School of the University of Pennsylvania, I received a letter from Dr. Thomas P. Gerrity, dean of the school, telling me of his own children's reactions when he and his wife discussed the presentation they had both heard:

> Over the weekend, we were talking with our children about your videotape of the three boys besting each other by their predictions of how high they could throw a ball. My son Jimmy, who's four, volunteered that he could throw the ball even higher than any of them. And our youngest daughter Erin, who is almost three, said, "Daddy, I'd throw the ball to you or Jimmy!"

So there it was: Jimmy, at four, claimed he could top the boys, while three-year-old Erin reframed the activity as an invitation to display connection to family members.

None of these examples, I should stress, implies that boys are purely competitive and girls purely cooperative. The boys were very cooperative in how they competed, and girls can be very competitive in their efforts to match a popular girl.

One woman who heard my lecture commented that this new insight made her wonder whether she was giving her son the best advice. She had cautioned him not to fight with his friends or put them down. "You want them to like you," she told him. Yet, with this new perspective, she realized that she was teaching him girls' norms. She might still want to give him the same advice, but it would be more helpful to him if she acknowledged that his friends might not share that view. Watching boys at play, you can see that many find it funny and fun to put each other down and to fight—though there are certainly lines over which a boy can step and truly anger his friends. (There are boys who never seem to master the level of aggression that is acceptable to most other boys and are avoided because they play too rough.)

## "It's Nothing to Do with Who Wins": Whose Norms Are These?

An example of a mother teaching her daughter norms common among women appears in an article by Alyson Simpson, an Australian researcher who tape-recorded her own family playing a board game. The family includes her husband; her six-year-old daughter, Heather; and her four-year-old son, Toby. At one point Simpson chastises Heather for wanting to cheat. (When her throw of the dice yielded a result she did not like, Heather demanded another turn.) But the mother's lesson to her daughter was not only that one should not cheat but also that one should not care so much about winning. She says, "That's what a game is, Heather. It's luck, it's chance, it's playing. You're supposed to be having fun. It's nothing to do with who wins." This view of competition is far more often heard from women than from men.

In the same article we see how a mother can be puzzled by her husband's style. Simpson reports that Heather won the game after all. While Heather is still in the flush of victory, her father asks, "So did I win because I came in last?" Though she gives her father a puzzled look, Heather answers, "Yes."

Simpson was troubled; she suspected that Heather was willing to give up her victory in order to be "Daddy's girl." Simpson also wasn't sure why her husband declared himself the winner. She wondered, "Is he trying to show her that the value of the win is not so great after all? Is he subverting the idea of who the winner is by suggesting it is an arbitrary decision? Is it a power game to make her prove her loyalty? Is it him being just as silly as Toby . . . ? I don't know the answer for sure." I don't know for sure either, but my guess is that it was none of the above but simply teasing—a common way that men show affection.

Fiction writer Joan Silber captures what might have been this father's perspective in a short story, where she notes a father's reaction when his daughter is entering the brat stage. "Bob is thinking how he misses the time when Lisa was smaller," Silber writes, "when you could make up anything and she believed you." I suspect this is the sort of fun the father was having with Heather when he said he'd won because he came in last. He was teasing her—and she was just young enough to be fooled.

Heather's way of resolving the situation is a classic example of a girl trying to make everyone equal—with stunning creativity. As Simpson describes the scene, Heather "arranges all the pieces, naming them all as winning." Pointing to the pieces in turn, Heather exclaims, "The first to win, the second to win . . ." In other words, she redefines *win* as "finish," so everyone can win.

Apparently reminded of a ditty she has heard Heather sing, her mother asks, "What's the funny rhyme that you say, Heather? Is it first—" Heather recites, "First the worst, second the best," and her mother completes the rhyme, "Third the one with the hairy chest." At this everyone laughs.

Watch what Heather does next. After singing this ditty, which reframes the winner as the worst, Heather says, "First the worst, me and Toby second the best, and Daddy's the one with the hairy chest." She assigns to no one the stigmatized role of "first the worst," names both her brother and herself "second the best," and teases her father for having a "hairy chest." It seems that Heather has learned her mother's lesson—that winning isn't important—as well as her father's lesson that teasing shows affection.

## Comforting Insults, Insulting Comfort

Differing habits with regard to teasing often cause frustration between spouses. Harriet organized an evening of self-improvement events at a community center in her town. She was pleased that her husband, Lenny, attended with her. As people gathered before the events began, she introduced her husband to the woman who would be leading a workshop on "using your voice," especially in singing. One of the purposes of this workshop was to encourage women who were reluctant to sing because they had been told they didn't sing well.

Harriet had decided to attend this workshop because she was in that group: She still recalled with pain her high school graduation, when the choral director told her and one other student to just mouth the words while the senior class sang the school's anthem. When Harriet said she was looking forward to singing in this workshop, her husband quipped, "Please spare us."

Harriet was hurt by this remark, and the workshop leader reacted the same way. Later, while leading the workshop, she repeated Lenny's remark as an example of how people can discourage others from using their voices.

It is easy to share Harriet's reaction: to cringe at the cruelty of Lenny's quip, especially since this was an event that Harriet had organized and they were talking to a visiting leader whom they did not know well. You could say that his remark was a power maneuver, bringing his wife down a notch just when she was flying high. Yet another view is possible, and I would put my money on that one. Playful insults and teasing put-downs are a common way that men and boys show affection and intimacy. In this view Lenny's remark was a connection maneuver. Being women, however, both Harriet and the workshop leader were less likely to see the insult in that light.

Sometimes it's not self-evident whether a remark is truly meant to be hurtful or meant in the spirit of friendly teasing (or ambiguous or both at once). Between women and men, teasing is risky because playful insults are a common way of showing affection among boys and men but less so for most women—at least most American women. My husband tells me that one of the first things he learned about me was that he had to curb his impulse to tease me because I would be hurt rather than touched.

There are cultural differences here, too. For example, sociologist Sandra Petronio writes that she learned in her Italian American family to use playful insults to show affection, but when she moved to Minnesota she found herself continually apologizing and explaining, "I was only joking." The same discovery was made by a Greek woman who came to the United States to study. She found that the more comfortable she felt with new friends, the more likely she was to playfully insult them—until she figured out that American women were more likely to be offended than charmed.

If women and men tend to view teasing differently, then mothers' and fathers' ways of relating to their children are open to different interpretations as well. For example, in a study of mothers and fathers talking to their preschool children, psycholinguist Jean Berko Gleason found that fathers were tougher on their sons than on their daughters. Some fathers addressed their sons in "disparaging terms" such as "dingaling," "nutcake," "Magoo," and "wise guy." Fathers also tended to threaten their sons; for example, one said, "Don't go in there again or I'll break your head."

But how are we to interpret these findings? Does the fathers' "toughness" mean that they are literally giving their sons a hard time, or is there a metamessage of affection in their words, as when a man says to someone he's teasing, "Oh, I'm just giving you a hard time"—meaning "My intentions are friendly; I'm just teasing."

Calling your child insulting names can be a sign of affection—or even protection. In this spirit many cultures of the world resist praising children for fear of jinxing them with the evil eye. Linguist James Matisoff explains that "the evil eye" is a widespread folk belief that evil spirits can attack through another's glance. Because evil spirits envy good fortune, a sure way to lure them is by praising. Therefore, to protect children, parents in East European rural Jewish tradition replace compliments with insults. Matisoff explains that in this tradition no woman would dream of saying, "Oh, what a beautiful baby." Instead, she would indicate her admiration by saying, "Yech, what an ugly thing!" In the same spirit, linguist A. L. Becker tells me that it is not unusual in Burma for children to be given names like Ugly Little Frog to ward off evil spirits.

## Making a Joke of Disaster

Joking can also be a way of warding off evil—or at least dealing with it. And this conversational ritual, too, is more common among men than women, sometimes leading women to feel that their brothers forgot to grow up. This difference describes how Lynn felt when she posed a serious question involving their aging father to her two adult brothers—both successful professionals, fathers, and respected members of their communities—and they began singing a goofy song from an MTV cartoon show!

Their father, in his early eighties, was in a nursing home, suffering from senile dementia. The nursing home staff asked the family if they would authorize an autopsy on their father's brain following his death to determine whether the dementia had been caused by Alzheimer's disease. Their mother deferred the decision to her three children, and Lynn, the oldest, conferred with her brothers. Although it was upsetting even to contemplate someone cutting into her father's brain, Lynn was in favor of the autopsy because Alzheimer's is believed to have a hereditary component. She also felt that their father would have supported this decision, since he had been a surgeon who regularly convinced his patients' families to permit postmortem examinations.

When Lynn broached the subject with her two brothers, they began singing "Pinky and the brain, brain, brain, brain!" She tried to get them to be serious, but they kept interrupting and making jokes. (In the end they signed the authorization.) To Lynn it seemed that her brothers had reverted to childish behavior. But joking is a way that some men (obviously not all) deal with the most upsetting subjects. The reference to a brain had suggested the song they both knew—and singing and laughing together created rapport, sending a metamessage: "We're in this together."

A man who was surprised by another man's using an absurd joke in the face of tragedy is J. D. Dolan, who wrote a heartbreaking memoir of his brother's death from burns suffered in a workplace explosion. As Dolan sets the scene, he is spending the night at the home of his sister and brother-in-law; the next day all three will drive to Phoenix, where his brother is hospitalized. Dolan is about to go to sleep on their couch when his brother-in-law, Ernie, offers him bedtime reading:

> "Are you *sure* you don't want to read yourself to sleep?" Ernie said, and handed me what he'd been holding behind his back.
>
> It was a comic book. . . . I didn't get it at first, . . . and then looked closer. On the cover, sneering, ready to lunge, was a villain—a monster, really—his skin a patchwork of deep scars. The scars of somebody who'd been burned.
>
> Ernie was grinning at his inside joke. Our joke.

It was Ernie who had called Dolan in Paris to tell him of the accident and urge him to fly home; it was Ernie who picked him up at the airport when he arrived. His making a joke of Dolan's brother's burns—"our joke," man to man—did not mean that Ernie was making light of the tragedy. It was his way of creating a connection with Dolan in the face of it.

## "How Was Your Day?" Power Lines—or Connection Lines

At dinner tables across the United States, families enact a daily drama of Telling Your Day. (According to Shoshana Blum-Kulka, an Israeli sociolinguist who compared Israeli and American dinner-table conversations in her book *Dinner Talk,* it is a peculiarly American ritual. Other cultures have other verbal rituals, such as the one A. L. Becker tells me he encountered many a morning in Southeast Asia: Telling Your Dream.)

The telling-your-day ritual is set in motion when mothers turn to their children and say (when the family includes a mother and a father), "Tell Daddy what you did in school today," or "Tell Daddy about our trip to the zoo. What animals did you see?" Anthropologist Elinor Ochs and her students, who recorded dinner-table conversations in middle-class American families (the same study in which they recorded the argument between a mother and father about pony pictures that I discussed in Chapter 4) captured many "telling your day" stories.

Ochs and her student Carolyn Taylor also noticed a pattern: In a majority of the instances their video cameras recorded, fathers responded to the stories by passing judgment, assessing the rightness of their children's actions and feelings, setting up a constellation the researchers call "father knows best." For example, when eight-year-old Josh, who has been doing homework, announces, "I'm done," his father asks in a "disbelieving tone," "Already, Josh? Read me what you wrote." It is the father's prerogative to question whether Josh really is finished.

In the families Ochs and Taylor observed, mother usually knew what the children had to say. This was true not only of mothers who had been home with the children during the day but also of mothers who worked full-time, because generally they had arrived home earlier than the fathers and had already asked the children about their days. The fathers could have asked "How was your day?" during dinner, but in these families they usually didn't.

Ochs and Taylor uncovered a fascinating and telling pattern. Children were most often the ones whose behavior was judged by other family members, and children rarely questioned or judged others' behavior. This puts children firmly at the bottom of the family hierarchy, since the one who is judging is one-up. Fathers most frequently judged others' behavior—and their own behavior was rarely held up to scrutiny and judgment. This put fathers firmly at the top of the hierarchy—a natural position for parents in a family.

But mothers were not up there along with fathers. Mothers found their own behavior held up for judgment as often as they judged others. So fathers were in the position of judging their wives' actions in addition to their children's, but mothers judged only their children's actions, not their husbands'. In other words, the storytelling dynamic placed mothers in the middle of the hierarchy—over the children but under the father.

The system is even more subtle: Ochs and Taylor found that mothers did question their husbands' statements—but not their actions and feelings. Mothers who took issue with fathers' statements were usually defending themselves against their husbands' judgments of them. The researchers illustrate this with an example in which a wife tells her husband that her mother bought her a dress; the husband criticizes the purchase, and the wife defends it.

Patricia says that her mother bought her a dress to wear to a wedding. Her husband, Dan, challenges, "I thought you had a dress." Patricia explains, "Your mother bought me it. My mother didn't like it."

"You're kidding," Dan responds. "You're going to return it?" Patricia explains that she can't return the dress his mother bought her but not to worry—it wasn't too expensive, and she'll wear it to dinner the night before the wedding.

This could have ended the interchange, but Dan continues to question his wife's actions: "Isn't that a hell of a waste?" Patricia repeats that the dress wasn't that expensive, and that her new dress "is great." Thus she is challenging her husband, but only to defend herself against his negative judgments. This is very different from initiating a challenge, as he did by questioning her mother's gift in the first place.

There is, I suspect, an unstated competition by proxy going on here: Whose mother's dress is number one? It is possible that Dan felt his mother was being exploited or rejected. But these factors, though interesting and important for understanding family, are beside the point here.

Another difference between mothers and fathers that Ochs and Taylor noticed is that fathers passed judgment not only on what their wives did at home or during recreational activities but also on what they did at work. Fathers, however, typically didn't tell about what happened in their workplaces, so mothers could not pass judgment on them.

The authors also observed that mothers often questioned their own actions. An example comes from the family that argued over the pony pictures. Recall that the mother, Marie, owns and runs a day-care center. At dinner she tells of a client who was taking her child out of the center and paid her last bill. The client handed over more money than was needed to cover the time her child had spent in day care, so Marie returned the excess. But she later wondered whether she had made a mistake. After all, her policy required two weeks' notice before withdrawing a child, and this mother had not given notice. Perhaps the client had intended the overpayment to cover those two weeks and Marie should have kept it, enforcing her own policy.

The father makes clear that he endorses this view: "When I say something, I stick to it unless she brings it up," he says. "I do not change it." So Marie's action is called into question. She herself raised the issue of whether she handled the situation in the best way; her husband then added to her self-questioning.

Ochs and Taylor found that this pattern was common: If mothers questioned their own actions, fathers sometimes "dumped on" them by reinforcing the conclusion that the mothers had not acted properly. In contrast, the authors found that in the rare instances when fathers questioned their own actions, mothers did not add their own questioning voices.

Ochs and Taylor identify a common dynamic in middle-class American families by which the family is a hierarchy with the father at the top. And they show that this dynamic is "facilitated . . . by the active role of mothers who sometimes (perhaps inadvertently) set fathers up" to take the role of judge by encouraging their children to report their days to their fathers.

For me the most important word in this quotation is *inadvertently.* I suspect that this dynamic—so familiar, so compelling—may be the tangled result of gender differences in assumptions about the place of talk in a relationship. When a mother asks her children what they did during the day, she is engaging them in rapport-talk, creating closeness by exchanging details of daily life.

If Father does not ask, on his own, "How was your day?" it does not mean that he is not interested in his family or does not feel—or wish to be—close to them. It just means that he does not assume closeness is created by this kind of talk.

When Mother prods a child, "Tell Daddy what you did in karate today," she is, it is true, initiating a dynamic by which Father will assess the child's actions and thus be installed as the family judge. But I would wager that this is an inadvertent result. I would bet her goal was to *involve* the father, to bring him into the family circle that she feels is established by rapport-talk.

From this point of view, the father-knows-best dynamic is as much a misfire as are the two most common sources of frustration in conversations between women and men. The first is the classic marital conversation in which a woman tells a man what happened during her day—what she did, whom she met, what they said, what that made her think, what that made her feel—and he doesn't know why she's telling him. (Like the taxi driver, he thinks, "What she says just doesn't make any sense.") Then, full of hope, she turns to him and asks, "How was your day?" and he says, "Fine" or "Same old rat race." Eventually, she complains, "You don't tell me anything," and he can't imagine what she expects him to tell.

The second source of frustration is closely related. In telling him about her day, she includes problems that arose or actions she questions. She is doing troubles talk, bringing up a problem just to talk about it. Like the taxi driver and many other men, he may well think that she is *asking* for advice—and that he is giving her what she wants when he tells her how to fix the problem. She protests, "Don't tell me what to do." And he protests, "Why do you want to talk about it if you don't want to do anything about it?"

These gender-related patterns create the father-knows-best family dinner dynamic that Ochs and Taylor identify. Father is taking the role of judge because he figures that's why he's being told the stories. Fathers are less likely to talk about work because they don't want advice about how to solve problems there, so they see no reason to talk about them. Many men feel that rehashing at home what upset them at work forces them to get upset all over again when they'd rather put it behind them and enjoy the oasis of home. They may also resist telling about problems precisely to avoid being placed in the one-down position of receiving advice.

Thus I believe that on the few occasions Ochs and Taylor found in which fathers questioned their own actions, it is no surprise that mothers did not further dump on them—not because they felt they had no right to judge but because they probably took these revelations in the spirit of rapport-talk rather than as invitations to pass judgment. The unintended result of these clashing rituals is that mothers find themselves sliding down the family hierarchy without knowing how they got there.

A final comment on Ochs and Taylor's study is perhaps the most important of all. At the same time that they report and illustrate these patterns, the authors emphasize that not all families are alike. This is crucial to keep in mind, just as it is enlightening to recognize the dynamics set in motion by the "How was your day?" ritual. Ochs and Taylor found, for example, that over half of the instances where a father targeted a mother came from one family. In that family the mother also targeted the father, but far less often. In another family where they found the father targeting the mother, they found the mother targeting the father just as often. The researchers also observed a family in which neither parent questioned the other's actions but both did so with their children. And in yet another all the challenges were aimed at one child.

I am sure all readers can discern such unique patterns in families they know or inhabit. The crucial point is to understand how patterns of telling and judging stories balance the dynamics of hierarchy and closeness in families—and how patterns of gender can drive the engine without anyone realizing it.

## "Do You Get My Drift?" Indirectness Comes Home

A verbal move that often creates confusion in both personal and work relationships is using indirectness when telling others what to do. Family members need to get each other to do things just as surely as do colleagues at work. And sometimes their ways of going about this can be frustrating—or opaque—to each other.

Cindy was increasingly distressed because her son continued living at home after graduating from college and beginning to work at a full-time job. His upkeep was straining her tight budget. After about three months she sat down to talk with him: "I think it would be fair for you to pay rent now," she said. And he replied, "I'm leaving soon anyway."

After this conversation Cindy was greatly relieved that she had finally confronted her son and settled the matter. She expected to begin receiving rent immediately. As time passed and no rent appeared, her anger mounted. After several more months it erupted. In the ensuing quarrel it emerged that her son had heard her statement as an expression of her opinion, not a request for action. He had walked away from their pivotal conversation satisfied that the issue of paying rent, though raised, had been left in abeyance for a while longer.

Cindy assumed that expressing her opinion entailed a request for action: As the parent and the owner of the house, all she had to do was make her wishes known; her son would feel obligated to honor those wishes. Her son's interpretation, in contrast, was not so different from the way many men react to women's statements of feelings. Because he would make a request directly, he does not recognize her statement of preference as a request.

Knowing that men often honestly miss indirect requests, Cindy would have done better to end the conversation by seeking a commitment to act. She may not have been comfortable giving an order ("Have a check for me on Monday"), but she might still have voiced her understanding: "Then we agree you'll start paying rent?" or asked for a commitment: "When can I expect a check?"

There is no telling how much of parents' frustration with recalcitrant teenagers is exacerbated by gender differences in ways of speaking. Several years ago I had students in a class keep notes on personal experiences and observations that related to course readings. The class had read, in my book *Talking from 9 to 5,* about women at work telling others what to do in ways that were obvious to them but could be called indirect by those who missed the message. In response to this insight, a young man named Scott Sherman was reminded of an encounter with his mother:

> On a wintry Illinois morning, my father had gone out to work while my mother and I had stayed at home. At breakfast, as we were looking out the window at the snow accumulation, my mother remarked about how much snow was on the sidewalk, and how long it would take to shovel it. I agreed with her, and then proceeded to finish my meal. After breakfast, I began enjoying my day off, lounging around the house and watching television. As I relaxed, Mother was cleaning around the house. Some time later, she came at me in a rage. She screamed that she was working around the house, and that the least that I could do would be to shovel the walk like she had asked me. This attack then infuriated me, for I felt as if her accusations were unjust. Not only did I not realize that she was cleaning the house, but I was certain that I had never been asked to assist her in anything. I retorted that I would have been willing to do whatever was asked of me, but that since she hadn't requested anything, I hadn't done anything. This ignited an argument that ended in my mother running outside to start shoveling the snow herself. Obviously, I went out and relieved her of the job, but the miscommunication was definitely due to my misunderstanding of her indirect request.

The scene of a mother becoming angrier and angrier as she works to clean the house while her strong, idle teenage son is watching television must be played out daily in American homes. Just knowing that their sons' maddening laziness might result in part from a misunderstanding would be a relief to many mothers.

Of course, this miscommunication is not based solely on words. It is probably accurate to say that Scott misunderstood his mother's indirect request and also that his mother mistakenly assumed that calling attention to the snow on the walk was a self-evident way of requesting that he shovel it. But in addition Scott's mother probably expected her son to notice, on his own, how hard she was working and offer to help her out, to do his part. Part of the logic behind indirect requests is a conviction that you should not have to ask—that the others would volunteer to do what needs to be done if only they understood that need.

This perspective emerges in another conversation recorded by PBS cameras in the home of the Loud family. Pat and Bill are having a talk with their son Grant. At one point Pat compares Grant with his younger sister: "Delilah cleaned up the kitchen four or five times yesterday, did a whole bunch of dishes. How many dishes did you do yesterday?"

"If somebody asked me to do them," Grant replied, "I would've done them."

This must have seemed a lame excuse to his mother. I doubt anybody told Delilah to do them either. Yet Grant must have regarded his mother's complaint as unfair, just as Scott Sherman was infuriated by his mother's anger at him for not doing something that, in his view, he had not been asked to do.

Many women tell me that their sons object to being asked to do things in indirect ways, whereas their daughters don't. "I talked to my son and daughter the same way," one mother (a British mother, it happens) told me, "but they reacted differently. I'd say, 'How would you like to clean your room?' My daughter might not do it, but she never objected to the way I asked. My son always gave me an argument: 'No, I wouldn't *like* to clean my room,' he'd say. 'If you force me, I'll do it, but I wouldn't *like* to.' I never knew why he reacted that way; I didn't see anything wrong with the way I asked." There was a simple explanation: The way she asked was more common for girls and women than for boys and men.

## Men Can Be Indirect, Too

It's important always to bear in mind that though women in the United States, on average, are more likely to utter and correctly interpret indirect requests, this pattern is not universal by any means. For one thing, cultural differences impinge. I have written about the greater tendency of Greeks and Greek Americans, both male and female, to use indirectness when making requests. For reasons of cultural influence or just individual personality, there are daughters as well as sons who object to their mothers' indirectness.

There are also families in which fathers are more likely to make requests in an indirect way, and mothers more likely to be direct. Sherry's family was one.

Sherry was taking her parents, who were in their eighties, to the airport, a two-hour drive. About halfway into the ride, her father asked, "Do you need gas?"

Pleased to show her father that she was responsible and had planned well, she answered with satisfaction, "No, I filled the tank before I picked you up."

A little while passed; then her father spoke again. "When you lose your gallbladder," he said, "it changes everything." He had had his gallbladder removed the year before.

"Really?" she asked. "How so?"

"Oh, everything," he said. "For example, when you have to go to the bathroom, you really have to go pretty soon or the consequences are disastrous."

Suddenly Sherry put two and two together. "Oh, that's why you asked about my needing gas!" she said. "You want me to make a rest stop!"

"Well I just thought," he said, "that if you stopped for gas, I would take advantage and use the facilities." Hesitant to impose by requiring the driver to stop, and modest about revealing potentially embarrassing details of his bodily plumbing, Sherry's father had couched his request as a neutral question. It was his daughter who had missed his meaning, though she hastened to comply as soon as she got the point.

## Your Money or Your Love

Many issues that arise in families are not, at bottom, about language, but they are negotiated through talk, so women's and men's ways of talking in a close relationship play a role. One of the most important of these issues is money.

Nancy and Eric own a summer home by a lake. Although they

look forward to a time when they will spend many weekends at the lake, right now they spend only a week or two there each year. The rest of the time they rent it out, because they need the rent money to make the mortgage payments on the home. Nancy loves the house and yearns to spend more time in it, but she deprives herself for the good of the family. One day Eric announces that he is buying an SUV. Nancy is devastated. She is tempted to strike back with retaliatory spending: "If he's going to do that, I should go buy something I want." (She resists that temptation.) She feels, "I've been a fool to deprive myself if he won't deprive himself."

Nancy and Eric regard the SUV purchase as situating them differently on the connection-control grid. On the control continuum, Nancy assumes that because they are equal partners, each should consult the other about decisions that affect them both. But he would feel imposed on—uncomfortably controlled—if he had to check with his wife before buying something. That would remind him too much of having to ask permission of a parent or a boss, making him feel one-down. She should trust him to take into account their finances when he makes a decision.

Nancy also feels, "I care about the family, but he's only looking out for himself." In this sense, the deepest hurt is the violation of connection: "I would not make a decision like that on my own, because I see us as a team. If he is acting on his own, I feel stranded. Where's my team?"

It's not that Eric does not value their closeness. It's that he doesn't feel their closeness is threatened when he makes a decision on his own. (You have to ask, though, how he'd react if she made a similar decision on her own; if he wouldn't like it, then his desire to resist being controlled reflects hierarchy, not equality.) So in addition to being a power struggle over who controls the money, it's also a connection struggle about what these maneuvers mean in terms of closeness: What do they say about our relationship? What do they say about our love?

Nancy and Eric did not often have disputes about money. Another couple, Frieda and Denny, did. Their experience illustrates another element that often underlies such arguments—that the families we grew up in provide a background against which our current dramas play out.

In Frieda's family extravagance was a form of celebration, a way of enjoying life. Denny's family regarded extravagance as morally suspect. This difference lays the groundwork for ongoing conflict. Both wife and husband are reacting to perceived metamessages about their relationship: He thinks, "You know how I feel about spending, yet you still insist on it." And she thinks, "You know how much this means to me, yet you begrudge me the pleasure."

Their family histories set the stage for the conflict in a deeper way, too. Frieda's parents always talked with scorn about penny-pinchers, as Denny's parents did about big spenders. The way we heard people being talked about when we were growing up plants assumptions about how various behaviors are to be judged. Children determine that they will or will not behave certain ways in order to avoid—or earn—being talked about in those tones. With echoes of their parents' judgments in their ears, Frieda and Denny both fear, "I married someone who has grave character defects, so what does that say about me?" Neither expresses these deeper concerns, because they seem so damaging. Yet their reticence prevents them from getting to the heart of their disagreement.

## Home Is Not Gender-Neutral

Women's and men's differing assumptions about the meaning of talk impinge on just about every issue, including money. When Eric makes a major purchase without consulting her, Nancy ends up feeling she is not as important in the family as he is. In other words, she sees herself receiving less consideration, as if she were one-down in the family hierarchy. When a family includes children of both sexes, many aspects of family life can make sisters feel that way, in comparison to their brothers; some are expressed in language, and some are made up of ways of talking.

Family is not an equal-opportunity institution. Living with siblings of the other sex can be an immersion course in inequality. Consider the study I mentioned earlier in which researchers found that fathers issue more prohibitions and negative statements to boys than to girls. This is not surprising, since boys in every culture that has been studied are more physically aggressive than girls (though cultures differ in whether they encourage or discourage aggression in boys—or girls). Still, the pattern can be seen as a way that families are tougher on boys.

Brothers and sisters often notice—and resent—the different treatment that siblings of the other sex receive. Brother is allowed to stay out at night as late as he likes; sister has a curfew. Sister is given rides at night; brother is not. For better or worse, many girls who grow up with brothers see them getting more freedom, or having greater career expectations placed on them. This doesn't mean that all children who have siblings of the other sex see them getting unequal treatment; it just means that many do, and those who have no other-sex siblings don't.

In her study of how parents talk to their children, Jean Berko Gleason also found that parents—both mothers and fathers—interrupt their daughters more than their sons. Girls often find it hard to be heard in their families. You can see this in a conversation the sociologist Sam Vuchinich analyzed from another point of view: how the conflict ended.

In this example two brothers and a sister, all in their thirties, are talking about their parents. Carl says that their father, Jack, is happy, but Sue and Ray disagree; in their view he is a chronic complainer. Watch how the sister's voice is drowned out. (Her attempts to speak appear in bold.)

CARL: I think Jack is basically happy. I don't think it takes that much for him.

SUE: Just something to bitch about.

CARL: Oh God. He—he really is not that bad.

RAY: [*Exclaiming loud disagreement*] AH-H OOOOOHHH!

SUE: **[*to Ray*] That's what I tried to tell him. He didn't—**

RAY: [*to Carl*] When you must—you must— They—they must calm down when you were there or something.

SUE: **I said I—I—**

CARL: NO. NO! That's—that's just the way they talked over the years and it wasn't really any different when we were growing up.

The conversation continues—between Carl and Ray. Sue says no more in the excerpt Vuchinich presents. Sue addresses Ray, but Ray addresses Carl. Sue's two attempts to speak are cut off, and she attempts no more.

It is impossible, based on this short excerpt, to say for sure that Sue is not given a chance to talk in this family. Perhaps in this instance her brothers were simply more excited about what they had to say. Perhaps in other conversations she talks over them. My own research has shown that what I call high-involvement speakers freely talk over each other, trusting others to persist or withdraw depending on how badly they want to raise a topic or complete a point. But this excerpt struck me as a possible example of a kind of inequality that can be created through talk in a family.

No matter how much we might wish it were not so, being a girl or a boy in the family makes a difference, just as ways of talking that tend to typify men and women play a role in almost any conversation. If we want to understand what goes on when family members talk to each other, we have to consider the influence of gender. Just as conversational style differences between women and men can cause confusion and disappointment in even the best relationships, so can they frustrate the members of even the strongest families. Understanding the gender patterns of talk can help dispel some of the frustration and make strong families even stronger.

Six

# "You Guys Are Living in the Past"

## Talking with Teens

LAUREN WAS STANDING with her thirteen-year-old son, Dylan, and his friends at his middle school graduation. She saw a piece of lint in his hair and reached to pick it out. Dylan winced and jerked his head away: His mother was treating him like a baby in front of his friends. Lauren was rocked back. Countless times in his young life she had reached into her son's hair with the privilege of closeness and the confidence of rank. This reaction was new. They were entering an era when he would interpret all her gestures completely differently from what she intended. Not only would he resist being taken care of but he began being embarrassed by the parents he had once revered.

John Anning had always relished the long bike rides he and his daughter Emily took through the rolling hills of Redwood City, California, where they lived. But when Emily entered seventh grade, she refused to wear a helmet because she thought it looked funny. John would not let her ride without it, so the bike rides he cherished came to an end. Then John and his wife, Linda Lehr, told Emily about the exciting family trip to New York City they had planned for the coming summer. Instead of being thrilled, as she would have been just a year earlier, Emily wept inconsolably at the prospect of being torn from her friends for two whole weeks.

In another family it was the mother who cried when she realized her close-knit family of three was beginning to unravel. She and her husband sat down to watch television as usual one evening, and she beckoned their teenage son to take his place between them. Though he briefly obliged, it wasn't long before he stood up and announced that he wasn't interested in watching television with his parents anymore. He preferred to spend the evening in his room, at his computer. With that he made his exit, leaving his mother and father a family of two.

Welcome to the world of teenage children and their shell-shocked parents.

## The Storm Before the Quiet

A father of seven commented that he and his wife regard as their "glory years" those in which all of their children were out of diapers and not yet adolescents. The downside of changing diapers many times daily is self-evident, but the challenges of adolescence are more complex. First, the double meanings of caring and criticizing that complicate everything said in a family kick in with a vengeance. As children are beginning to find their way in the world on their own, parents see an ever-growing need to provide guidance. But the children's view is very different, as Emily Anning, at fifteen, explained from the perspective of her friends: "Their mom tries to give them helpful advice that's critical advice. Especially if they know it might be true, they're hurt by it, so they get mad."

Parents' jobs heat up when children become teenagers and get more and more involved in the world outside the home. (Indeed, many teenagers seem to be focusing all their energy on spending as much time as possible outside the home.) So parents feel more than ever the need to protect their children and teach them what they need to know to function in society. Yet just as the need to protect them from harm becomes especially urgent, children are least open to instruction and protection. As a result, it becomes harder and harder to find the right balance between connection and control.

Teenage years can be like the storm before the quiet—the storm created by these conflicts before the (relative) quiet when children move out on their own. I asked a father of adult children what it's like having his children grown. He said, "It's great, because I can just enjoy them, and not have to be teaching them all the time." This father was expressing his pleasure at moving toward a relationship more focused on equality rather than hierarchy, socializing with his children—enjoying their company—rather than having to instruct, take care of, and worry about them. He recalled that the switch occurred around the last year of high school and the first years of college—toward the end of their teenage years.

Parents spend the first dozen years of their children's lives taking care of them; you might say they are in a caretaking frame, where *frame* refers to the larger goal or activity speakers are engaged in when they say or do something. As children get older the emphasis gradually shifts to enjoying their company, a socializing frame. But the shift can't happen overnight: You don't go to sleep one night in the caretaking frame and wake up the next morning in a socializing frame, the way Dorothy finds herself in Oz rather than Kansas. There is a period when it's all a muddle—you can't figure out which frame you think you're in, which your child thinks you're in, and which you should be in.

Students in one of my seminars were discussing this dilemma. A woman whose own children were still in elementary school pointed out that teenagers want to be equals in a socializing frame but their parents put them in a caretaking frame. The stepmother of a teenage daughter reminded her: But when you treat them as equals in the socializing frame, they want to get back into the caretaking frame—to be taken care of.

Parents hope to get from children what children crave from parents: unconditional love and approval. And most parents (or grandparents or other adults in the caretaking role) get it, more or less, until the children become teenagers. Then it vanishes. Suddenly nothing a parent says or does is right. "If I say one thing," a mother says of her teenage daughter, "she'll be crushed. If I say another, she'll be angry. If I say nothing, she'll know I disapprove. And if I praise her, it seems to make her angriest of all. 'You can't judge!' she says. 'You're completely biased!' " It's an acute case of "I can't even open my mouth."

Linda Lehr also recalls that her daughter Emily objected to being praised as much as to being criticized: "She'd say, 'I don't like it when you think I'm so smart and so pretty and I'm so good at things.' " Linda finally figured out that Emily objected to her parents' praise for the same reason that she began doing her usual top-notch job on homework—then refusing to hand it in. She didn't want to feel better than her peers. And she heard her parents' praise as an attempt to distance her from her friends. Emily, too, was struggling to find her balance: If she was smarter than her peers, she wasn't as close to them, and fitting in was her most important goal. (Eventually, with Linda's help, she found a way to be close and fit in without hiding her abilities: She started a peer-tutoring program.)

For their part, parents are hurt by their teenage children's judgment of them. "Don't you have any jeans?" one boy asked of his father, who he thought dressed too conservatively. "I can't go to the beach with you," a girl told her mother, "because you don't shave your legs." I recall the depth of humiliation I felt as a teenager when my mother chewed gum and folded it over between her teeth—her front teeth! It was as if the world was shining a spotlight on me, and my mother was in the spotlight with me, so any failing would be exposed to universal scrutiny. Teenagers judge their parents harshly because they themselves are feeling so harshly judged by the world. But for parents the pain of being judged by a family member is compounded by the shock of reversal: The child you always protected and cared for is now installed as your judge.

Another reversal takes place around this time, too. The world into which children are born is wildly different from the one their parents know. Parents take for granted that their greater experience in life gives them a perspective that their children lack and can benefit from, and in many ways this is true. But in other ways the world in which parents' experience was gained is so different from their children's that the parents' wisdom isn't of much use. For example, Albert Macovski, professor of electrical engineering and radiology at Stanford University, recalls that his parents warned him he'd be making a big mistake if he went ahead with his plans to become an electrical engineer because it was too hard to get into the electricians' union. Working-class immigrants from Poland, his parents had only one frame associated with things electrical. The worlds of engineering and of universities were outside their experience.

Although this confusion was particularly apt to occur in an immigrant family, the rapid development of technology and the equally rapid evolution of society turn almost all families into cross-cultural experiences, with parents and children having grown up in different worlds. In many middle-class American households a child as young as eleven is the in-house authority on the family computer, which baffles and confounds parents who are helpless before it. My father, at ninety, commented to me, "I used to explain things to you; now you are always explaining things to me." This reversal becomes overwhelming as parents age, but it begins when children are in their teens—their *early* teens.

## "What Are You, Crazy?" Conflicting Assumptions, Clashing Frames

"Someday you will realize I have clay feet," my father wrote me recently on e-mail—that magical medium that opens up new lines of communication—"and then you'll be disappointed." He was responding to the love and admiration that I was using e-mail to express. "Don't worry," I replied by return message. "I know about your clay feet. When I was a teenager, that's all I saw."

For example, during my last term at college (I was twenty: no longer a teenager but close) I shared an apartment off campus with two female classmates. After I graduated I lived for several months in my parents' home, where my mail was duly forwarded. One day a letter arrived addressed to Jay Lovinger, c/o me. My father, normally an oasis of rationality and calm, was beside himself.

I could not understand what upset him. I explained the situation: Jay wasn't my boyfriend; he was just a friend (in fact, a friend of my boyfriend, who had graduated the year before). Jay had returned for a visit to campus. Because my roommates and I lived in an apartment rather than a dorm, he stayed with us, "crashing" on our living room couch. This explanation did not pacify my father. I pressed: What possible harm could come from my receiving a letter addressed to Jay? My father offered the following scenario: Someday I would meet a boy I wanted to marry. The postman would tell the boy's parents that I had received a letter addressed to another boy in care of me, and they would not let him marry me.

My father has no memory of this; he laughs when I recount it. "That's ridiculous," he says, which is certainly what I thought at the time—though then his (rare) anger as well as his illogic sent me into a tailspin. Looking back, I now understand that he was speaking in code to refer to a world order that had made sense in his time. In my father's youth, young men and women had friends of the same sex and sexual attachments to members of the other sex. The idea of young women and men being just friends made no sense to my parents; there was nothing in their experience to prepare them to understand it. So a friendship with a boy was ipso facto sexual, and this, ipso facto, threatened my life chances. To my parents, my happiness would be determined by whether or not I married, and my marriageability depended on my virginity. Receiving a letter addressed to a boy in care of me was code for having had sex. In my sixties world (the year was 1966), friendships between young men and women were common; virginity was not a requisite for marriage anyway; and early marriage was not a requisite for happiness. (Quite the opposite, with half of all marriages ending in divorce, a wedding hardly meant a happily-ever-after guarantee.)

My father and I could not work out our conflict at the time because the dispute was over bedrock assumptions about how the world worked. Put another way, receiving that letter called into play fundamentally clashing frames for male-female relations. Even as we stood in the same room, we were standing on completely different ground.

## Clashing Frames, Isolating Alignments: Every Teen Is an Island

I still recall the letter incident because I was so baffled by it, and so infuriated by my father's irrationality. Many arguments between parents and teenage (or young-adult) children can be traced to the irrationality that each sees in the other. Often that impression grows out of clashing frames—differing sets of expectations or assumptions—that come of having grown up in different worlds.

When the teenager is female, the unstated (or stated) issue is often sex. Parents see their daughters' sexual vulnerability, but protecting them entails curtailing their freedom—and this is the aspect against which many daughters rebel. And here is an arena in which gender inequality becomes inescapable. Fifteen-year-old Emily Anning put it succinctly: "Parents are less strict with boys. They let them stay out later and go places more. With girls, it's 'Whose house are you gonna be at, where are you going?' Boys have more freedom."

Given this backdrop, one of the biggest sources of conflict between teenage girls and their parents is dating. Let's start with a fairly tame example. This conversation took place in a blended family: Denise, who is fourteen; Denise's father, Jim; and Jim's wife, Anna (who is not Denise's mother). There is another family member present—Jim's twenty-four-year-old daughter from his first marriage—but she takes only a small part in the conversation.

Alignments are key in this conversation, in addition to framing. Denise is the center of attention—wrapped in connection. But she is also isolated, in a way, by the alignments created. Throughout this discussion Denise's father, stepmother, and half sister are aligned with each other first because they have experience dating, which they draw on in giving Denise advice, but also because they share assumptions about dating. So alignments result from the patterns of framing: both the framing of the adults as givers of advice and Denise as receiver (placing her in a one-down position) and their common experience of the world and how it works.

This is how the different assumptions about dating surface. A homecoming dance is coming up at Denise's all-girl school. She wants to go with a particular boy, but she hasn't asked him yet. In fact, she's hardly spoken to him. Her stepmother, father, and half sister all agree: She should talk to the boy first, then decide whether to invite him to the dance. Denise resists; she clearly assumes that it is not required or appropriate for a girl who likes a boy to talk to him. This fundamental difference in framing—in their assumptions and expectations about male-female relations—is what makes the conversation go round and round like a carousel, the same words continuously replaying.

(Readers will find one or the other assumption more reasonable depending on their age or experience with children of this age. One mother was surprised when her eleven-year-old daughter announced she had a boyfriend, but she was even more surprised to learn that they had never spoken. *Boyfriend* meant that her daughter liked the boy—from a distance. It was a category that had meaning for the girls who talked to each other about which boys they liked.)

The conversation begins when Jim asks Denise, "What are you planning to do with Ben? Because if you don't ask him today, there's no point." His wife, Anna, then says, "Denise doesn't even know him, Jim. She hasn't even talked to him!" Denise objects, "Yes, I have, a few times." But when Anna asks, "What have you talked about?" Denise replies with the noncommittal teenage opener "Oh, what's up?"

" 'What's up?' " Jim asks. "What else?"

Denise disappoints him by laughing. "He just looks at me."

Then Anna reasserts her view: "I know. She doesn't even— You won't even say 'hi' to him."

Jim suggests that Denise "just go and have fun," but Denise says she doesn't want to go to the dance alone. Anna points out that Denise's friend Melissa will be there, but Denise says that Melissa is going with "a good friend of hers that's a guy." This gives Anna the opportunity to reinforce her assumption: "See? So she *talks to* boys."

Denise then asks all the adults present—her father, her stepmother, and her older half sister—how they got their first dates. They all recall that the dates were with people they already knew—people they had talked to. Then Anna and Jim continue to give Denise advice, predicated on the same assumption. Jim reminds her, "You haven't talked to him so far and I've been—we've been encouraging you for some weeks."

"How do you know he's not a jerk?" Anna asks. "You've never talked to him." Later she repeats, "I think you should talk to him even before you think about asking him, Denise."

Jim then offers a specific plan: "Maybe you should do this. Suppose you were to *talk* to him tonight, and I don't mean 'Hello how are you?' but I mean like corner him and talk to him, and talk about things, and we've given you enough topics, and then, like, then maybe calling?" Turning to Anna, he asks, "What do you think? Then she could call him, and ask if he wants to go?"

In reply, Anna goes back to her main point: "I think she needs to talk to him."

The conversation takes on an almost comic character as the adults repeat each other's words, reinforce each other's views, and generally align with each other to advise Denise based on their frame: Girls and boys first get to know each other by talking, and then—only then—one invites the other to a dance. But the adults never succeed in getting Denise to accept their view, nor do they learn why she resists, or whether this is how it is done in Denise's group.

In reading the transcript I kept wishing that the adults would take a break from telling Denise what to do and spend some time asking her about the world she lives in. It's easy to understand why they don't; that's the nature of assumptions: They seem self-evident, so you don't question them and don't think to explain them. But therein lies a key to conversations between adults and teens: To the extent that the adults have more experience of the world, it is quite right for them to give advice. But to the extent that the world in which teens move is a different one from the world of adults—different even from the world in which adults were teens—it would be helpful for adults to ask their teenage children to explain (insofar as they can) the world as they see it. After listening and grasping the way this world works, adults will be in a better position to offer advice that might actually be taken.

In the end Denise solved the problem in her own way—a rather ingenious way, taking advantage of telephone technology. She did call the boy she was interested in, but it was a three-way call, with a friend silently on the line. When Denise learned that the boy already had a date for homecoming, she went to the dance with a boy she had known for a long time, just as her friend Melissa did. So Denise took the advice of her father and stepmother by calling the boy she liked and by going to the dance with a boy she already knew. But she did not try to get to know the first boy before asking him, and she found the courage to make the call by enlisting the support of a close friend in a way the adults had not thought of.

Considering the unanimity with which the three adults aligned—not intentionally but just because they shared both experience dating and assumptions about male-female relations—you get a glimpse of how a teenager might feel like the lone member of a tribe living in a family where everyone else speaks a different language.

## "I Don't Know What You Thought It Would Be": What's a Date?

When a girl enters her teen years, nothing can spark as much conflict as relations with boys, given the complex interweaving of social pressure, the girl's longing for attention and approval from her peers, and the parents' responsibility to protect their child from premature sexual experience.

The PBS documentary *An American Love Story,* which follows a year in the lives of Karen Wilson, Bill Sims, and their two daughters, offers a rare opportunity to listen in on a dispute about just this issue. We heard, in Chapter 5, the conversations in which Karen was questioning twelve-year-old Chaney, who had just returned from her first "date"—a brief walk in the park with a boy. Now let's listen in on the negotiations, which continued over several days, that led up to that date. A student in my seminar, Alla Yeliseyeva, examined what Karen and Chaney said during that difficult time. Mother and daughter were speaking from completely different frames—contrasting (and conflicting) sets of assumptions about what Chaney would do when meeting the boy.

Unlike Denise in the previous example, Chaney had talked to "the boy" (as he is referred to throughout), but she had never seen him. They had been introduced by her best friend, Nelly, and had become acquainted by telephone. Chaney has now arranged to meet the boy in person: They have set a time and date for him to come to their home. On this, mother and daughter agree. But it emerges that they have very different ideas about what will happen next—clashing frames, or conflicting expectations, about what sort of date is planned. Karen expects the meeting between Chaney and the boy to be rather like a play date, in which two children get together in one child's home, with a parent present. Chaney's idea is more like an adult date, in which a boy comes to a girl's home and takes her out.

These clashing frames first come to light as Karen asks when the boy is coming and remarks, "I get to see him? We'd better not eat all the snacks Daddy bought for you all." Chaney's response catches her mother off guard:

CHANEY: We are not staying here.
KAREN: What do you mean?
CHANEY: Huh?
KAREN: What do you mean you are not staying here? Who said that you could go on the street with the boy?
CHANEY: Uh-oh! [*laughing*]
KAREN: Ah-ah! [*laughing*]

Though mother and daughter are laughing at this point, they do not keep laughing for long; it soon becomes clear how deep and irreconcilable their clashing frames are. Chaney says, "I thought you said I could."

"I did not say that you could," Karen clarifies. "I said, 'Bring him here, we're going to look him over.' "

Trying to accommodate her daughter's wish not to stay home with the boy, Karen suggests that she could go with them—a reasonable enough plan for two children but unacceptable given Chaney's idea of her date.

"No, please don't follow me!" Chaney wails—reframing the meaning of "going with" (a connection maneuver) to "following" (a control maneuver).

Karen points out this discrepancy: "I am going *with* you. I'm not following you."

But Chaney persists in rejecting the proposal: "No, please don't go with me. Please! Please!"

In frustration Karen says, "I don't know what you thought it would be." The answer, unstated, is "a date"—in the adult sense. Because Chaney never wavers from this assumption, and Karen never wavers from her assumption that Chaney is too young for that type of date, their negotiations take on a repetitive and circular character, like the conversation between Denise and her family about the homecoming dance.

Implicit in Karen's and Chaney's conflicting frames for Chaney's date is a second clashing assumption: In the caretaking frame Karen feels she needs to be present to protect her daughter, who, at twelve, is still a child, though she looks much older than her age. But Chaney knows one thing for sure: She does not want her mother there. At the same time Karen probably feels hurt because Chaney is distancing from her. These conflicting frames play a role in Karen's assumption that Chaney will entertain her guest at home, as opposed to Chaney's assumption that home is the last place she wants to be for this important encounter.

The matter is not settled in this conversation. Because the different perspectives are not opinions but assumptions—expectations that are taken for granted—they are difficult to articulate. They are like rocks in the road that mother and daughter keep stumbling over.

"What's the matter with your home?" Karen asks.

"I don't want to stay here," Chaney answers, though this isn't really an answer.

"Yeah, just tell me why," Karen presses.

"Because you're here," Chaney answers, honestly.

Karen suggests, "What if we stay in back?"

This does not satisfy Chaney, who responds, "You are still *here*."

At this Karen is incredulous: "We are supposed to go away and let you and the boy be in the house alone?"

"No, I didn't say that," Chaney replies. It's true; she didn't. What she said was that she wants to go out with him, alone.

The interchange that follows captures dramatically the contrasting assumptions that underlie everything Karen and Chaney say. The activities Karen proposes all come from the play-date frame. Chaney rejects Karen's suggestions because they do not fit the adult dating frame.

In trying to explain why she wants to go out with the boy rather than entertain him at home, Chaney asks a rhetorical question: "What's the good of him coming if we can't do anything?"

Karen tries to come up with things they could do. "You could play Ouija board," she suggests.

"Oh no!" Chaney rejects that idea.

"You could eat," Karen goes on. "You could listen to records, you could watch TV."

Chaney greets these suggestions with sarcasm: "Oh, what fun!"

"Isn't that what you normally do?" her mother asks.

"At home, yeah," Chaney says, unconvinced.

Still trying to get Chaney to explain her basic assumption, Karen asks, "Okay, so what is so important about us being here?"

Unable to explain, Chaney ends the conversation in a way that teenagers often end conversations with adults: "Nothing," she says. Then she says: "I— Never mind." And she walks out of the room.

If Chaney doesn't (or can't) explain to her mother why she is determined not to entertain the boy at home, neither does Karen explain to Chaney why it is not acceptable for her to go to the park with him. Karen just repeatedly reminds Chaney, "You're twelve years old!" To Karen, this is prima facie evidence that it is not appropriate for Chaney to be alone, unsupervised, with a boy.

Because this disagreement grows out of conflicting frames—differing assumptions about what kind of "date" Chaney should have—talking about it just leads to angrier and angrier fights, as neither puts into words the basis for her assumptions. What Karen doesn't say, probably because she thinks it's obvious, is that being alone with a boy would put Chaney at risk for sexual behavior she is not old enough to handle. What Chaney doesn't say is that having her parents there to protect her sends a metamessage that she is a child just when she wants to feel grown up. Like many teenagers, she probably feels she can't be herself, her own whole person, if her parents are watching. (In the end, as we saw in Chapter 5, the boy failed to appear when the family was gathered to greet and entertain him at home. Instead he showed up unannounced on another day—and Chaney went for a walk with him to the park.)

## "Why Not Bring Them Here?" To Go Out or Stay at Home

The battle over going out versus staying home is one waged in many families with teenage children. A mother who had always made birthday parties for her children at home was baffled when her son insisted on taking a group of friends to a bowling party—and didn't want his mother there. A mother whose daughter insists on meeting her friends at the local Starbucks suggests, "I can make you coffee here"—and is met with a look of devastating disdain from her daughter, to whom coffee is not the point: getting out of the house is.

All these conflicts arise because the parents are in the caretaking frame—just the frame their teenage children want to escape. Parents want teenagers to stay home to make sure they're safe. But teenagers feel they can't be themselves at home; just having their parents there means they're being treated like children—the metamessage they most want to avoid.

In addition to worrying about their safety, parents are reeling from being rejected by the children whose love they had taken for granted. When a teenager stalks out of the house, refuses to go on the family vacation, or retreats to a bedroom and slams the door, parents are hurled back to their own teenage years, when they felt rejected by the peers who counted most, and nothing they did seemed to measure up. Once again a father is the geeky boy who gets the cold shoulder from the pretty girl, or he's the clumsy kid the boys choose last for their team. Once again a mother is the girl left out when the popular girls have a sleepover party, or she's the wallflower no boy will ask to dance.

## A Monster in the House: Mothers and Teenage Daughters

Though teenage years are difficult for almost all families, there is a special circle of purgatory reserved for mothers and their teenage daughters. In her song "Different Tunes," the folksinger and songwriter Peggy Seeger captures this unique drama, especially the scene in which the daughter is perennially walking out:

> Why won't you tell me where you go?
> Wish for once you'd stay at home.

Herself the mother of a daughter (as well as two sons—so she knows how the struggles differ), Seeger explains that she based her song both on her experience with her own daughter and on "conversations with other mothers and their teenage daughters. Most of the mothers said the same thing: at somewhere between eleven and sixteen, their daughters turned into monsters." But the assessment was mutual: "The majority of the daughters referred to their mothers as ferocious, interfering, dictatorial, judgmental, et cetera—i.e., monsters." (Reassuringly, Seeger notes that in most cases, including her own, the war ended in mutual peace within three or four years—but an awful lot of suffering can result from three or four years of war.)

Seeger's song presents the mother's and daughter's views in counterpoint. The lines just quoted come in a verse in which the mother describes how her daughter appears to her:

> Dressed in black from head to toe,
>   talks for hours on the phone.
> Why won't you tell me where you go?
>   Wish for once you'd stay at home.
> Looks at me so blank and cold,

a look that cuts me to the heart.
Where's the child, the friend I had,
the daughter like the morning star?

As Seeger describes it, the mother is mourning the loss of closeness ("Where's the friend I had?"). This closeness is just what the daughter is casting off, as her refrain reflects:

I can take care of myself, you know.
I'm not a baby now. Leave me alone.

Though the daughter doesn't want the displays of connection and affection that frame her as a child, she does want the caretaking a child is entitled to. The mother's voice says:

Shakes me off when I try to touch her,
throws herself at all the boys,
just can't think with her music blaring,
she can't live without that noise,
I'm in the kitchen making dinner,
washing dishes, in the dirt,
"Mum, have you seen my satin blouse
and fixed the zipper on my skirt?"

In a sense, mother and daughter are holding the same elephant leg, but they are grasping it from different angles. As the mother is wondering, "Where's my child?" the daughter is protesting, "I'm not a child anymore."

In addition to mourning the loss of closeness to her daughter, the mother is concerned about her daughter's safety—in particular regarding her sexual vulnerability. These two concerns dovetail when the daughter leaves the house:

Where are you going? When will you be back?
You're surely not going out looking like that?

"Like that" usually means wearing skirts too short, pants too tight, and blouses too revealing—in a word, looking too sexy.

(One mother recalls the helpless dread she felt seeing her daughter walk out in a see-through lace blouse—with nothing but her bare skin under it.)

The daughter, knowing what her mother means, sings:

> Mum goes all coy about the boys.
> She thinks I do more than
>     I do.

(This line took me right back to my father's distress at my receiving a letter addressed to Jay Lovinger in care of me.)

Seeger's song captures the hurt caused on both sides by the clashing frames: The daughter wants to be treated like an equal while the mother sees she still needs protection. And the daughter wants to put distance between herself and her mother, who defines their relationship by its closeness.

## "Mum Thinks We're Doing It All the Time": Love or Promiscuity?

There is evidence that the same clashing frames are causing tremors in families around the world. Peggy Seeger was raising her daughter in London. The situation is similar in Sweden, according to a glimpse we get in an article by Swedish sociolinguists Karin Aronsson and Ann-Christin Cederborg.

The conversations that Aronsson and Cederborg examine took place during family therapy sessions involving a fourteen-year-old girl called Lisa, her mother, and a therapist. Much of the dispute involves Lisa's boyfriend, Erik. In addition, the mother complains that Lisa "has terrible aggressions," "becomes very angry," and refuses to obey the rules her mother sets. (For example, Lisa takes the 11:00 P.M. bus home rather than the 8:30 bus she is supposed to take.)

The researchers point out that the disputes about time and rules reflect two different stories by which mother and daughter interpret Lisa's relationship with Erik: The mother sees her daughter's actions as part of a promiscuity story, whereas the daughter sees them as part of a love story. *Story* in this sense is another way of talking about frames—sets of assumptions and expectations that give an overall meaning to what is said or done. By seeing herself as a heroine in a love story, Lisa interprets her own actions as she would those of an adult in a committed romantic relationship—or a marriage. She wants to escape her mother's control. Seeing her daughter's actions as evidence of promiscuity, her mother is in a caretaking frame, attuned to her daughter's sexual vulnerability.

These different story lines, or clashing frames, account for many of the conflicts that Lisa and her mother reveal in the therapy session. The mother, for example, worries that Erik, who is seventeen, "exploits her to do certain things and I think that he perhaps exploits her sexually, and that's what I wish to protect her from." But the act of protecting her daughter frames Lisa as incapable of taking care of herself—an insult, from Lisa's point of view. Her mother makes it explicit: "She's so weak that she can't resist."

Lisa's response is as passionate as it is inarticulate: "You are really all blown in your head." More specifically, she protests, "I don't obey him. I do what I like."

Her mother, however, remains adamant: "He has an enormous influence on you."

Also at issue is the amount of time Lisa spends with Erik. "I think it's really strange that it has to be that often," the mother says.

Lisa retorts, "But you see your husband every day." In other words, Lisa frames herself and Erik as a couple in love, comparable to a married couple.

Another aspect of time that looks different to mother and daughter is how long the pair have been a couple. "I've been with him a really long time," Lisa says. But she finishes the sentence with an embarrassed laugh: "all of three months." And that is where the love story gives way to a promiscuity story, as her mother adds, "Compared to others, well you know that's an eternity."

Time has very different meanings for mother and daughter in another way, too. The mother believes that there are times of day when her daughter should not be with her boyfriend—late at night (which is why she wants her to come home on the 8:30 bus) and during school hours. The daughter protests that she visits her boyfriend only during free periods (after all, that's why they're called free—you're supposed to be able to do what you want) and only when he is ill (though she admits, under pressure from her mother, that he has been "ill" quite a lot lately).

The disputes about time also reflect the mother's concern about Lisa having sex with Erik. In Lisa's view, "it doesn't really matter what time it is." She tells the therapist that she has decided not to have intercourse with Erik and that she has the strength to say no, but "Mum thinks we're doing it all the time." Proceeding from her frame, Lisa sees herself as an adult in love who is able to judge when to see her boyfriend. Proceeding from the caretaking frame, her mother sees her as a child who should be in school during the day and who will be more vulnerable to sexual exploitation at night.

Aronsson and Cederborg cannot know whether or not Lisa has had sex with Erik, though they note that her protest could imply that they do it, just not "all the time." Part of Lisa's outrage comes from the metamessage of her mother's disapproval, and also from what she sees as irrationality in her mother's assumption that sex is determined by the hour of day. Yet what else do parents have to go on if not the hours that their daughter is out and the way she behaves—openly rebellious or obedient and respectful? Still, these clues do not always lead to accurate conclusions.

Two sisters, now in their fifties, laughed as they told me how misguided their own parents had been. One was the "good girl" who never disobeyed; she wore clothes her parents approved and went on proper dates with neatly dressed boys who picked her up and returned her home at appropriate hours. The other sister was the "bad girl" always at war with their parents as she dressed in her father's old shirts (this was the sixties) and ran around Greenwich Village at all hours of the night. The reason they laughed, in retrospect, was that the good girl was having sex with her well-dressed boyfriends during respectable hours, and the bad girl was spending the disreputable wee hours with a group of friends listening to poetry readings and singing folk songs in dimly lit cafés. (On the happy-ending side, both sisters turned out just fine, as far as I could tell.)

Now that I am an adult listening in on these conversations involving teenage girls and their mothers, I see the mothers' point of view most clearly: The girls seem so vulnerable to sexual exploitation, I want to shout, "Wait, just wait! There will be plenty of time when you get older to have a boyfriend and fall in love."

But I also remember how lonely I felt when I was a teenager. The only ones who understood were my friends—and the Beatles, who sang the line I loved because it reflected how I felt: "She's leaving home after living alone for so many years." They got it!—how living "at home" actually felt like living alone. My parents had each other, but I had no one who cared more about me than about anyone else in the world—and no one, it seemed, who spoke the same language I did.

In retrospect, I think it would have gone a long way if I had reason to believe that my parents understood the way I felt, but I never tried to tell them. I have no memory of their asking me, either. Understanding each other's point of view is a goal nowhere in evidence in these conversations between teenagers and adults. The teens are focused on escaping their parents' control and disapproval, and the adults are understandably focused on getting the teens to behave in ways that keep them safe. But that goal might be more easily reached if the adults tried to understand why their children act—and feel—the way they do, and let them know that they understand.

## "You Guys Are Living in the Past": The Sound of Two Frames Clashing

It is not only teenage girls who throw families into a war zone. Teenage boys do, too, though the behavior in dispute tends to be different—focused less on sex, more on rule breaking, but similarly on the hours and the company they keep and how they spend their time. For example, let's listen in on an Australian family that was televised for a documentary shown on public television in Australia and Britain. David Lee, a University of Queensland professor, analyzed an argument among the mother, Noeline; Larry, her live-in partner; and Michael, her son from a previous marriage.

The argument erupts as Noeline, Larry, and Michael are planning a party to celebrate Michael's sixteenth birthday. Once again, as Lee shows, the key to the conflict is clashing frames—in this case contrasting expectations for parties—that grew out of different experiences of the world. Michael wants someone posted at the door to turn away uninvited guests. Noeline and Larry fear that physical violence might erupt, and they repeatedly warn that they don't want any fighting in their house. The dispute never gets settled because the clashing frames go unstated.

The trouble starts during an amicable discussion about the upcoming party, when Michael mentions that he will ask his older brother, Paul, to come over and guard the door, "so people don't crash the party." Noeline assures him, "They won't crash the party, sweetheart. You can easily put them off." This basic difference is the one that drives everything said thereafter. And right there at the start, Michael expresses a conviction that threads through the dispute: The adults are speaking from knowledge of a world long past. "Oh yeah, yeah, maybe twenty years ago, Mum," he says. "Today if— There'd be easy another forty people if you didn't have a person at the gate."

You can see right here why the conflict won't easily be resolved. Michael is *assuming* that a party requires someone to turn away uninvited guests at the door. We know it's an assumption—something he takes for granted—by the way he raises the issue. Contrast it with how he asked, earlier, "And can I have a DJ too? Is that okay?" Asking permission to have a DJ indicates that Michael knows the idea might meet with disapproval; it's negotiable. In contrast he does not seem to foresee that asking Paul to guard the gate will be problematic. He takes it for granted as part of his "party frame."

But Noeline has no such expectation. The progressing argument can be traced to that spark. Again and again, as their conversation repeats itself like a tape loop, Michael's conviction persists that his parents don't understand the world he lives in because their experience is of a different world.

## Sarcasm, Threats, and the End of Communication

Listening to the argument that ensues, you'll hear all the tactics we saw in Chapter 3 that get in the way of settling family arguments: sarcasm, yelling, and insults in place of explaining assumptions and separating messages from metamessages.

Noeline challenges Michael's idea of having Paul guard the gate. "Don't you think," she asks, "it's a little bit dramatic saying you've got to have a bouncer at a private person's party?"

Rather than explaining further, Michael responds with sarcasm ("Okay. Fine. We'll leave the gate open") and an implied threat: "You just see. You—you think I'm so stupid. But if you—you look around and open your eyes, you'll see. We'll wait till the night."

What really angers Michael is the metamessage ("You think I'm so stupid"). He's got a point. The adults won't take his word for what is needed or appropriate at his party. Michael resorts to sarcasm because he doesn't seem able to explain his assumption, other than to say he'd be embarrassed.

In a later conversation Larry questions Michael about how many guests he's planning to invite and repeats his concern that the party not turn violent. (The emotional temperature is turned up, as he uses the curse *bloody.*) "This is our home," Larry says. "We're certainly not going to start bloody having fights or bloody well trouble in this joint." He goes on to say that if there might be fighting, the party will be called off "because the cops will only come once or twice. Then they'll leave you on your own, if you keep ringing them, if there's trouble here."

Michael again responds with sarcasm, casting Larry's image as ridiculous: "Oh yeah, there's going to be gang warfare in my backyard, is there?" Here, as throughout the episode, Michael maintains that there will be no fighting, but by using sarcasm, he ensures that Larry will be angered rather than reassured.

When Noeline asks, outright, "Why do you need a bouncer at the gate?" Michael tries to explain: "I'm just saying, well say I invite three guys, they bring a friend along. He's—he's a guy that I don't like . . ."

To Larry the solution is simple: "Well tell them not to bring friends, you've invited them." Noeline repeats Larry's words, linguistically creating their alignment as a team against Michael: "Tell them not to bring friends."

Noeline and Larry's advice sounds reasonable enough, but apparently it seems unthinkable to Michael, who replies, "Oh, how am I going to do that?" Larry begins to shout that if everyone is going to bring friends, then there isn't enough room. Ironically, this is exactly Michael's point. But rather than saying so, Michael replies, "Forget about it, man. You're an idiot, man." By introducing an insult into the argument, Michael pretty much guarantees what comes next: Noeline shouts at her son for calling Larry an idiot. Then Michael walks out.

Michael's outburst is reminiscent of Lisa telling her mother "You are really all blown in your head." And walking out of the room is just what Chaney did when she couldn't explain to her mother why she wanted to go out with the boy rather than entertain him at home. I suspect that teenagers become verbally abusive—or sullen and uncommunicative—because they can't explain their frames in a way that makes sense to their parents. In this conversation Michael's frustration is understandable, because his parents keep insisting that he limit the number of guests at his party but reject the way he proposes to do this.

The topic comes up again later. "We had your damn party over at the park," Noeline says. "We didn't have gate-crashers."

"Party over at the park," Michael replies. "How old was I, Mum? Eight?"

"Six," says Noeline.

By harking back to a party Michael had when he was six, Noeline is pretty much admitting that she has no reference point for the kind of party he might have now. Absurd as this sounds from Michael's point of view, parents who have been giving parties and caring for their children for so many years would understandably assume that what worked in the past should still work. This is just the sense in which children becoming teenagers can find their parents completely unprepared.

Noeline goes on to caution that she doesn't want anything in the house wrecked by fighting, and Michael protests, "All I said is that you got to have someone at the gate to stop people I don't want coming in here. That's all I said. I never said anything about fights."

## What a Difference a Word Makes

Where *did* the idea of fights come from? As David Lee points out in his analysis of this argument, it came from a word.

Recall the first conversation, when Noeline said, "Don't you think it's a little bit dramatic saying you've got to have a bouncer at a private person's party?" Using the word *bouncer* was Noeline's way of showing that she thought Michael's request was silly. (In a similar move Michael said that Larry was predicting "gang warfare in my backyard" to exaggerate and ridicule Larry's concern.) Bars employ bouncers to expel troublemakers when fights break out or threaten to break out. So the idea of fights crept in with Noeline's choice of the word *bouncer*—pulled in tow by association with that word. How frustrating it must have been to Michael, who couldn't point to where that idea came from, other than to say, accurately, that it came from someone's "imagination."

The source of confusion—the associations with the word *bouncer*—is not spoken or traced, so the argument resurfaces and recycles without getting resolved. When Noeline says, "If someone came to my front door to a party that weren't—wasn't meant to be here, I'd go and say, 'You can't come in.' Can't you do that?" Michael simply replies, "You guys are living in the past." When she urges him to make a list of invitees, he writes "NO-ONE" and walks out of the room.

Reading this transcript, I wanted to plunk the parties down and make them lay their frames on the table by putting their differing assumptions into words. Michael knows (or believes), based on experience of the world he lives in, that the only reasonable way to keep unwanted people out of his party is to have someone other than himself turn them away at the door. Noeline and Larry assume that the only reason anyone would need an outsider to turn people away is because they would start fights or destroy property.

Perhaps there is an unspoken association by which a group of boys suggests violence, just as the scenario of a girl alone with a boy suggests sex. In any case, it does seem here that Noeline and Larry don't really listen to Michael. But what good does listening do if you are hearing about a world you have never experienced and cannot imagine?

Michael, Noeline, and Larry were a working-class family living in Australia. Yet the clashing frames for parties that they encountered are strikingly similar to those experienced by an upper-middle-class family living in the affluent Washington, D.C., suburb of McLean, Virginia. With no one at the door to turn away uninvited guests, a teenager's party swelled out of control, more or less as Michael had predicted for his party.

When her daughter Kim was in eighth grade, Terry planned a birthday party for her, just as she had planned parties every year of Kim's life. But the party that resulted was unlike anything Terry had experienced. Although thirty of Kim's friends were invited, sixty youngsters showed up. And there was no way Terry and her husband could keep track of the antics of sixty teenagers fanned out through their home. Plus, here were prepubescent boys attempting to mix with girls exactly as they would with other boys—for example, trying to start a conversation with a girl by throwing food at her. It was a scary evening—and dramatized that when children become teenagers they and their parents are entering a world their parents know little about.

## Whose Side Are You On? How Teens Affect Adults' Relationships

Another key to Michael's dilemma in dealing with his mother, Noeline, and her partner, Larry, is alignment. When all three are present, Noeline aligns herself with Larry by questioning why Michael wants someone at the door and by warning him against violence. Noeline and Larry thus present themselves to Michael as a team, united against him. But when Michael walks out of the room, Noeline shifts her footing. Turning on Larry, she shouts, "For God's sake, he *can* have a bloody birthday party."

Larry retorts, also shouting, "Of course he can. But if there's going to be bloody a million people here, we haven't got the room."

"Of course we haven't got the room," Noeline shouts back. And then she adds, taking her son's side, "He's not stupid." This is just the position Michael was taking earlier: He is responsible enough to know how many people the house can accommodate and should be trusted to keep it to that limit. Even questioning him on this point implies that they think he's "stupid"—that he doesn't see what's obvious.

Now Noeline is aligned with Michael against Larry. She even threatens to leave. "One of these days," she says, "I'll pack me bloody bags and I'm going out of here. Truly. It's more drama living in this house than out of it."

When Larry says (quietly), "I don't know why," Noeline repeats his words, but loudly: "*I* don't know *why.*"

Like so many family members, Noeline really doesn't know why everything leads to a fight. It is painful to see her getting caught between Larry and Michael, between her life partner and her son. But it struck me as sad, too, from Michael's point of view, that he didn't get to see his mother side with him. Such alignments cause children distress in any family, but they carry special weight in stepfamilies. Since Noeline was Michael's mother long before she met Larry, Michael probably feels extra keenly the pain of being isolated when he sees his mother aligned with Larry.

Of the many differences that can lead to friction in families, one of the most potent is disputes about how to deal with children. In the PBS documentary, the mother, Karen Wilson, remarked that when their older daughter, Cicily, was unhappy at college, the father, Bill, was inclined to yield to her desire to drop out, but Karen insisted she stick it out for at least the first year, after which she could, if she liked, transfer to a college closer to home. Karen's own history played a role; her parents had allowed her to drop out of a college she disliked, and she never went back to complete her education. "I fought with Bill much more than with Cicily over not letting her come home," she said.

Karen Wilson and her husband, Bill Sims, had a solid marriage. Indeed, it was their enduring commitment to each other that gave the series its title, *An American Love Story.* Imagine the challenge that teenage children present when parents are already at war. A man who was divorced from the mother of his teenage daughter commented that he and his wife had to be "super-careful" because when they differed about how to deal with their daughter, they had a tendency to lose sight of her entirely: She would become a battleground on which they fought with each other. "Children are sacred territory," he said, "because the stakes are so high."

## Mom and Dad Together—at Cross-Purposes

When there are two adults living with a teenager, the struggles among them are especially complicated because there are three people involved—and, consequently, three separate relationships: one each between an adult and a teen, but also one between the two adults. And relations between the adults are irrevocably altered by their differing reactions to the child.

In homes across the country, if not across the world, arguments like these are wreaking havoc among parents and adolescent children, but it's difficult to pin down how things spiral out of control. Rarely do you get the chance to go back and trace what was said. Once again the television documentary featuring the Loud family provides such an opportunity—a rare glimpse at the shifting alignments among a teenager and his parents.

The conversation we'll look at next is particularly fascinating because on the surface the parents present a united front to their teenage son. But examining the conversation closely shows that, subtly, the parents are at cross-purposes with each other. This pattern takes on special resonance given the knowledge that Bill and Pat have decided to divorce. When one parent tries to pin their son down, the other pries him loose. Watching how this happens allows us to see how shifting alignments, in addition to clashing frames, confound loving parents in their attempt to deal with their teenage son. It also highlights the need for parents to be attuned to each other's ways of talking in addition to their child's.

Bill and Pat Loud are having a talk with their seventeen-year-old son Grant (the third of five children). The summer before his senior year of high school is drawing to a close. Bill had arranged a summer job for Grant in his construction company. But Grant is not showing up for work every day; he is going in only three days a week, and he doesn't want to continue even that. Furthermore, according to Pat (who is home during the day with her children), when Grant is home all he does is play music with his band and hang around the house.

Bill and Pat both disapprove of their son's behavior, but Pat focuses on Grant's behavior at home, while Bill focuses on his behavior at work. Pat and Bill also have different ways of expressing their disapproval. Pat is the direct one, whereas Bill tries to make peace, buffering her criticism but also offering his own in a more indirect way.

## "It's Not That I Don't Want to Work"

Parents and son are sitting beside the family pool in their Santa Barbara, California, home when Bill says, "I was talking with your mother, y'know, and I told her that you weren't very interested in doing any more work."

Grant says, "Um."

To parents of teenagers, especially teenage boys, this response may sound familiar. (One woman who lives with five teenagers—her children and stepchildren—commented that she has become expert at interpreting the grunts of her teenage sons. It's an art, she said—one that reminds her of learning to interpret the sounds her babies made before they could talk.)

Bill continues in a way that has the appearance of support and understanding but also has an unmistakable underlying message of accusation, which Grant picks up. "I don't blame you," Bill says. "I think that's a very honest reaction. There's nothing wrong with that kind of feeling. It's a natural thing to feel like you don't want to work."

Ignoring the apparent support, Grant zeros in on the accusation, and denies it. "Dad," he protests. "I don't—it's not that I don't want to work, it's just a—"

Grant never completes this self-defense, because Pat cuts in and cuts to the chase. "What kind of work did you have in mind, then, Grant?" she asks. "Watching television and listening to records? Playing the guitar? Driving the car? Eating, sleeping?" Her words heavy with sarcasm (that verbal strategy we have seen a lot of), Pat put her finger on what is bugging her.

Now you want to hear what Grant will say in response, but you don't get to, because this time Bill cuts in. "No, uh, listen, Grant," he reassures his son, "you are a very good boy. We are very proud of you."

So Grant doesn't respond to either accusation: his father's that he doesn't want to work or his mother's that he does not do anything constructive when he's home. Nor does he accept his father's reassurance "We are very proud of you." Instead, he responds, "Yeah, I know you're not."

## "That's Where We're Different: I Don't Like to Work"

This pattern repeats itself throughout the conversation. A few turns later Bill indirectly confirms that he is not really proud of his son. Once again he levels a serious accusation, but indirectly. "The way I figure," Bill says, "is that I work like a son of a gun to keep everybody eating and doing and buying the gas and driving the cars, and doing everything they want to do, see? I work like a dog. I work about twelve, fourteen hours a day. Not that I don't—I don't mind it. I *like* to work y'know. I got broken in when I was twelve."

"Well that's where we're different," Grant says. " 'Cause I don't. I don't like to work."

Here is another pattern we saw in Chapter 3—one that turns up in most arguments that go nowhere. Grant picks up on a side point his father made and avoids the main point. When Bill said that he likes to work, he was simply trying to head off the impression that he was complaining or self-pitying. His main point was that people *have* to work in order to live, and Grant is now old enough to pitch in. Grant ignores that point by focusing on whether or not his father *likes* to work. (In the process he contradicts his own earlier denial, "it's not that I don't want to work.")

Once again Bill begins by seeming to accept and approve of Grant's honesty. "Well that's—that's a good natural reaction," he says. He goes on, however, to show that he is neither accepting nor approving: "But if you don't want to work then you shouldn't want all the things that work— Leisure is no fun unless you offset it with a little work."

Then Bill moves on to the point he was getting at: "But Patty and I were talking about your present problem, not wanting to do *anything* this summer. Which is *fine*. That's fine."

Bill frames his disapproval as being in Grant's best interest: that he won't enjoy his leisure if he doesn't work. And Bill calls Grant's not wanting to work "a problem." So when he says (at the start), "That's a good natural reaction," and (at the end) "That's fine," Grant knows it isn't really fine and his father doesn't really think his reaction is good. Grant and his parents clearly have vastly different frames—conflicting assumptions—about how he should be spending his time.

Grant then protests: "I didn't say I didn't want to do anything this summer." So Bill asks what he wants to do. Grant offers a vague denial: "I have been busy all summer."

Instead of asking what he's been busy with, Bill again offers surface reassurance—"Now you have been, I have been very proud of you. I have been *damn* proud of you"—before repeating the question, "But what do you want to do, Grantie?"

Notice that Bill calls his son Grantie—an affectionate nickname—just when he is challenging him most directly. But again, rather than giving Grant a chance to answer, Bill answers for him, suggesting that all Grant wants to do is play with his band. Grant indirectly acknowledges this while anticipating his father's objection: "Every time I say that, you always give me some deal about that's no way to make a living and—"

Grant knows his parents don't approve of what he really wants to do: play music. Once again it's his mother who gets to the point, dismissing his plans to form a band, since the friends he plays music with are no longer in town: "Well 'cause everybody is gone now, let—let's forget the band business anyway." Then she levels a serious accusation: "But the fact is that—when you are home— Well I have a couple of things. First of all, you either have a desperate misunderstanding, or it was an out-and-out blank lie that you told us when you said that you weren't supposed to go back Thursday. Dave was expecting you."

"I said I didn't know I was supposed to go back," Grant replies.

Pat's response is ironic. "Oh," she says, "how can I be wrong all the time?"

Since no one can be wrong *all* the time, Pat's question implies that Grant must be wrong at least *some* of the time—and maybe, just maybe, this is one of those times. But her husband defuses the tension by making a joke: "Well, honey, that happens to all of us at one time or another." They both chuckle at this, dropping the matter of whether Grant was expected back at work when he did not show up.

Pat then returns to the issue most salient for her: Grant's behavior when he is home. She says, "Then when you come home, all you do is sit around and strum that guitar."

"That's not true," says Grant.

Pat concedes, "Okay, you eat a lot, and you sleep a lot."

"No I don't," says Grant.

Pat adds, "And you watch a lot of television."

"No I don't."

"And you don't do anything to help anybody around here," Pat goes on. "Then you get in that car and use Daddy's gas card and go someplace. Now I am getting mad."

Pat builds up to a crescendo when she says, "You're an awful big baby. You really are."

And at that point Bill steps in to buffer the effect of his wife's accusations. "Well, y'know," he contradicts, "he is a good boy and I think that uh—"

Though Pat and Bill ostensibly are aligning with each other in confronting Grant, in fact they work at cross-purposes, as each cuts in when the other is about to demand a response from their son.

## THE UNKINDEST CUT

Finally, Bill issues a challenge. "Grant," he says, "if you don't want to work down there, it's okay, but I think you ought to move down to Mark's or someplace, y'know, and support yourself." With these words, in his calm, nonconfrontational way, Bill makes the strongest threat a parent can wield: He is, in essence, threatening to throw Grant out of the house.

But Bill immediately takes back the threat. He says, "So maybe if you stay here it's okay, but you probably have to get out in the morning and—"

Grant cuts in and says, "Well I'd rather *not* stay here is the whole thing."

Neither Bill nor Pat asks him what he means by that. Instead Bill says, "Well fine, Grantie, that's—I mean, it's your life, I can't control you. I think you are making a *big* mistake by not going along with the program and putting in five days a week in there while everybody—"

Here Grant makes explicit his contrasting assumption: "The program was *three* days a week, which I was *putting in all the time.*"

"That program is *your* program," Bill disagrees. "That wasn't *my* program. And the guy needs you for five days."

At last the unresolved difference is on the table: Grant maintains he was supposed to work only three days a week at the job his father arranged for him, whereas Bill believes it was a full-time job.

## CONFLICTING WORK ETHICS

Underlying this conflict is a deeper difference—conflicting assumptions about work. This emerges in what comes next. Bill asks, "What's wrong with working five days? There's nothing else to do, Grant. Really nothing else to do. You might as well apply yourself."

Grant disagrees: "Well when you are digging *cement* for *five* days a week, you can find something else to do."

Bill responds, "Well for two days—you got two full days off."

*"Oh, two full days!"* Grant scoffs. "Let's not kid each other, Dad."

Here's the rub. To Bill, a man has to work to support his family. Period. Working five days a week with weekends off is normal. To Grant, it's unacceptable to spend five days of his life doing something that's both difficult and meaningless (like "digging *cement*"). That's why "two full days off" sounds absurd to him: The word *full* is trying to make something out of nothing.

Now that Bill has laid his true difference with Grant on the table, guess what happens? Pat cuts in and gets back to her point—how Grant behaves when he's home. She picks up Grant's words to lead him back: "Well let's not kid each other that you've tried to find something else to do."

The conversation ends with Bill proposing a deal: "Why don't we do this, Grant? We've only got two more weeks. Why don't we give it until just the first of September and then quit. How about that? Put in two or three weeks of *five* days a week, and then quit. And then you'll have two weeks. If you want to go on a vacation, I'll promote you to some kind of a vacation or some kind of a trip. 'Cause *school,* Grant, is going to start September the fifteenth."

"You don't think that *I know* that?" Grant replies.

And then Pat says, "Well I really am glad to know that you are going to go down and give it another try. I thought you might feel differently about it."

Grant does not say whether he is buying into the deal or not, though his mother speaks as if he did.

## Just Listen

If clashing frames cause everyone frustration in this as in the earlier example, one reason Grant and his parents made so little headway is that they didn't really listen to each other. They simply rejected claims that conflicted with their own frames. Though their frames—their assumptions about work and the value of activities like playing music—will continue to clash, it would be more constructive to lay those frames on the table, putting assumptions into words. By really listening they could even help each other verbalize assumptions that normally are simply taken for granted as self-evident.

When speakers align with each other, they often repeat each other's words. One way to show you're listening is to repeat the words—or rephrase the ideas—the other person is saying. This provides a firm basis from which to proceed, as each understands the other's position. Much of the looplike character of arguments comes from each person saying the same thing over and over. Once each party has repeated the other's point, the temptation to keep saying it disappears. You have to move to something else—like what to do about it.

In this example Bill and Pat each had slightly different perspectives on Grant's behavior. Though they seemed aligned with each other, in fact each prevented Grant from responding to the other's challenges. They both would have made more headway if each had given the other a chance to pursue his or her argument to a conclusion, forcing Grant to respond.

In the end the parents didn't get a firm commitment from their son to change his behavior. It's important to end a discussion with *all* parties saying outright what action they have agreed upon.

## How Did I Do?

After this discussion the cameras remained with Bill and Pat, who continue talking to each other. Their conversation shows the couple's own uncertainty about how they're handling their jobs as parents. Bill begins, "Well I think we had a very successful talk, Patty. I think we made a few points, don't you?" Pat reassures him: "Yeah, you did very well. I must commend you on that, Bill. You finally did something right."

Ouch. This last remark clearly has a lot of history. Not only Grant's acceptability but also Bill's was on the line in the conversation. I doubt that children suspect the extent to which parents themselves feel they are on shaky ground. And if there are two parents talking, then they are seeking approval from each other at the same time that they are negotiating whether or not they approve of their child.

Bill reveals the logic behind his own approach, which is to stay calm and defuse the situation when Pat gets angry. He says, "Well I always remember when my father used to talk to me, and he used to cry and get so serious y'know, I always—and I always wondered y'know, Why is he crying? y'know. You—you don't listen to people who get that emotional." Pat shares Bill's concern—and self-criticism—as she replies, "That's right. Y'know I just get shrill and mad and—" At this they share laughter, cementing the agreement between them, aligned in their stance toward their son.

Mothers and fathers have good reason to be more worried than ever about whether they are measuring up as parents. The parameters for proper behavior are becoming more and more diffuse, just as more parents work full-time outside the home and there are more influences inside the home over which they have limited control, such as television and the Internet. In addition, psychology, which has become widely established as a popular moral code, holds parents personally responsible for their children's failures and personalities. Bill and Pat Loud, raising teenagers in the early seventies, were swept up in the first wave of this gathering storm.

## The Deny-Everything Approach

Returning to the son's point of view, I was struck by how little Grant revealed about his world. His parents did most of the talking—not surprising, I suppose, since they were the ones who had a complaint about him. Let's look more closely at the verbal maneuvers Grant used in response to his parents' challenge. Then I'll contrast Grant's approach with that of his brother Lance, in a different conversation.

Grant's chief tactic in responding to his parents' accusations was simple: Deny. Deny everything. Here are a few of his responses taken together:

Dad, I don't—it's not that I don't want to work.
I didn't say I didn't want to do anything this summer.
That's not true.
No I don't.
No I don't.
I am *not* trying to run away from responsibilities.
That's not true. That's not true.

By offering denials in place of substantive defenses, Grant gives his parents little to respond to. For their part, they do not encourage him to speak more, nor do they wait to listen to his answers. By working as a team, Bill and Pat actually make doubly sure that Grant does not explain why he acts the way he does and resists acting the way they want him to.

Grant's denials could all be valid, viewed from his frame: He wants to work, to do something, and to be responsible—but it must be work that is personally meaningful. From his parents' point of view, shirking work until you "find yourself" is no different from shirking work, period. If these clashing frames had been verbalized, perhaps his parents could have helped Grant find work he considers meaningful, or demanded he contribute financially, so the need to earn money would take on reality in his own world.

## The Aikido Approach: Don't Deny; Intensify

Grant Loud is one of five children, all teenagers except the oldest, Lance, who has just turned twenty. Lance has recently returned from a stay in New York—and he is unemployed. Whereas Pat and Bill had a joint "talk" with Grant, Pat alone sat down with Lance. But Lance's response was very different from Grant's. Whereas Grant denied every accusation his parents directed at him, Lance used what I call the aikido approach.

Aikido is a self-defense art that turns an attacker's power back against him—not just rolling with the punches but making sure that the attacker hurts himself with the power of his punch. In other words, if someone comes at you full force, and you roll in the direction of the attack and then roll out of the way, the attacker will hit the wall or the ground and hurt himself with all the force that was aimed at you. Just so, Lance accepts and exaggerates his mother's criticisms, leaving her defenseless.

Pat begins with a question not unlike the one she and Bill posed to Grant. "And you," she asks, "what are your plans? I just want to know. Just, y'know, out of idle curiosity."

Of course Pat isn't asking out of "idle curiosity." I suspect she puts it this way to downplay her question so it doesn't come across as too confrontational. Lance makes no attempt to defend himself. "Well," he says, "I really can't think of anything to say about that."

Reminding Lance of his own prior words, Pat says, "You tell a lot of people you are going to San Francisco."

Lance does not try to maintain that his plan makes sense. "I know, that was silly," he says.

Just as Grant has a fantasy of starting a band, Lance has a fantasy about making a film: "I'd like to give the film that I just—I made today—it's gonna be really awe—, it's gonna be so awesome."

Pat throws the cold water of realism onto Lance's plan: "It sounded to me to be, perhaps a bit redundant? Like it might have been done before that—"

Here comes the aikido move: Rather than deny his mother's criticism, Lance embraces it. "Oh God, yes," he says. "That's exactly the way it sounded to me as a matter of fact." He then explains: "But you see, I had written this original plot, but Alonzo was going to star in it, and he didn't want to star."

Pat knows enough about Lance's life to ask a pointed question: "Why did you wait until he left to start it then?"

Again, aikido: Lance agrees, "Yeah, I knew. Well anyway you are right, you are right, and I am to blame as a matter of fact."

Lance then intensifies the reverse pressure on his mother: He turns her criticism of him on this one issue into a general condemnation of his character—and takes it to his bosom. "But still, you know me," he says. "And you've lived with me for twenty years and you know that I screwed up on it." In the aikido spirit, Lance turns Pat's disapproval into something he wants rather than something he denies: "You can feel sorry for me. I mean I love people to feel sorry for me."

"I don't feel sorry for you," Pat says. "I feel a little bit tired."

Now Lance turns the tables as he tells his mother that her approach is ineffective. "But there is no use in feeling tired of something," he says. And when she reframes her stance by saying, "I've been waiting around for you to do something," he simply repeats his advice: "I know, but you see, there is no use in feeling tired."

It's instructive to see how different Lance's approach is from his brother's—yet how similar the effect. Pat gets little resolution from her talk with Lance. It is harder to get angry at someone who uses the aikido approach, because he is not presenting a hard wall of resistance against which you can strike. But the challenge for Pat is much the same: to focus on what actions Lance plans to take in the future.

## Reframing to End the Impasse

In all these examples of parents and teenage children, the conflict could be traced in part to differences in framing—different assumptions about the world that were hard for either party to put into words. If clashing frames hold the key to understanding conflict, then reframing can hold a key to resolving (or at least beginning to resolve) the disputes.

What we are willing to do or not do is shaped by how we define the meaning of that action. Usually it is the metamessage—what it means to us that we do (or someone else does) something—rather than the action itself that determines how we react. Let's take the complaint common among teenagers that their parents nag them. First I'll explain how it works with couples, then I'll show how this insight can help resolve disputes with teenagers.

Many men, when asked the source of dissatisfaction in their marriages, reply, "She nags me." Women rarely make that complaint about men. Instead, one of the chief complaints I hear from women about the men in their lives (and from parents about their teenage children) is that they put off doing what they promised to do. "He started building bookcases for me," one woman said. "I was glad, because we really could use those bookcases. But then he never got around to finishing them, so not only don't I have the bookcases, but I've been stepping over the boards and nails for months. He says he'll do it when he has time, but when he wants to figure out some new computer game, he always has time for that!"

What turns women into nags and men into recalcitrant shirkers? When he volunteered to build her bookcases, she felt loved. But when he put off finishing them, she felt let down: "He doesn't love me as much as I thought; he isn't as 'together' a person as I thought." And even worse: "Oh my gosh, I have a shirker for a husband, so I must not be as valuable a person as I thought." All these doubts lend urgency to her reminders that he finish the job.

But now his radar system begins to beep. "I started this job because I love her and wanted to do something for her, and because I thought it would be fun. But now she's nagging me about it, and that takes the fun out of it. If I hop-to the minute she tells me to do something, I'll be a henpecked husband. So I'm not going to do a stick of work on that bookcase until I'm good and ready!" The more she urges him to finish the job he started, the more he feels that the only way he can avoid being a henpecked husband is *not* doing what she tells him to do. (This is the mutually aggravating spiral I discussed in Chapter 4 as complementary schismogenesis; each person's way of talking drives the other into ever-escalating forms of an opposing behavior.)

Reframing can work magic. Ironically, she would stand a better chance of getting him to do what she wants if she didn't keep reminding him. Then he would feel freer to "choose" to do it himself. Even the most recalcitrant people—teenagers—can change with reframing. Here's an example.

Jennifer wanted permission to go on an overnight trip with a mixed group of friends. Her mother knew that her father would disapprove. In the past she would have argued Jenny's case for her, but doing so put her in an intensely uncomfortable position, caught between her husband and her daughter. So, instead, she told Jenny she would have to get her father's approval herself. Her mother did, however, offer advice: "He gets upset with you when you don't do the dishes right after dinner. And he gets upset when you put off finishing your homework. So before you talk to him, why not do those things, so he'll be in a better frame of mind." Jenny did these things, and it worked. Reframing transformed for Jenny the meaning of doing her homework and her chores. Now she saw these as part of her own strategy to get something she wanted rather than as a response to a parent's nagging.

Parents, too, can act differently if they reframe their view of a situation. Another mother also felt herself caught between her husband and her teenage child. The father was in a permanent state of disapproval because their son never seemed to live up to his potential. He didn't do homework, watched too much TV, stayed out too late with the wrong friends. The father's view was that his son had to shape up, and he never ceased to tell him so. But the son's view was that his father just criticized him all the time.

Both parents met with their son's teachers during an open school night. The mother had prepared for the meeting by asking her son to write out his own assessments of the teachers and what he thought his parents would hear from each of them. He put his teachers into three categories: those he liked and was fairly sure would speak positively, those in the middle, and those at the bottom, whose classes he knew were a big problem. About one teacher he wrote, "She hates me." Sure enough, the meeting with that teacher was not going well. She said that the boy had started out doing fairly well, but as the term progressed he became more of a problem, not applying himself. As the mother listened, her blood pressure rose—not because of her concern for her son's progress but because she could sense her husband's disapproval of their son gaining force with each of the teacher's complaints. She looked at the notes her son had given her and decided to do something dramatic. "Well, let me tell you what he told me," she said to the teacher. "He said you hate him."

This made the teacher draw back in surprise and become defensive. "There are twenty-three students in that class," she said. "I can't give personal attention to each one." But the mother wasn't worried about the teacher's response. She was more focused on her husband's. And the effect on him was remarkable. Seeing the teacher stiffen against his son's honest assessment, he aligned himself with his child rather than with the teacher. "I've noticed something about Sammy," he said. "He does better when he's encouraged." By instigating this realignment, the mother had also inspired a reframing, by which her husband viewed their son's behavior with more understanding and less judgment.

Reframing is key, because it breaks the cycle. A parent disapproves of a child's behavior, but the more he expresses his frustration and tells her how to improve, the more she feels criticized. "Nothing I do is right," she feels, "so why bother?"

Another way to break the cycle harks back to Chapter 3: Instead of arguing against the illogical claims teenagers make, parents might try to understand the logic by which their children's statements make sense to *them*. In some cases parents might talk less and listen more. And in order to show that they've heard, they might repeat back the child's point of view. It's a truism that many teenagers feel misunderstood. They might more readily accept parents' injunctions if they feel their parents have listened and understood their point of view, even if they don't agree with them in the end. (By the same token, it would be fair to insist that children repeat the points being made by the adults they're talking to—though most teenagers can do this anyway.)

Illogical as it may seem, another way to break the cycle is to show more approval rather than less. Candice Carpenter, cofounder and CEO of iVillage.com, an on-line network in which women exchange support, insight, and advice, gives this example: A number of women were exchanging messages about problems with teenagers. They made a pact that for a month they would not criticize their teenage children about anything. You might think this would only make things worse: Without direction and encouragement, why should the children improve? But the effect was the opposite. At the end of the month the teenagers had all improved. The mothers had broken the cycle of disapproval and recalcitrance.

Clearly it is unrealistic to refrain from any kind of criticism, but this is one of many ways that parents can break spiraling cycles. John Anning found another way to break a cycle of frustration with his daughter Emily. "She knew she could yank my chain,"

John recalls, "by saying that she might not go to college; she might just work at Burger King, have a baby, get tattoos and piercings. I'd be alarmed, as she wanted me to be. I'd get indignant—after all we'd provided! I'd try to argue her out of it, and it'd escalate." But one time John didn't bite: "I just said, 'Yeah you could do that. I'll always love and support you whatever you do, though you might want to keep your options open.' " Voilà. When she stopped getting the reaction she sought, Emily stopped making such declarations. John broke the cycle by going along with Emily's scenario rather than opposing it—a kind of aikido approach.

Children, too, can break the cycle. At fifteen Emily Anning commented on herself at twelve: "In seventh grade, I thought I was like old and really cool. . . . I thought I was older than I really was. I thought I was mature enough to do everything, and resented when my mom didn't want me to. She got more protective because I acted like that. I realized I would have more freedom and get to do more things if I didn't fight them."

Parents and teenagers can console themselves that teenage years don't go on forever. (In some families the storm hits later—but then, too, in most cases, it eventually passes.) But the lesson of reframing to find a way out of disputes caused by clashing frames will be of use in all conversations—especially those taking place in the pressure cooker that is family.

## A Brief Interlude II

# "Call Me by My Rightful Name"

IN OUR NAMES are our selves. Because we wish so much for our families to see us for who we really are, we want them to call us by our rightful names (to borrow the title of Michael Shurtleff's play). Sometimes this means slightly altering the names given to us; sometimes it means adopting names we have chosen for ourselves. A change of name can indicate taking on a new identity—or reclaiming an old one.

Teenagers are especially apt to feel that they don't fit in their families—that the adults they live with don't *really* see them, don't understand who they really are. One way some young people claim the selves they think they are, or want to be, is to change their names, or the spellings of their names. Boys refuse to be called Bobby, Lenny, Richie, or Billy. Henceforth they will be Bob, Len, Dick, or Bill. Girls adopt new names or sometimes just change the spelling of the old one. Debbie becomes Debi, Kelly becomes Keli—and the dot over the *i* becomes a whole little circle.

I was called Debby between the ages of five and twenty-nine. I began to chafe at this name when I was twenty-five. I was studying toward a master's degree in English literature at Wayne State University. One of my professors had a wife named Deborah. How I envied her the dignity of our full name. It seemed to me that she had earned the right to be Deborah, like the majestic actress Deborah Kerr. She must be adult, serious, accomplished—or just plain lucky. Being called Debby made me feel childlike, frivolous, and insignificant, like the diminutive actress Debbie Reynolds. At five feet nine inches, I couldn't cut it as cute. Yet I felt powerless to change what I was called—or who, inside, I felt myself to be.

At the age of twenty-nine, I saw my chance. Having recently separated from my first husband, I moved across the country to attend graduate school in California and took back my father's surname. And I asked everyone to call me Deborah. It was a tough sell; many people didn't want to make the change. Hardest of all was getting my parents to switch. They made a valiant effort, though even now, twenty-five years later, they backslide at times.

The funny thing is, now that I'm firmly Deborah in my mind, I find it charming and homey to be called Debby by my parents, other relatives, and really old friends—but not by anyone else. When others call me Debby, my ire rises. It feels as if they are either claiming inappropriate familiarity or putting me down. I know these reactions are irrational: Many Deborahs go by Debby; how is a stranger to know that I don't? But the name itself, in its diminutive form, has evocative power far stronger than this logic.

I said that I was Debby from the age of five. Before that I was Diane. How did this happen? My mother cannot bear for me to tell this story in her presence, because it makes her feel so guilty. But here it is.

When I was born, the third daughter after my sisters Naomi and Miriam, my father had chosen the name Deborah for me, and my mother had agreed. But while my mother was in the hospital, her older sister visited her and counseled that the name Deborah was harsh. Why not name me something softer, like Diane? Convinced, my mother entered Diane on the official records. My father, committed to Bible names, never approved. (He had even picked out the name for a fourth daughter: Rachel.) But it took him four years to assert himself, which he did just in time for them to register me in kindergarten as Deborah.

Such a simple thing, a name change. But when I think of it, an odd discomfort creeps over me, and childhood unhappiness comes tumbling back. Among my earliest memories is my distress that two people, both teenage boys—Stevie Rattien, who lived three houses down to our left, and Bobby Berger, who lived across the street—refused to make the switch. I have few other memories of Stevie or Bobby—all that remains is my frustration that they refused to call me by my rightful name.

I have always liked the name Deborah better than Diane, mostly because it goes with my sisters' names. But that doesn't change the peculiar feeling it gives me to think that it wasn't always my name. I have no memory of the moment my parents told me Diane wasn't my name anymore. Did it feel as if they were telling me they didn't like the little girl I was and wanted me to be a different little girl? I remember feeling bereft because I no longer had a song. My sister Miriam, called Mimi, had Maurice Chevalier singing to her, "You are the sweetest little cutest little Mimi." When I was Diane I thought "Danny Boy" was my song, since Danny could be a nickname for Diane. As Debby I had no song. Other than that small disappointment, my only clue to how I felt about the change was how upset I was that Stevie Rattien and Bobby Berger kept calling me Diane.

A young woman who was successful in enforcing her new name is described by her sister, Micah Perks, in her memoir, *Pagan Time*. Perks presents her younger sister, Beky, as shy, pliable, and silent. Later in the memoir Perks and her sister, both grown, visit their mother together. Her younger sister has transformed herself into an assertive adult:

> My mother suggests we all go to the lake. My sister nixes this. My sister has learned to speak up, with a vengeance. . . . Nobody calls her Beky, she's Bekah now. She doesn't want anything to do with the baby sister routine. Don't mess with her.

Bekah's taking control of her life is embodied in her choosing—and enforcing—her rightful name.

One of the most heartbreaking and riveting personal stories to come to light in recent years, John Colapinto's *As Nature Made Him*, tells the life of David Reimer, a child whose genital organ was destroyed in a surgical accident when he was nine months old. His parents were told by doctors that their baby had no chance of living a happy or normal life. Then they encountered a doctor at the world-famous Johns Hopkins University who gave them hope:

If they changed the boy's sex, he would grow into a happy, normal girl. When he was eighteen months old, the baby's testicles were surgically removed. From then on he was dressed as a girl, given girls' toys, and called Brenda Lee. But the child's life was torment. Girls avoided Brenda because they thought she played too rough, and boys avoided Brenda because they had no interest in playing with a girl. At the age of fifteen, Reimer was told the truth of his birth. And the first thing he asked was, "What was my name?"

David Reimer, at thirty-five, recounted this memory on *The Oprah Winfrey Show.* I knew the story because I had read Colapinto's book. But hearing David himself repeat the question he asked, I felt myself choke up. He says it simply, but the emotion is overwhelming because the question implies so much. By asking his name, he was asking, Who was I? Who was I before these dreadful things were done to me, to mask who I am? David went on to say, "It's one thing when you lose a part of your body. It's another when people try to change you to something that you're not and then try to convince you in your mind that you are." All that knowledge was contained in the question "What was my name?"

David is the name Reimer chose for himself (though he let his parents make the final choice) when he determined to resume life as a male, because of the courage suggested by the biblical David, who, against all odds, faced down a giant. That, after all, is what David Reimer had done because, as Colapinto shows, it was by sheer force of the child's inner strength that he resisted all the adults who pressured him to undergo further sex-change surgery. Somehow, inside, David never lost sight of who he really was. And that against-all-odds conviction and courage were captured in the name he took.

For others, taking a name different from the one given to them at birth is a way of expressing and experiencing inner shape-shifting. One example is Donna Williams, a woman with autism. In her books *Nobody Nowhere* and *Somebody Somewhere,* Williams explains that her autism prevented her from interpreting others' speech in an authentic way, or translating her own feelings into speech. So she adopted two personas, Carol and Willie, whom she thought of as her "characters," to speak for her. Willie went for interviews; Carol held down jobs. Willie was a speed reader who accumulated facts to impress people; Carol smiled, cocked her head, and filled the air with social chatter. Willie was strong, feared nothing, and was always in control. "As Carol," Williams explains, "I never had to understand anything that happened. I just had to look good." Williams had to go through a long and difficult process, with the help of a therapist, to give up the protection of Willie and Carol and face the world as herself—Donna.

As a young, attractive woman, Williams was the object of a great deal of sexual attention from men. In the character of Carol, she allowed men to have sex with her, all the while separating herself from the experience by not being Donna. Another woman who becomes someone else when engaging in unwanted sex is Sue Silverman, who, in her memoir of incest, recalls her growing up as a sequence of names. In order to withstand her father's violations of her body, in her mind Sue became someone else when he was molesting her: Her body became Dina, and Sue withdrew. As she got older her father's nightly visits became more violent and turned to rape. From then on, when her father visited her at night he found Celeste. Silverman writes:

> Erase Celeste. Erase Dina. Erase me—whom I appear to be—and there is yet another girl, a little girl, someone else, but she is the one person I can't see. This little girl is a faint smudge, as transparent as a shadow, her body hiding inside a flower petal, or her heart hidden deep inside a rock. For this little girl must hide. It is far too dangerous for her to come out.

This little girl is Sue. As an adult Silverman was helped by a therapist whose ability to see and to save her is encapsulated this way: "Finally someone remembers my true name and calls to me: *Sue, come home.*"

For both Donna Williams and Sue Silverman, the names their parents gave them represent their real selves, which they had to struggle to reclaim. For others, the names their parents gave them become metaphors for the feeling that their parents see them not as who they really are (or who they want to be) but as who their parents want them to be.

A man complained that his college-age son, upon returning

from his junior year in France, had changed his name from Andrew to Guy, pronounced the French way, with a hard *g*, "Gee." The father told this in a spirit of disbelief: "I gave him the name Andrew, and it's a perfectly good name. There's no way I'm going to call him Gee." Hearing this, I was sympathetic with the father's plight: The name his son had chosen was hard to say, seemed affected, and, in the father's view, had nothing to do with the son he had raised and loved. But I could also imagine the son's point of view: "He can only see me as who he wants me to be."

And that, in the end, says a lot about family. Parents give us our names, which tell us who they think we will be. As we grow we develop our own ideas of who we are—or who we would like to become. And we want the people who continue to have the most power—our family—to see who we are and tell us we're okay that way, even if the paths we have chosen for ourselves are not the ones they would have chosen for us, even if the names they gave us are not the ones we have chosen for ourselves.

# Seven

# "I'm Still Your Mother"

## Mothers and Adult Children

DORIS, AT SIXTY-TWO, is standing in the closet of a hotel room, surveying the clothes she brought on this visit to her parents. Each time she reaches for an outfit, she draws her hand back, as she hears her mother's voice in her ear: "You're wearing *that*?" This has been her mother's reaction to what she wore on each of the previous three days. All the clothes that seemed perfectly fine when she packed them now appear shabby, ill-shaped, inappropriate. Paralyzed, she is unable to choose any outfit at all. The lesson is clear: No matter how old we are—even when we are almost old ourselves—our mothers' disapproval causes pain (which can easily turn to anger).

But switch to the mothers' point of view. A joke describes four Jewish women talking. The first exclaims, using a Yiddish expression of dismay: "*Oy.*" The second matches the expression and ups it: "*Oy vey.*" The third completes it: "*Oy vey is mir,*" which translates roughly as "Oh, woe is me." The fourth admonishes her friends, "Ladies, I thought we agreed we wouldn't talk about our children." The message of this joke is parallel: Children are the source of mothers' woe.

Mothers complain that their children don't pay enough attention to them, don't do things right, and are hypersensitive, so the mothers feel, "I can't even open my mouth." The same themes show up in grown children's complaints about mothers but with the focus reversed: Mothers are too demanding, too meddling, and, above all, too critical—even (or especially) when they protest, "I only say this because I love you."

It's easy to see one or the other perspective, depending on whom you're talking to and who you are. It's difficult to keep both perspectives in mind at once, yet it's essential—if not to keep both perspectives in mind at the same moment, then to consider both in retrospect and in metacommunicating—in order to avoid the hurt that results as mothers and their adult children find their footing on the control-connection grid that I described in Chapter 3. In a way the mother-child relationship is the central one in a family, the one through which we can understand all other family relationships, because it is in the mother-child constellation that the intertwined desires for connection, approval, and control mix together in the strongest brew.

## Chief Critic, Chief Judge

I asked Marge, a woman with grown children, about her parents. She responded with half a dozen examples of her mother's never-ending criticism. I could tell by the swiftness with which Marge offered these remembered conversations that she had told them many times over. All these recollected comments had the same implication: Her mother was critical of Marge's appearance.

Marge's mother would say, for example, "Why don't you ask Sally where she gets her shoes? They're very attractive." (Implication: Your shoes are unattractive; Sally knows how to shop and dress; you don't.) The post office was her mother's ally: Clippings arrived with pictures of women and recommendations like, "This is how young women are wearing their hair now; I think it would look good on you." (Implication: Your hair is a mess; you're out of touch with the fashion.) Visiting several weeks before her mother's death, Marge received a rare compliment: "I see you've finally lost your butt." But the very next day, when Marge wore a different skirt, her mother took the approval back: "I see now it was an illusion."

Marge's husband once tried to explain to his mother-in-law why her remarks were hurtful to Marge. "From your point of view," he acknowledged, "you are just giving helpful advice. But Marge hears it as evidence you think she's doing everything wrong." "That's right!" her mother agreed. "She takes everything as criticism!"

Marge herself made an attempt to change their interactions. During one of her mother's two-week visits, she said, "You're here for only two weeks. Why don't we try to just do things together, and enjoy each other's company?" Her mother's response was straightforward, clear-sighted, and plaintive: "But I only have two weeks!" In other words, I have only two weeks in which to set you straight, get you on the right path, help you improve yourself. They were back where they started.

Marge and her mother were caught in the web of confusion created when message and metamessage are not distinguished. Marge's mother—like many parents—was focused on the message level: "I just said you'd look good in this haircut. Why are you getting so upset?" Marge heard the metamessage: "I don't think your hair looks good the way it is; I don't think you are attractive." And in an ongoing relationship—which every family relationship is—any comment draws meaning not only from the current context but also from a long history of comments that define the relationship, like barnacles on a rock that cannot be scraped off. Since Marge had had years of evidence that her mother disapproved of her appearance, she was primed to interpret any new comment as yet another criticism to add to the list.

Marge and her mother were also struggling to find their footing on the control continuum between hierarchy and equality, and on the connection continuum between closeness and distance. Marge's mother was focused on the closeness: "I am trying to help you because I care about you." She would not stop a stranger on the street, hand her a newspaper clipping, and say, "I think this hairdo would look good on you." But, like many people who are positioned high on a hierarchy, her mother seemed oblivious not only to the metamessage level of her "suggestions" but also to the power she had over her daughter: Disapproval would be much easier to take from a stranger than from a mother, because our parents are our first and primary judges. We want above all to feel that they think we're okay.

Ironically, Marge's mother probably felt powerless: She could see all these ways her daughter could make herself more attractive, and Marge simply refused to do them. It was probably this feeling of powerlessness that made her so relentless—and made her feel she could not afford to waste a moment of her two-week window of opportunity to help Marge improve. Also ironically, if she felt she was safely on the closeness end of the connection continuum when she helped Marge improve, her comments pushed them toward the distance end, as Marge reacted with anger and hurt.

We hold these nuggets of hurt like family heirlooms: bits of conversation in which our parents' disapproval is set like a birthstone in a ring. We clutch them to our hearts, where the edges continue to scrape, but we can show them off, to communicate, encapsulate, the hurt we know we felt.

## Come Here—Leave Me Alone: Reframing a Mother's Attentions

Marge's recollections of her mother's criticism seem to leave no doubt that her mother was at fault: She obviously was criticizing her daughter's appearance and refusing to acknowledge how that criticism would make her daughter feel. But I heard these conversations from the daughter. They might come across very differently from the mother's point of view. Sometimes mother-daughter relationships are never-ending tugs-of-war between wanting to be close and feeling angry when that closeness doesn't guarantee approval. One mother commented that there was a period when her daughter called every day from college—and got annoyed at her mother each time. Much as the mother appreciated her daughter's staying in touch, she didn't enjoy being snapped at—especially when it was the snapper who had initiated the calls.

Sarah Vowell, a radio commentator, captures a moment when a daughter suddenly sees her frustration with her mother from her mother's point of view. Vowell's monologue begins with a gothic interpretation of her mother giving her a home permanent when she was young:

> I'm sitting at my desk, quietly "minding my own" as they say in the rap songs, when my torturer darkens the doorway. She drags me into a cramped bathroom, shoves my head under a faucet, shines a blinding light in my eyes, cinches my neck in plastic sheeting, and comes at me with scissors. She douses me with chemicals and makes me sit there, dehydrating under the plastic while the acid stings my flesh. And so, when I look up from my desk and see her standing there with the scissors, I shudder.
>
> "Hi, Mom," I say. "Guess you think I need a haircut?"

Vowell recalls that as a girl she was an embarrassment to her mother, a former hairdresser, because she was "all scuffed shoes and stringy hair and lint." Now, as an adult, Vowell is an embarrassment to herself: Thanks to her youthful appearance and high-pitched, childlike voice, she comes across "so young and innocent and harmless" that she doesn't get the respect she deserves. Determined to acquire a more "menacing" appearance, she contacts a group of goths who offer makeovers. "Goths," Vowell explains, "are the pale-faced, black-clad, vampiric types" of young people whose appearance she envies.

During the makeover, Vowell is "willing and able to do something with them that I was never able to do with my mom: namely, sit still while they poke and prod and paint me without complaint":

> I sit in a chair and Monique curls my hair while Terrance fusses with my lipstick and Mary paints my nails black. All at once. I find I enjoy this loving, methodical attention.

And then comes the revelation:

> What if all those years my mom wanted to do just this—sit me down and fiddle with my hair—not because she wanted to torture me or because she was embarrassed about how I looked or

because she missed her job? What if she wanted to do this for me to show me that she loves me? If all along she was trying to give me the feeling I'm getting from these strangers?

I thought *she* was the oppressor and I was the victim, but it can be just as true the other way around.

Sarah Vowell conveys the paradox of mother-daughter relationships—an intensified form of all close relationships: the paradox of connection and control, the come-here-leave-me-alone dynamic that makes some daughters call their mothers every day and get angry at them each time. When the attention came from strangers, Vowell could see the pleasure of being fussed over—a pleasure she could not appreciate when the fussing was done by her mother. Then she could see only her mother's disapproval of her appearance, and the intrusion of her attentions. Ironically, she could accept the goths fussing over her precisely because she didn't care that much about their opinion of her, and because there was no history between them.

## "You're Still My Baby"

Age, no doubt, was the key to Sarah Vowell's insight. As an adolescent she could not see that perhaps her mother was seeking closeness rather than (or in addition to) correction. Many tales of parents' criticism come from the teenage years, when our parents' disapproval reflects our own fears that we will not make the grade in the outside world. That's why our parents' comments bring back the anguish of those years. For example, one Mother's Day, Cheryl arranged to do something that she knew her mother really enjoyed: go shopping together. But as the day unfolded, Cheryl wondered, "What could I have been thinking?" When, in a dressing room, her mother said, "Those pants don't flatter you," the pain of Cheryl's adolescence came rushing back, the floodgates opened by the familiar lilt of her mother's helpful judgment.

Many adults become like children when they return to their parents' or grandparents' homes. A woman I know who is so firm and supercompetent that she intimidates me once commented that despite her having told her mother innumerable times over the years that she has become a vegetarian, her mother continues to serve her meat. Surprised, I asked, "What do you do?" I was even more surprised by her reply: "I eat it, of course." Tough as she is in the world outside, when she goes back home she is once again a child subject to the authority of her mother.

Grown men are subject to their mothers' authority as much as women. Aaron is fifty-five. His eighty-five-year-old mother is visiting. Aaron is preparing dinner, and his mother is keeping him company in the kitchen. As they talk he reaches into the pot and pinches a string bean between his fingers, raising it to his mouth to taste. Thwack! His mother slaps his hand. Telling this story, Aaron laughs and says, "She knows what's right and what's wrong, and that was wrong." I responded, "And you laughed, of course." He paused, so I gave him another choice: "Or did it make you angry?" "I laughed about it later," he said. "At the time it made me angry."

## Who's Making Whom Miserable

No one captures the complexities of communication between mothers and daughters better than the novelist Amy Tan. In Tan's *The Joy Luck Club,* Waverly Jong is distraught: The evening before, she introduced her Chinese mother to the American man she plans to marry, and her mother's only comment was to ridicule Rich's freckles: "So many spots on his face." After a sleepless night Waverly marches to her mother's home determined to confront her about "her scheming ways of making me miserable." But she finds her mother asleep, looking so helpless and small that Waverly fears her mother is dead. When her mother awakens and asks what's wrong, Waverly "didn't know what to do or say. In a matter of seconds I had gone from being angered at her strength, to being amazed at her innocence, and then frightened by her vulnerability."

Waverly goes ahead and confronts her mother, but the conversation does not go at all as she expected. Her mother claims to have meant no harm when she spoke the truth: Rich does have spots on his face. Then she looks "old and full of sorrow" as she protests, "So you think your mother is this bad. You think I have a secret meaning. But it is you who has this meaning. Ai-ya! She thinks I am this bad!" Waverly ends up feeling guilty for having hurt her mother: "Oh, her strength! her weakness!—both pulling me apart. My mind was flying one way, my heart another."

How poignantly Tan dramatizes the power of mothers over daughters—power created in part by daughters wanting their mothers' approval so badly. But what's the view from the other side of judgment and advice? Children have power over mothers because mothers are held responsible for all their children's failings. And this explains in part why mothers are so eager to set their children straight.

## Mothers Are to Blame—for Everything

"BAD MOTHER" says the sign that a kindergarten teacher pins on Mrs. Johnson in a hilarious scene from the musical about women's lives *A . . . My Name Is Alice.* Poor Mrs. Johnson has been squatting on a kindergarten chair while her daughter Janie's teacher sits at the big desk, delivering damning judgments. Janie was humiliated, the teacher says, because she brought Pepperidge Farm cookies to the bake sale, while the other children brought cookies that their mothers had baked. And she holds up Janie's artwork—a pig made out of a Clorox bottle—as irrefutable evidence that the child has psychological problems that are her mother's fault!

It isn't only children's teachers who pass judgments on mothers, blaming them for their children's failings. In a study of giving and receiving advice, Andrea DeCapua and Lisa Huber present examples of unsolicited and unappreciated advice offered by strangers in public. In both cases the advice was addressed to a mother, instructing her on how better to care for her child. In one example, an older woman approached a young mother standing in a checkout line and said, "My what a fat baby! You know, he really does need to lose some weight. Do you watch what you feed him?"

Strangers feel free to approach mothers when they appear in

public with children—and to offer advice on how better to care for them. Being open to unsolicited advice also leaves mothers vulnerable to accusations—even by strangers—that they aren't doing their job right. And these judgments can trigger genuine self-doubt. One mother who frequently got advice like that from strangers actually began to worry about whether her baby was overweight—at the age of six months—simply because she had those bulging cheeks many babies are born with.

Mothers feel these judgments even when they are unspoken (maybe even when they are unintended). And mothers are more likely than fathers to feel that their children's misbehavior reflects badly on them—perhaps because others hold mothers more responsible than fathers. The difference in a mother's and a father's reactions emerged in the following conversation.

Sheila was aghast when her daughter, nearly three, had a screaming tantrum directed at Sheila's aunt. "Weren't you just so humiliated when she started screaming at Aunt June?" she asked her husband, Dan.

There was a brief pause before Dan answered: "No."

Sheila went on, "I just feel horribly embarrassed when she goes off—when she does that."

"I don't," Dan said simply.

Sheila continued, "Like it's some reflection of our bad parenting."

"I don't think we are bad parents," Dan reassured her. "I think we're good parents, and I think she's very two."

Sheila then wondered aloud "why she's more two now that she's almost three."

Dan amused them both with his reply: "Well, my impression is that three is not much better than two."

Note the difference in how Dan and Sheila regarded their child's tantrum. Sheila was embarrassed and humiliated because she feared that her aunt would attribute the child's tantrum to their failure as parents; she assumed Dan was feeling the same way. But, as so often happens in cross-gender conversations, he wasn't. (In this case the contrast seemed especially salutary, as Dan was able both to reassure Sheila and to lighten the mood with humor.)

The knowledge that they will be blamed for their children's failures gives urgency to mothers' determination to improve their children. They are attuned to the metamessage—what this says about the kind of parent I have been. One of the biggest challenges to mothers of grown-up children is trying not to feel responsible for every move their adult children make.

## A One-Person Parenting Industry

Part of the reason we are so critical of mothers is that we expect so much of them. Putting so much individual responsibility on mothers for the upbringing of their children is not the norm in human history. Sarah Blaffer Hrdy, an anthropologist, notes that in much of the human world as well as the animal world, allo-mothers are the norm: Females share child rearing with relatives, neighbors, and older children. One mother as the sole parenting industry for her children is an aberration. As Arlie Hochschild shows in her book *The Second Shift,* mothers in most middle-class American households do the lion's share of child rearing, even when both parents work full-time.

Author Stephanie Coontz recalls a mind-opening experience she had while visiting Hawaiian-Filipino friends on a Hawaiian island. She was sitting with a group of mothers and keeping an eye on her toddler, who was playing with other children. Suddenly she realized that she was the only mother continually jumping up to tend to her child. In fact, she was the only mother keeping an eye on her child. But the other children were not being neglected. The other mothers were keeping an eye on the floor around their feet, tending to whichever child came into their floor space. In this way all the children were tended to while each mother had a more manageable task.

Middle-class American mothers often feel they are expected to be the sole sentry in a twenty-four-hour watchtower. One mother was distraught when she heard her teenage daughter's voice on a cell-phone voice-mail message: "Mom. I'm at the hospital. We had an accident. We're all fine. But call me! Right now! Why don't you have your cell phone on?" In an essay in *Newsweek,* the mother,

Nicole Wise, notes that, after recovering from her initial "self-flagellation and guilt-wallowing," she realized that having her cell phone on would not have prevented the accident. She had incurred her daughter's wrath by being unavailable for an hour. Thanks to the new technology, she was "supposed to be instantly reachable and immediately responsive every moment of the day and night."

## Now You See Her . . . : The Invisibility of Mothers

Ironically, mothers' very availability can lead to a kind of invisibility. In many families, what Mother does is taken for granted (after all, she is always there), in contrast to Father's attentions, which seem special because he is so busy, his time so valuable, and his presence something special, like Sunday compared with weekdays. And there is evidence that this pattern is widespread.

Anthropologist Hildred Geertz describes a complex system by which Javanese speakers must adapt their language to just the right level of respect balanced with familiarity. Children learn that when they speak to siblings and cousins, they must use forms that show more respect to older ones than to younger ones. They learn that strangers—as well as those who are older or higher in rank—must also be addressed with respect. But, Geertz points out, "Most people continue to speak to the mother in the same way as they did as children," that is, with verbal forms that show more intimacy but also less respect.

I recall my surprise when I observed my first husband, who was Greek, using a similar pattern in addressing his parents. When talking to his father, he always used the formal, polite forms of the second-person pronoun and verbs. But when he talked to his mother, he used the informal, familiar forms.

What a lot this contrast says about mothers: From the perspective of the connection continuum, do people feel so close to their mothers that they resist switching to respect language, which implies distance? Or, from the perspective of the control continuum, does it mean that Mother doesn't merit the respect Father gets? I suspect it means both at once.

You don't have to look to Java or Greece to detect this pattern. In a study based on tape recordings of American families at home, Susan Ervin-Tripp, Mary Catherine O'Connor, and Jarrett Rosenberg examined "control acts"—that is, how people spoke in order to get others to do their bidding. The researchers found that "effective power and esteem were related to age"—except when it came to mothers. When children asked their mothers to do something for them, they spoke without deference. Here again, we could conclude that children have less respect for their mothers or that they feel closer to them—or (as the researchers suggest) that they have come to expect their mothers to fulfill their requests.

Mothers are pervasive and ignored, always there and often unnoticed. Consider a poem called "Epiphanies," about those moments when you suddenly get an insight that transforms your life or the way you think about it. The poet, Stephen Fellner (or the voice he creates in his poem), is waiting for an epiphany, wondering how it might present itself:

> Would it want me to lavish praise upon its presence like Zoloft or Prozac,
> or would it prefer to go unnoticed, unmentioned like your mother's advice you take for granted?

What caught my attention is the way this poem describes a mother's advice: desirable, yes—as desired as an epiphany. Yet you don't notice or mention it; you just accept it as your birthright.

## The Many Faces of Mom

Mothers are often taken for granted, while fathers' time is more valued precisely because mothers are working so hard to accomplish so much. Shari Kendall had a family tape-record four dinner conversations in their home and was able to capture some of the many roles the mother embodied. The mother is Elaine, the father is Mark, and their ten-year-old daughter is Beth.

Among the roles Kendall was able to identify in Elaine's talk were these: Head Chef (she oversaw the preparation of food); Hostess (she offered and served food); Caretaker (she helped Beth); Teacher (she taught Beth how to prepare a taco); Miss Manners (she monitored Beth's dinnertime etiquette, reminding her each evening to say the blessing and ask to be excused); Facilitator (she kept the conversation going); Moral Guardian (when Beth told about what happened during her day, Elaine passed judgment on how people in the story behaved); Conversationalist (she engaged in social talk with Mark and Beth); Social Secretary (she juggled Beth's social schedule); and Manager (she made sure Beth got to places she needed to be both on time and properly equipped). It is breathtaking to watch Elaine balance these multiple and often competing tasks.

For example, in the following excerpt, the three are discussing the location of a restaurant, when Elaine switches from Conversationalist to Miss Manners without missing a beat:

ELAINE: 'Cause there's something else on the other corner by Jackson's.
BETH: Yeah, not over by Jackson's.
ELAINE: Do you know what that is?
**Wipe your chin off please.**
BETH: The one that's by . . . Chicken, whatever, Boston Chicken?

Elaine admonishes Beth to wipe her chin, where food has apparently fallen, while continuing the conversation about the location of a restaurant.

In another sequence Elaine carries on a conversation with Mark while she helps Beth get ready for her horseback riding lesson. The family is discussing destinations and distances:

ELAINE: It couldn't be any further than when we drove to Ohio.
MARK: No, about six hours.
BETH: Excuse me!
ELAINE: **Okay, go ahead and get your vitamins and go up and brush your teeth 'cause you're gonna probably have to leave about a quarter after or so.**

BETH: The only weird thing is—remember when I rode Whiskers?

Kendall points out that balancing these two tasks takes a lot of attention and energy, even though they wouldn't be counted in a time-use study. This burden comes clearer when we contrast Elaine's many roles with Mark's two: Conversationalist with his wife and Playmate with his daughter.

## Comparisons at the Heart of Hurt

Knowing that they are often passed over, mothers can overreact to any remark that indicates their children undervalue them. One mother was riding in a car with her teenage son, Andy, who was talking about how much he liked his friend's mother, Mrs. Harris. As Andy spoke, his mother began to squirm: Irrational jealousy was seeded and started to grow. Did he think Mrs. Harris was a better mother than she? Her discomfort blossomed when he said, "Mrs. Harris is the sweetest woman in the world." "What am I?" his mother blurted out. "Chopped liver?" Andy looked at her with genuine puzzlement. He was talking about Mrs. Harris. Who said anything about her?

We all compare ourselves with others in our minds, making lists of attributes and giving ourselves checks or demerits as we rate others. When someone speaks ill of a third party (he was loud, she was petty), we privately reassure ourselves (I would not have said that; I'm not loud, I'm not petty—or, more troubling, I could have said that; I hope people don't think I'm loud or petty). And when we hear someone else praised, we secretly wonder whether we would merit similar praise (and fear we wouldn't). This is such a common response that the Turkish language has a fixed expression to allay people's fears. Anyone who praises someone who is not there is likely to add *Sizden iyi olmasin,* "May she or he not be better than you," to reassure the person who *is* there. Because English does not have this sensible expression, Andy didn't think to say anything to reassure his mother, who heard her son praising Mrs. Harris in a way that seemed to exclude her.

Comparisons are often at the heart of hurt. Many parents try to inspire their children to better behavior by offering good examples: other children. Usually the result is simply instilling an aversion to the child held up for comparison. The irony is that in many cases the child who provides the example does not really live up to the model either. The difference is the magnifying glass of close relationships: The parents know the other child only from outside appearances, whereas they know their own child's weaknesses from close, daily observation. My father tells of such an incident, in which he was the child held up as a model—but he was only putting on a show.

As an adult my father became acquainted with a cousin whom he had met only once, when they were both small children in Poland. This cousin had harbored resentment from that one meeting because, for a long time after, their mutual grandfather had used the visiting city cousin as a remonstrance: "Why aren't you religious like your cousin Eli?" But the story behind that meeting shows how mistaken his grandfather was.

My father was living in Warsaw with his mother's family. This cousin was living in Kielce, where my father's father was from. When my father was six his mother took him to visit his father's family. The favorable impression was made when the cousin (who did not normally wear a skullcap) tried to snatch the skullcap off my father's head. As my father tells it, "To prove how serious I thought it was, I hauled off and smacked him." The irony is that my father did not normally wear a skullcap either. But when his mother took him to visit his deceased father's relatives, she had warned him that his grandfather was very devout, so he had better wear a yarmulke at all times. When he fought his cousin who tried to knock it off his head, it was his mother's anger that he feared, not the Almighty's.

## "I Don't Have a Necklace Like That": Comparisons Across Generations

In families who are very close across generations, comparison can implicate not only mothers but also grandmothers. "Why do you hate me?" Loraine's grandmother asked. Loraine was thrown for a loop. "What do you mean?" she asked in turn. "I invite you to stay with us for two weeks every summer. I send you gifts and visit you. How can you say I hate you?" "You take your parents and your in-laws on vacation every year," Grandma said, "but you never take me on vacation!" I doubt Loraine's grandmother would expect to be taken on vacation if she didn't have to confront the comparison of Loraine's generosity toward her parents and in-laws. It wasn't so much that she needed to go on vacation with Loraine and her husband as that she didn't want to settle for less love than Loraine was willing to give to others.

Nina also took her parents on vacation, to the Southwest, where they were shopping in a jewelry store. Nina saw a necklace she thought her mother-in-law would like and decided to buy it for her. Her mother looked hurt. "I don't have a necklace like that," she said. So Nina felt she had to buy one for her mother, too. But she was annoyed. After all, she was taking her mother, not her mother-in-law, on this trip. A gift for her mother-in-law was, in a way, a consolation prize. Had her mother thought about it rationally, she would probably have reached the same conclusion. But reactions to comparisons are emotional, not rational. They are sudden outbursts of the fundamental imbalance in relationships that we are always trying to right—or, more accurately, trying to weight in our favor.

Since many women gauge their relationships, including those with their children, by where they are placed on the continuum between closeness and distance, they can be hurt by reported conversations that indicate an in-law (or stepmother) is closer to their children than they are. That's what happened in the following example.

Doreen was happy in her job as office manager to a real estate agent who had her own one-person business. At first it seemed like an incredible bonus when Doreen's daughter Connie fell in love with her boss's brother and announced they were getting married. Doreen was also delighted when Connie and her future sister-in-law, Doreen's boss, really hit it off. But as the wedding date neared, the rapport between Connie and Doreen's boss began to rankle. "Isn't it great that they're going to Hawaii for their honeymoon?" Doreen's boss asked casually. But Connie had not discussed her honeymoon with her mother. Time and again her boss would refer to information that Connie had not told Doreen. It made Doreen feel so left out that she was considering quitting her job. At least she wouldn't be reminded daily that her daughter was having conversations with her future sister-in-law that Doreen wished she would have with her.

## Mother as Communication Central

Family alignments are created in part by conversations: who tells what to whom? In many families, Mother is the Chief of Communications: All information passes through her, and this makes her the hub of the family wheel. As the daughter Cicily commented on the PBS documentary *An American Love Story,* "Dad is a man of few words. Mom will go on forever." This apportionment of speaking parts is common in two-parent families, especially with regard to personal talk, one-on-one. (A man recalls that dinners at his home consisted of everyone listening while his stepfather held forth, but that was more like a lecture, or what I call report-talk.)

I once asked a large class of college students whom they talk to when they call home. The vast majority said their mothers. Their fathers, they said, get on the phone only if there is some business to talk about, like a tuition payment that didn't arrive or a request for money—in other words, report-talk. Author Jane Bernstein recalls that, when she went away to college, she addressed letters home "Dear Mom and Dad," but only Mom replied. Even when she was home on a visit, her mother spoke for her father:

> Sometimes during the visit my mother would say, "Your father is delighted to see you." Or: "Your father says you look well."
>
> It was as if he lived in a different country and spoke another tongue, and my mother was his sole interpreter.

When she was an adolescent, this made Bernstein angry. When she was older, it made her sad.

Children themselves sometimes choose to use their mothers as intermediaries in communicating with their fathers. Recall the incident in which twelve-year-old Chaney sought permission to go out with a boy. Chaney herself told the filmmaker, Jennifer Fox, "Mommy is the messenger. I talk to Mommy." And Chaney was clear on why this was: "If I get Mommy to let me go," she said, "then she'll convince Daddy." In the end (as we saw) Chaney did go. And she wondered how her father reacted. So she asked her mother, "What'd Daddy say?"—even though her father was at home at the time she asked.

Many people recall their fathers as absent—away at work, or away at home: in a workshop, garage, or study. (Jane Bernstein's father was always "off somewhere, working at his desk, or watching a game on TV.") Even if they are physically present, fathers are often remembered as silent. A clue to this mystery emerged when my class discussed whom they talk to. One student said that when her parents divorced, her father began calling her to get the news directly that he used to get through her mother.

This provides another view: It may not be that fathers have no wish to talk to their children; it may be that they don't know how to get into the kinds of conversations mothers have with children—especially daughters. Or perhaps they don't feel the need, knowing their wives will collect information and pass it on. One man who had two adult children—a son and a daughter—commented that he kept up with what was happening in both his children's lives through his daughter. Not only did he feel more comfortable talking to his daughter about personal matters, but so did his son.

In other words, one of the reasons that mothers often hold the post of Chief of Communications is that many men as well as women feel more comfortable talking about personal matters to women. The playwright Jeffrey Solomon, whose play *MotherSON* is about his mother's coming to terms with his being gay, commented in a post-play discussion that he was fourteen when he admitted to himself that he was gay, twenty-four when he told his mother—and twenty-six when he finally told his father. The play dramatizes numerous conversations with his mother, as she struggles to understand, accept, and finally take pride in his identity.

An audience member asked Solomon about his father, and the playwright answered that once he had told his father, "my dad never wanted to talk about it again." Then he added, "*I* didn't want to talk to him about it!" As he said this Solomon shook his shoulders and then his entire body in a mock shudder, indicating how repellent he found the prospect. Many gay men have told me of first coming out to their mothers. After that, some say, they relied on their mothers to tell their fathers. According to Shari Kendall, the loving, understanding mother and the unaccepting father that must be brought around by the mother (sometimes successfully and sometimes not) are stock characters in gay and lesbian movies.

When children have a problem, if they tell it to a parent, they're most likely to tell their mother—even if the problem is the father. One mother lamented this situation in her family. "Carly gets very upset with her father," she said, "but she tells it to me. I ask her, 'Why don't you tell Daddy?' and she says 'I can't.' " But this creates problems for the mother. "I get knots in my stomach," she said, "when I get caught between my daughter and my husband." She dealt with the problem by encouraging her daughter to confront her father directly, with her mother standing by for support.

The scene might go like this. After dinner the three of them remain at the table. "Why don't you tell your father what you told me?" the mother suggests. Reluctantly, looking down, after much hesitance, the daughter does so—emboldened by her mother's pressure but also by her reassuring presence. The mother encourages her to explain further and encourages the father to give her a chance to finish and expand. Eventually, this mother told me, her daughter learned to deal with her father directly.

E-mail may be changing this pattern. One woman commented that, since hooking up to e-mail, she began "talking" regularly to her father. Here, my own experience has been similar: at ninety my father learned to use e-mail. Now I know that although I may not talk to him when I call on the phone, I can "talk" to him on e-mail. Maybe this is because he is more comfortable with e-mail than with the telephone. My father is reticent in conversation but eloquent in writing, where he can gather his thoughts and choose his words. In addition, however, alone at his desk on e-mail, he has the lines of communication to himself. Usually he quickly passes the telephone to my mother when I call, but my father, too, will talk at length if I happen to call when my mother is not at home.

## Watch What You Say: Keeper of Family Secrets

A family is like a small corporation with a big public relations department, often headed by the mother. Just as corporations (and politicians) get in more trouble because of cover-ups than because of the information they wanted to hide, so individuals often find that keeping a secret is more damaging than revealing the information would be. Yet being a member of a family means keeping secrets. In this way the power of information to create alignments is learned early on.

Rosalind recalls that as a child she wrote what she did each day in a journal and regularly showed her mother what she had written. On New Year's Day when she was in third grade, her mother decided that the family would have breakfast in the dining room rather than the kitchen, to observe the grandeur of the occasion. Little Rosalind duly wrote in her journal, "This morning we had breakfast in the dining room, which was very unusual." When she showed her mother what she had written, her mother reacted with dismay. Warning Rosalind that this would give the wrong impression about the family, she made her daughter change what she had written by crossing out the *un*.

The incident stuck in Rosalind's mind because she had written the truth and was made to feel she had done something wrong. Worse, her mother had made her write a lie: It was *not* usual for the family to eat in the dining room. Recalling the incident, Rosalind stressed how unlikely anyone would have been to read a third-grader's daily journal. Was her mother crazy, or what? I doubt Rosalind's mother was so deluded as to think her daughter's diary would be read by their neighbors. But Rosalind would have many opportunities throughout her life to reveal images of her family to the world. By making her change the words in her journal, her mother was teaching her a lesson in family presentation: "Bear in mind," the lesson went, "the impression you're giving others about our family, and make sure you don't give a bad impression—regardless of the facts."

Many parents give their children the feeling that they should not reveal family secrets. The talk show host Diane Rehm writes in her memoir *Finding My Voice* that she felt, as a child, that she was living two lives: one inside her family and one outside. One source of difference was language: She spoke English outside and Arabic at home. But most troubling to Diane was a vague sense that she had to be careful what she said without knowing exactly what not to say. "There was a constant admonition 'not to tell' anything about our family which made me uneasy, afraid that I would somehow say something I shouldn't say that would violate the rules as they were laid down."

Finding the line between what information should stay in the family and what should go out is a challenge to all children. I recall my shame when my junior high school Spanish teacher drilled the class by asking each pupil, in Spanish, "Where do you comb your hair?" All the children who went before me answered either *"en el baño"* (in the bathroom) or *"en mi dormitorio"* (in my bedroom). When my turn came, I answered, without hesitation, *"en la cocina"* (in the kitchen). My teacher's response was swift: "If you were my daughter, I wouldn't let you comb your hair in the kitchen!" Mortified, I stammered, "But it takes a long time to comb my hair because it's so long" (my hair reached my waist), "and the radio is in the kitchen." The teacher seemed grudgingly to accept this explanation. But I felt I had unwittingly revealed a shameful truth about my family—a distasteful lack of cleanliness of which I hadn't even been aware until that moment.

Growing up, learning to move back and forth between the outside world of strangers and the inside world of family, is a process of learning to manage information: what to reveal, what to hide. In this our parents are our guides. But for many, like Rosalind as well as Diane Rehm, becoming an adult means questioning the information our parents wanted kept secret, because secrets have their own built-in liability: a metamessage of shame.

## Take Care: You Represent the Family

Having to keep something secret makes it seem awful—so awful that you can't let anybody know. This is a theme that is echoed by many lesbians and gay men recalling the enormous relief they feel when they "come out," that is, stop keeping their sexual orientation a secret. Sometimes families place unfair demands on sons and daughters in this way. One young man, for example, came out to his mother, who accepted his being gay but asked him not to tell anyone in the extended family. This undercut her acceptance: If it was really okay to be gay, why should it be kept secret? Even more destructive, when he went to college in a faraway city, he met and was welcomed by cousins. But he was not able to get close to them because, in order to keep his word to his mother, he had to keep his private life hidden.

In a sense this young man had to choose between loyalty to his mother and loyalty to himself. From his mother's point of view, he represented her to the extended family, so it made sense to ask that he present an image that she felt reflected positively on her. It is common for mothers to ask their children not to reveal aspects of their lives that the mothers feel would embarrass them. One woman, for example, was chagrined to tell her relatives that her son had been fired from his job as a stockbroker and was unemployed. She felt redeemed, however, when she was able to announce that he had entered law school. When he decided that he did not like the law after all and dropped out of law school, his mother waited years to pass the news on to her relatives.

My own mother had to tell her relatives, within two weeks, that two of her three daughters had separated from their husbands. When her third daughter announced that she, too, was separating, my mother implored her to keep it secret for a while. She could not bring herself to make yet a third compromising announcement so close to the other two.

## Be Happy—Do It for Me: Child as Redeemer

Not only do parents feel that their children represent them (a warranted impression, given how others regard parenting) but also many parents see their children's lives as opportunities to redeem their own.

Many of us feel we have been given an assignment to make up for our parents' losses. In some cases we accept these assignments with relish; in others we reject them. Many of my professional women friends had mothers who regretted having given up their careers when they married and encouraged their daughters not to make the same mistake. As far as I know, my friends are glad they took this advice. A daughter who resists making up for her mother's losses is the heroine of a Scottish play by Liz Lochhead, *Perfect Days.*

Barbs is a divorced woman with a successful career who wants to have a baby. Her mother, who does not want to hear about her daughter's dissatisfaction, blithely tells Barbs that she reported to a friend, "Our Barbra's perfectly happy."

"I'm not," Barbs corrects her.

"Aye you are!" her mother insists. And she explains why she believes her daughter *must* be happy: "Wish I'd had your chances. Career. Travel. Own home. Wish I'd done something with my life instead of just frittering it away bringing up you and Our Billy."

Barbs tells her mother, "I refuse to pretend to be happy so you can be happy about how happy I am."

Barbs's mother wanted her daughter to have the opportunities she did not have. Another woman, Norma, felt that her mother resented her having opportunities that her mother had missed. When Norma decided to spend a summer in London, her mother made this explicit: "I never went to London, so why should you?" Norma's mother, moreover, wanted Norma to marry and have children, just as she did. She made it plain that she was worried sick that, at thirty-eight, Norma was still single. Norma did just what Barbs refused to do: She pretended to be happy about being unmarried so her mother would be happy. But it never worked. Norma's mother was convinced that she was miserably lonely and miserably childless, so she resolutely ignored any evidence to the contrary, despite Norma's futilely parading such evidence before her. Her mother's view never changed because it was based not on Norma's life but on her mother's.

## The Solace of Mother

Thus far I have been discussing how metamessages about connection and control complicate communication between adult children and their parents, especially mothers. But it would be misleading to imply that these complications define most mother-child relationships. For many people the image of mother is almost sacrosanct in their experience, their memories, or their imaginations because of the solace a mother's care represents. In this sense, again, the mother-child relationship is the one most central to family, because it represents most strongly the comfort and protection suggested by the very word *family*.

I have seen people of every age—sixty-year-olds, eighty-year-olds—cry when recalling their parents now gone, especially their mothers. At family gatherings my aunt Millie, who kept her beautiful singing voice into her eighties, often sang "My Yiddishe Mama," bringing tears to everyone's eyes with its nostalgia for a mother's self-sacrificing love. In Taiwan a teenage boy who lost his family in an earthquake doggedly sifted through the rubble in search of one small thing: a photograph of his mother.

Photographs can be particularly evocative, especially if they are childhood photos that capture the mother's outsized power and ability to provide protection from the child's point of view. We react so strongly to such pictures because, even when we are adults, the impressions made by our mothers when we were small are still embedded in our memories—and our responses.

This comes through in another song, "The Portrait," from the musical *A . . . My Name Is Alice,* sung by a woman looking at a picture of herself as a child with her mother. Recalling her mother, who is dead, the woman sings of a scene that encapsulates, perhaps more than any other, the idea of mother as protector: tucking her child into bed at night. The singer's mother tells her that she loves her—then leaves her in the dark. The song expresses the longing we all feel for a mother's protection: selfless, unconditional—and also the desolation we feel when our mothers must, in one way or another, shut the light and the door behind them, and leave us in the dark.

But how many of us actually received that completely selfless, unconditional love—or can really give it? Perhaps the intense nostalgia comes, for many, in the realization that we never had truly unconditional love from our mothers—or anyone else—nor can we provide it for our children.

I was talking to a friend about his mother's having taken care of her own mother in old age. "She didn't do it out of love," he said. "She did it out of obligation." I asked why that was. "Her mother didn't love her," he said. "Her mother didn't even like her. Her mother liked her brother but not her." I asked about his father. "My father's mother didn't like him either," he said. "When my father's family got together, she would just sit there; she never showed affection or interest in her children." Diane Rehm recalls that, to her and her sister, their mother "was a bitter, angry, depressed woman who had very little in the way of a positive emotional connection to us."

## Leaning on a Mother's Strength

There are, nonetheless, mothers who do provide that kind of solace, according to their children's memories. A man who credits his mother with unwavering love, support, and self-sacrifice is the black South African writer Mark Mathabane. When asked how he became a writer, given his childhood in the ghastly shacks of Alexandra, Johannesburg—where no books were in view and neither of his parents could read or write—Mathabane replied, "The seeds of this love for knowledge and for reading were planted . . . when my mother would gather us around the fire—usually we were wracked with pangs of hunger, because there was nothing to eat—and she would tell such mesmerizing stories, vivid images, deeply entertaining and instructive." It was his mother's determination that her children be educated, even though she was not, that laid the foundation for Mathabane's improbable success.

In his novel *The Grapes of Wrath,* John Steinbeck describes a mother's power to give strength to her family, and at the same time conveys the sense in which a mother represents a whole family—indeed represents, in our imaginations, the qualities of support, acceptance, and protection that we associate with the idea of family:

> She seemed to know, to accept, to welcome her position, the citadel of the family. . . . And since old Tom and the children could not know hurt or fear unless she acknowledged hurt and fear, she had practiced denying them in herself. And since, when a joyful thing happened, they looked to see whether joy was on her, it was her habit to build up laughter out of inadequate materials. . . . She seemed to know that if she swayed the family shook, and if she ever really deeply wavered or despaired the family would fall, the family will to function would be gone.

I saw this kind of strength in my Greek mother-in-law (my first husband's mother), who told me that she always made sure to appear composed and calm when she said good-bye to her sons: two who went to Germany to study and one who went to the United States to live. Only after they had disappeared from sight would she allow herself to cry.

## My Mother, My Rock of Gibraltar

Hope Edelman's book *Motherless Daughters* hit a nerve for many women who have mentioned it to me. "I miss her every day" is a comment I hear from many women whose mothers passed away. Often what is missed is someone who cares about the most mundane details of your life. A woman who called in to a talk show said of her mother, who had died, "She was my Rock of Gibraltar. I'd call her up to tell her I got a good price on toilet paper."

Odd as this detail might seem, it fits exactly with what Karen Henwood found when she interviewed mothers and their adult daughters in the United Kingdom about their relationships. They answered in terms of closeness, which they defined as confiding in each other about personal matters, including the minutiae "that would be too inconsequential to tell anyone else."

Interest in the most minute details of your life sends a metamessage of caring—and it is this caring that seems embodied in a mother's solace. The interest in small aspects of your life is understood to represent a far-reaching and all-encompassing kind of care. Sue Silverman, whose mother's protection was a rare occurrence, captures this aspect of a mother's solace in her memoir *Because I Remember Terror, Father, I Remember You.* Silverman recounts how her mother simply withdrew, feigning illness, when her father sexually molested and raped her. But she cherished a single memory in which her mother really was a mother to her, "the mother who knew how to listen, the mother who knew how to whisper the word 'sorry,' the mother who wasn't scared."

Silverman was in her early twenties, living alone. A man had just ended a romantic relationship with her. In emotional turmoil she sat on her couch with a telephone in her lap as "if it were all that remained of the relationship. It was all that remained of any relationship. . . . I was afraid to go to bed. . . . I believed, at that moment, I needed to hear my mother." Silverman dialed her mother's number, even though it was the middle of the night. Mercifully, magically, her mother agreed to talk—that is, to listen. After a few attempts to reassure her daughter ("One day you'll meet the right man," "You're a lovely girl"), she absorbed the depth of her daughter's distress and said, simply, after a pause, "Oh, dear. I'm so sorry." And Silverman recalls: "*Sorry,* I'd whispered to myself. *Sorry.* A word I'd waited to hear, a word to ease me through the night, a word to protect me until morning."

The word *sorry* provided protection and comfort because it meant that her mother understood—and cared about—what her daughter was feeling. That meant the daughter was not alone in the world, as she felt when her love relationship ended (and as she had felt throughout her childhood).

## The Other Side of Solace

Yet a mother's solace can have the opposite effect. One couple had to take their daughter home from college because she was having psychological problems. "It must be so hard for you," the mother said. But the daughter was angry rather than comforted. I suspect she saw her problems magnified in her mother's sympathy.

The mother-child relationship is emblematic of the inextricable double meanings of the two continua, connection and control. A mother's expression of sympathy or caring can hit that nerve. Not only does your mother's sympathy make you feel worse because it exaggerates the problem, but also, if your mother feels awful when you tell her about a problem, then you are guilty of causing her pain. This is the experience of a woman who had been unhappy in her job for some time, and had been unsuccessfully trying to get a better one, when she received yet another rejection from a company she had hoped would hire her. "I can't bear to tell my mother," she said. "Something about her pity is so heavy." Part of that weight, I think, is that her mother feels the disappointment so deeply that it becomes bigger. The metamessage is, "Anything that can hit my mother so hard must weigh an awful lot."

The other dynamic explains the experience of Carol, who finds that if she tells her mother of a problem, she is likely to hear the next day, "I was up all night worrying about what you told me. I feel so bad for you." I suspect that the mother's objective in saying this is to convey connection: "I care about you; I feel what you are going through; you are not alone in the world." But her mother's comments only compound Carol's distress, adding her mother's suffering on top of her own. In addition to worrying about her own problem, she has to worry about causing her mother to lose sleep. She ends up comforting her mother, assuring her that it isn't so bad.

Children don't all respond to expressions of sympathy—or any other maternal communications—the same way. Knowing that these liabilities exist, each parent-child pair must find their own comfort point for conversations. For some less sympathy will be more comforting: "That's hard, but I'm sure you'll work it out." For others more sympathy will yield more comfort. The only way to find the right blend is to metacommunicate; you can actually ask, "Is this making you feel better or worse?" or "What can I say or do to help?"

## Giving Comfort, Enforcing Discipline

Giving comfort is a two-edged sword because of the connection-control grid on which all family relationships are placed. The verbal act of comforting is at the closeness end of the connection continuum, because it grows out of and creates intimacy. But it is also at the hierarchy end of the control continuum when the one who offers comfort does so from a position of strength. Because this paradox is inherent in the mother-child relationship, comforting is, in a way, a quintessential maternal way of speaking.

That giving comfort is one of the main elements of mothering emerges in research on little girls at play. The other element of mothering that little girls were found to enact frequently is discipline. Though disciplining a child is clearly at the hierarchy end of the control continuum, it, too, creates connections. Seeing the power these two verbal acts of mothering have for the littlest children sets in relief the dynamics that drive all mother-child relationships. Let's watch how it plays out in the conversations of little girls.

"I'll be the mommy and you be the baby," little girls say to initiate play. One little girl whose talk was taped by her parents as part of their participation in my research project had two favorite scenes she liked to reenact with her mother, with their roles reversed. In one scene, which she never tired of replaying, the baby misbehaves and her mother disciplines her. In the other the child feels sad and her mother comforts her. Looking at these scenes provides insight into the power and the specific dynamics of the mother-child relationship, as seen through the eyes of a three-year-old—and as we continue to experience it throughout our lives. My research assistant Cynthia Gordon transcribed these conversations, identified the pattern, and worked out the analysis of them. I am quoting from her study.

During the period that the mother was taping her conversations, the little girl, called Natalie, was feeling sad because her friend Annie had moved away, and her mother had comforted her. Later the same week Natalie's mother was preparing her for a nap when Natalie turned to her and proposed, "Say 'Where's Annie?' and I will say 'She moved away.' "

Complying, the mother asks, in a high-pitched little-girl voice, "Where's Annie?"

"She moved away, sweetheart," says little Natalie, speaking in the same soothing tone her mother uses when comforting her. And, just as her mother had reassured Natalie a few days earlier, Natalie now reassures her mother (taking the role of Natalie) that she has another friend to play with: "Sarah will have to play babies with you," she says.

Gordon identified another occasion on which Natalie reversed roles with her mother—and replayed, word for word, with exactly the same lilt and flow, a conversation they had had earlier in the week. Natalie's mother was trying to carry on an important telephone conversation while her three-year-old was screaming for attention. In desperation the mother threatened, "If you scream while I'm on the phone you will have time-out."

A few days later Natalie proposes to her mother, "Be noisy while I'm on the phone."

Her mother obliges, wailing, "Mommy! Mommy! Mommy! I need you!" in a high-pitched voice.

At this Natalie tells her sternly, "If you scream, you will have to have a time-out."

In commenting on her findings, Gordon notes that the themes of these scenes—comfort and discipline—are the same two themes that sociologist Jenny Cook-Gumperz observed with two preschool British girls playing "mummies and babies." In "comforting sequences" they say to their dolls things like "shush" and "poor baby," while in "scolding/disapproval sequences" they tell their dolls, "naughty baby."

The dual acts of comforting and scolding capture the dynamics of connection and control as expressed by mothers toward their children. And both entail both dynamics. Comfort creates connection, but it also reflects hierarchy. Scolding reflects a parent's power, but it also creates connection. The fact that Natalie chooses these two scenes to reenact with her mother is testimony to the importance of these speech acts in her life. (It also shows that Natalie knows very well how a mother speaks and how a child speaks—even though she chooses to speak like a child when she is not role-playing her mother.)

## My Mother's Keeper: Reversing the Caretaker Role

Though we can't keep giving our mothers lines to say, or getting them to role-play with us, we all, I think, continue to balance and sort out these dynamics as we engage our mothers, and our adult children, in conversations throughout our lives. And there are often ways that mothers and adult children reverse roles, as the child comforts or cares for the parent.

Many children, especially daughters, feel their mothers' suffering as a burden it is their responsibility to alleviate. Stacey called her parents from a ski vacation and found them both in a good mood. When they heard where she was, her father quipped, "Do these things now, because when you're retired you won't have time." They all laughed at his joke. When she was hanging up Stacey said, "It's so great to hear you both sounding happy." Her mother immediately switched to a sighing voice. It was as if she feared that by allowing her daughter to see her happy she was losing some power over her. "I wasn't happy the last few days," she said glumly, and began to recount why. Stacey's own happiness began to drain away, replaced by the helpless feeling she got when her mother was unhappy and she couldn't fix it.

In her memoir *Daughter of the Queen of Sheba,* Jacki Lyden describes how she and her two sisters repeatedly rescued their mentally ill mother from one or another disastrous situation. No matter how many times they vow to stop bailing her out if she refuses to get psychiatric help, the sisters find they can't, because, as Lyden puts it, her mother is in her bones. She quotes her sister: "I feel like her problems are my problems. . . . I wake up, I'm with her. I go to bed, I'm with her. I've got my own family now. I'm supposed to be independent."

Jacki feels the same way. She describes a scene when her mother, in a manic phase, has invested money she does not have in yet another of her futile business schemes:

> One Saturday I stopped in and found my mother in her kitchen, surrounded by pyramids of carefully stacked purple coffee cups. She smiled at me. On each cup, she'd had her motto tastefully inscribed. "Think About Me," said the little cups. "Think About Me, Think About Me, Think About Me." Five hundred times over. "Think About Me."
>
> Oh, Mother, as if we could ever think about anything else.

Their mother's mental illness required Lyden and her sisters to take care of her at an earlier age than most children have to. Whenever a parent is ill, mentally or physically, this reversal takes place. Other situations, such as immigration, can bring it on, too: A child's ability to speak the language when a parent can't means the child speaks for the parent instead of the other way around.

For most adults, though, the reversal comes on gradually as their parents age. Marcia got a glimpse of such a reversal while visiting her grandmother in a nursing home. Grandma was blind, and her memory had deserted her along with her sight. She said to Marcia, "I told my mother that I don't like it here, but she said she can't help me; I just have to get used to it." At first Marcia thought that her grandmother had imagined a conversation with her own mother, dead so many years. But then she realized that she was referring to a real conversation she had had—with her grown daughter, Marcia's mother, who was her primary caretaker. Mother-daughter, daughter-mother—the relationship was the same, only her role was reversed.

Just as mothers can be invisible, their contributions taken for granted, so daughters sometimes feel that their attentions to their mothers are invisible. Because she was a lawyer, Judy found that her mother expected her to devote untold hours to doing her mother's taxes, looking over contracts, and generally serving as her private attorney. Occasionally Judy enlisted the aide of her husband, who was also a lawyer, when an area of law involved his expertise more than hers. Judy found that her mother expressed gratitude to her son-in-law but never to her daughter. On one occasion she even said, "I'll have to thank Arnie. I don't have to thank you!" On another, after Judy had invested a particularly large amount of time and effort in a matter that she was able to resolve in her mother's favor, her mother began a sentence, "Thank . . . ," and Judy was certain that at last the sentence would end ". . . you." Instead her mother completed the sentence: ". . . goodness it all worked out."

## "I Don't Know Why You Attacked Me"

Carolyn also felt that her mother, Elsa, did not appreciate her efforts. She had tried so hard to show her mother a wonderful weekend in New York, and her mother's response was to take her to task for one false note. The thank-you letter Carolyn received made her feel so bad she closed it in a drawer for days.

Carolyn had booked rooms at a comfortable new hotel, chosen a play she thought her mother would like, and hosted dinner at carefully selected restaurants. But one evening at dinner Elsa didn't like her food and sent it back. After bringing a replacement the waitress asked Elsa if it was okay now, and Elsa grumbled, "No, but never mind." Carolyn felt her mother was putting the waitress in a difficult position. "Either send it back again and let them fix it," she said, "or don't say it's not okay." The moment passed, but it was the one Elsa focused on in her note. She also thanked her daughter "for including me in the weekend," and enclosed a check to cover her part of the cost.

Carolyn felt that her mother was canceling out her efforts right and left. By thanking Carolyn for "including" her, Elsa was denying that Carolyn had planned the entire trip as a gift to her mother. Sending a check also canceled out the gift. But most hurtful was accusing her daughter of attacking her when Carolyn had made such a small and innocent remark. How could her mother let this one comment overshadow everything?

Carolyn allowed me to see her mother's letter. "I'm still not sure why you 'attacked' me at dinner Saturday night," Elsa wrote. "Was I really that rude to the waitress? (She even leaned into my ear and whispered, 'I'm with you.') Whatever, I hope I can be more careful in the future and you can be more tolerant." There is a plaintive, poignant tone to Elsa's hope that she can be more careful. Of course she can't, if she doesn't know what she did that was wrong. Her real plea is for Carolyn to "be more tolerant"—that is, less critical. The irony is that Elsa's complaint is exactly parallel to Carolyn's: Why did her daughter have to zero in on one false move?

Because we want so much to feel that our mothers—and our daughters—think well of us, any comment that indicates anything less than complete approval swells in significance, overshadowing everything else. And that is why the criticism I hear from mothers and about mothers is overwhelmingly about . . . criticism.

## Do It Over, Do It Better

I overheard two women chatting; one was knitting, and the other asked her how she had learned to knit. Her answer stuck with me: "My mother took up knitting when I was little," the woman said. "She knitted a sweater for herself. When I grew up she gave it to me, but it didn't fit. It was too tight. The wool was really beautiful, though—expensive wool, and I hated to see it go to waste. So I pulled it out and reknitted it myself, in the right size. I taught myself knitting in order to do that." What a powerful metaphor, I thought: a daughter pulling out the stitches her mother had knitted in order to get a sweater that better fits who she is. Just so, adult daughters tell me they were determined to be better mothers to their children than their mothers were to them. Pull it out, do it over: If you do it right, somehow you'll end up with a mother-child relationship that fits.

For many women becoming a mother is a way of establishing the mother-child bond that they never had, or that they had and lost. One such woman is Elizabeth Kim, author of the memoir *Ten Thousand Sorrows*. Kim lived with her mother in a tiny Korean village, isolated from the rest of the family and the village because she was the illegitimate child of an American soldier. When she was six she watched through the cracks of a basket in which she was hiding as her mother's father and brother hanged her mother to death because she refused to sell her mixed-race daughter into slavery. Kim was deposited at an orphanage and eventually adopted by an American couple. Sadly, they too were unable to love her and forced her at seventeen to marry a man who beat her daily. Kim saw only one escape from her boundless desolation: She defied her husband and became pregnant in order to re-create with a child the enveloping bond of love and protection that she had had for six years with her Korean mother. It was her determination to protect her infant daughter that gave her the courage to leave her abusive husband.

This moving story sets in relief the power of a mother-child bond to comfort not only the child but the mother. I have seen more than one mother-daughter pair who present an impermeable wall to the world—mothers who seem so besotted with their young adult daughters that, when the daughters are present, they have eyes only for them. In many ways they are like women in love. Mothers tell me they cannot make plans for a particular weekend because their daughter or son might visit and they are keeping it open. They call to cancel dates because an adult child has announced an unplanned visit. I have pondered this. I think it reveals how consuming a mother's love and devotion can be—for the mother as well as the child.

## Letting Gardens, and Mothers, Grow

Richard knew just how to observe Mother's Day. As he always did on this day of the year, he was working in his mother's garden, busily planting specially selected flowers for her, pleased that he was getting them in the ground early enough in the season. Then his mother appeared. Instead of expressing appreciation and admiration for his work, she said, "Y'know, I travel a lot now and I'm not really here to enjoy the garden as much as I used to. And a garden takes a lot of upkeep, with weeding and watering and all. If you really want to, you can do that, but you don't have to."

Richard felt hurt, undervalued, and resentful. He had knocked himself out to keep this family tradition: although he had just returned from a business trip, and would go into the hospital Monday for elective surgery, he made sure to get up early and head to his mother's house to work in her garden. He felt that she was minimizing his effort and failing to appreciate his sacrifice. He didn't say anything at the time—he just finished the job. But a few days later he confronted her: "I think you minimize things too much," he said. "It's okay to really enjoy things and take pleasure in them and express that pleasure." And he gave the garden as an example. "But I was just telling the truth," she said. So he got no satisfaction from the conversation.

Though Richard thought he was "confronting" his mother, in fact what he said to her was so abstract that its meaning was opaque. "You minimize things" could refer to anything. He would have gotten his point across more clearly, I think, if he had spoken personally and specifically: "I was hurt when you said that. I had gone to a lot of trouble to work in your garden, like I always do, and I felt as if you were minimizing my efforts." He might also have said, "I was confused. I felt like you were telling me that I should keep working on the garden at the same time that you were telling me it didn't mean much to you anymore. So whatever I did I couldn't feel good about it." Speaking about his particular experience and feelings rather than her "tendency to minimize things" would have been more likely to elicit a response that addressed his feelings—and hers.

I also think, though, that Richard's mother was trying to tell him this was no longer the best way for him to show his love for her. Her life had changed; perhaps the reason was, as she said, that she traveled more and wasn't home to enjoy the garden as much. Maybe she simply wasn't as "into" the garden as she had been. Perhaps it had to do with aging: Now in her seventies, she might find gardening work more tiring. Or perhaps as she got older, and no longer saw her life as limitless, she felt that weeding and watering were not the way she wanted to spend her remaining time on earth.

Richard felt that his mother wasn't appreciating his efforts, but in a way Richard wasn't listening to his mother, wasn't seeing that she was growing older and changing. It would have been easier for him to appreciate this if she had spoken more directly about it. But he could have made this easier for her by asking beforehand: "I want to do something for you for Mother's Day. Do you want me to do your garden, like I always do, or is there some other way we could spend the day that you would like better?" Even when she surprised him while he was busily gardening for her, he could have laid down his garden tools and said, "Wait a minute, Mom. I'm doing this for you. You tell me whether or not you want me to do it." Richard himself might feel sad if this Mother's Day tradition did not continue. Maybe *he* enjoyed working in his mother's garden. And maybe he would feel sad to think that his mother was aging and changing.

Parents often complain that their adult children won't let them change. Children don't want their parents to move from the home in which they grew up, or convert their old bedrooms into offices. They refuse to take their cartons out of the attic or basement and become angry at even the suggestion that their parents might throw them away. We are more focused on our parents as the repositories of our childhoods, which we want to hold on to, than on the sacrifices they made for us that they might no longer want to make—such as using their own bedroom or the dining room as an office so we could have a bedroom.

## My Mother, My Friend

Comedian Judy Carter tells this joke:

> I had a relationship that lasted thirteen years, and ended just like that. She said, "Let's just be friends." I said, "OK, Mom."

This joke captures something important about mothers and daughters.

Ruth Wodak and Muriel Schulz conducted a study comparing relationships between mothers and daughters in the United States and Austria. They found that it was typical for American—but not Austrian—daughters to say that their mothers are their best friends. The hallmark of best friends, for girls and women, is that they tell each other everything, especially secrets. But there is also an inherent conflict between being friends and being a parent. Friends, in theory at least, have no authority over each other—that is, no institutionalized authority. But parents have ultimate authority over their children—in obvious ways when the children are little but in continuing ways when they are grown.

An American woman living in Japan had this perspective brought home to her. While working in a small restaurant in Kyoto, she became close to the restaurant owner, a woman who showed her special kindness by giving her dinner, fixing her apron, and generally watching out for her. One day the American was visited at the restaurant by a relative, and she introduced the owner by saying, "This is my friend."

"Friend?" the owner reacted with disbelief and dismay. "I'm like your mother!"

To the American, *friend* had all the positive connotations of closeness that she wanted to convey. To say her boss was acting like her mother would have sounded like criticism. But in Japan, the parent-child relationship connotes closeness and caretaking without the negative overtones it has taken on for many Americans.

## The Queen of Biting Tongues

Colleen shared good news with her friend Gretchen: Colleen's daughter was about to get married and move out on her own. Since Gretchen had several adult children with whom she seemed to have excellent relationships, Colleen asked if she had any advice to offer. Indeed she did. Gretchen said, "You'll have to become the Queen of Biting Tongues."

This advice reminded me of something I heard from someone else. A friend who never complains about her mother introduced me to her parents at her fiftieth birthday party. I seized the chance to ask her mother how her relationship with her daughters (she has two) had changed since they've become adults with children of their own. She said that now when her daughters tell her that they plan to do something she doesn't think is a good idea, she says nothing, unless they ask her advice.

In addition, my friend's mother said, when she goes to her daughters' homes, she behaves like a guest: "I don't go into the kitchen, open the refrigerator, and say, 'Why are you keeping this here? This should go on the shelf!' My mother and mother-in-law did that to me. They would come into my house and say, 'That picture looks terrible there!' or 'That vase is ugly!' or 'Why did you paint your bathroom that color?' I know how much that bothered me, so I won't do it to them."

I think some parents would be hurt to feel that they have to act "like guests" in their own daughters' homes, because it would seem to negate the meaning of family. Focusing on the continuum between closeness and distance, they would find that a failure of closeness. But if you remember that you're also dealing with the continuum between equality and hierarchy, you can think of it simply as acknowledging the special power you have as a parent—and choosing to wield it with discretion.

EIGHT

# "Help Me—Get out of My Way"

## Sisters and Brothers Forever

A WOMAN I KNOW asked me what I was writing about. "Family communication," I said.

She seemed interested.

"Especially adult families," I added.

"Oh, yes," she warmed up. "Like dealing with aging parents. That's good."

"More like adult siblings, actually," I clarified.

"Oh Lord!" she exploded with emotion and energy. "Now you're on it!" And she followed up with a ten-minute diatribe detailing her frustrations with her sister and brother.

There are few relationships as close—or as hierarchical—as the relationship between siblings. The closeness is reflected in the way we use the words: "He's like a brother to me," "We're like sisters," meaning, "We are completely comfortable in each other's company; we know everything about each other; we love each other that much."

Having grown up together, having been there from the beginning, is what makes siblings close: They shared their childhoods. For example, in a story by Joan Silber, when the narrator needs someone to talk to about her boyfriend, she immediately thinks of her sister Tina: "I had gotten into several quarrels with Gene on the car ride back, and I couldn't tell how serious they were and I wanted to call Tina right away to ask her opinion." For women especially, a sister is a built-in buddy, ready for rapport-talk conversations by which to work out how they feel about people and events in their lives.

Yet there is also no relationship as hierarchical as the one between siblings. In many languages there are no words simply for "sister" and "brother." There are only words that reflect siblings' relative ages—and hence relative status. For example, in Sinhala, the language of Sri Lanka, a younger brother is *malli,* an older brother is *ayiya,* a younger sister is *nanggi,* and an older sister is *akka.* In Chinese families siblings address each other not by name but by titles that reflect the order of their birth: Third Eldest Brother, Fifth Younger Sister, and so on. This naming system puts into words the sense of where you are in the sibling hierarchy that pervades brothers' and sisters' relationships long after they are grown.

Even siblings of the same age—twins—can vie with each other over who's best and who's right. Keith did not have a twin brother, but he discovered this pattern in his friend Jesse, who did. Keith felt so comfortable with Jesse that he invited him to join his family for a week on their sailboat, which Keith himself captained. In this context Keith saw a new side of his friend: Jesse found fault with everything Keith did and started doling out small mocking jabs, little verbal rebellions. On the sailboat, where everyone's life was in Keith's hands, the behavior was not just irritating but downright scary. Sensing he was rattling his friend, Jesse said, with chagrin, "I'm treating you the way I treat my twin brother."

Several aspects of the setting could have brought out the competition: the family context, the audience of other relatives, and the hierarchy inherent in Keith being captain and Jesse a member of the crew. Whatever brought it out, treating his friend like a twin brother meant moving farther from the equality end of the continuum, more toward the hierarchy end.

Sisters and brothers are born into the same family, but it's a different family when each is born. Parents are first-time parents or experienced parents; live in different homes or different circumstances; have more money or less money—and if there are older siblings or stepsiblings, that, too, makes the family completely different. Illness or death, of a parent or child, also changes the family irrevocably, in different ways for different children. Parents speak differently to girls than they do to boys, and they speak differently to older siblings than to younger ones; older or younger siblings learn different ways of talking within the family; and these patterns of speaking take hold, influencing both how we speak and how we react when others speak for the rest of our lives.

Looking more closely at sisters and brothers—how the sibling relationship persists and develops into adulthood—sheds light on the interplay of connection and hierarchy that drives all family talk and family relationships.

## Birth Order Forever

Bessie Delany said of her older sister, "You know, Sadie doesn't approve of me sometimes. She frowns at me in her big-sister sort of way." Bessie was 101 when she said this, and Sadie was 103. The Delany sisters were immutably older and younger, those two small years between them so powerful that the gap continued to shape their relationship after they had both lived an entire century.

J. D. Dolan, in his memoir *Phoenix,* describes how he and his adult sisters—all older than he—continue to take the roles they learned as children in their dealings with each other. For example, having returned home for their father's funeral, they all accompany their mother to the funeral parlor, where she must choose a casket:

> Joanne, the oldest, led Mom from casket to casket, and they talked quietly, sometimes turning to ask a question. . . .
>
> June drifted around the showroom like an unmoored boat.
>
> Janice stared at one of the top-end caskets and twirled a strand of dark brown hair around her finger. . . .

Joanne, the oldest, was in place beside Mom, helping her make the decision. That left the other two sisters "unmoored," freed from the task but also adrift, since they weren't needed. And unneeded is just one step from excluded:

> We all went back into the funeral director's little office, where Joanne took the lead and started going through some of the practical matters of the burial ("And the difference between the two caskets is, this one's waterproof?"), weighing the costs and the options. June just sat there in high-idle, smoking a cigarette, and only once interjected a semihostile question ("*Which* casket is waterproof?"), as if we'd been trying to exclude her from the process.

Years later the siblings sadly gather again when Dolan's older brother is grievously (it turns out fatally) burned in an explosion. The author and his sisters, along with their mother, keep a two-week vigil at the hospital as his brother's condition worsens. Once again Dolan describes how each plays the role assigned by the order of birth:

> At times it did seem as if this catastrophe had reduced us to ourselves, as if we really did live inside the petty roles of childhood—Joanne the big sister, the peacemaker; Janice the middle child, with a middle child's resentment; June the youngest girl, her naïveté transformed into disappointment; and me the baby, who would rather be done with it quickly, then go outside and play—or, in this case, drive.

Despite these starkly different ways of dealing with their brother's devastating injury, the four siblings, with their mother, all gather at the hospital and keep vigil there until their brother John dies. Though the patterns formed by the order of their birth (and, of course, their individual personalities) created frustrations at this terrible time, they nonetheless faced the loss together, as a family.

## "You're Having That as Your *Meal*?" Birth Order at Dinner

Though tragedies bring out family patterns in particularly stark ways, the habitual ways of talking that reflect our places in the family emerge even in the most unremarkable, everyday settings. One evening three grown daughters had dinner with their mother at a restaurant. (Their conversation was taped—with everyone's knowledge and agreement—by one of the sisters.) When my research assistant Alexandra Johnston was transcribing the conversation, she had figured out which sister was the oldest by the time the family had ordered dinner. Let's see what she noticed.

When the youngest sister (I'll call her Yvonne for "Youngest") asked, "Does anyone want to split a dish? I don't think I can eat a whole meal," the oldest sister (I'll call her Olga for "Oldest") had the solution: "Well, take it home and eat it for lunch tomorrow. That's what I do." No one volunteered to split a dish with Yvonne, so she said she might have a salad. Olga then pointed out, "I think everything comes with salad." Olga also supervised their mother's decisions: Their mother recalled that she had been unable to finish her meal the night before, and Olga offered her the same advice: "Then eat it for lunch. That's what I do." Explaining that she had had a late lunch, Yvonne went for the salad after all—but not before her mother echoed Olga's reminder, "We're going to get a salad first," and Olga expressed disbelief: "You're having that as your *meal*? You're really not hungry?" Among the four women only the mother and the oldest daughter passed judgment on someone else's order—and Olga gave advice not only to her sister but also to their mother, in a rather direct way ("Take it home").

Offering advice and expressing concern are often perceived as the prerogatives of older siblings, and younger ones often object. A woman called to ask her younger brother how he was handling his financial problems and whether he had had any success securing a loan. "I'm his sister," she told a friend. "He's in serious financial trouble. I'm not going to pretend it doesn't exist. Of course I'm going to call and ask him about it." "Well what did he say?" her friend asked. "He blew a fuse," she replied. "He told me to stop trying to be his mother. That really hurt. I said I only bring it up because I *care* about him."

The resentment of a younger sibling when an older one gives advice can apply to older brothers as well as sisters. But when the older sibling is female, the parent who comes to mind is the mother. As this brother's comment shows, older sisters are caught in the same paradox we saw with mothers. The older sister, like mothers, is focused on the caring. But her brother, like children of any age, interprets her concern as criticism and interference. With siblings as with parents (especially when the children are teenagers or young adults), the younger sibling seems often to say, "Help me with this," then add, "Get out of my way!"

## Older Sister: Mini-Mom

Rita, the older of two sisters, picks their mother up and takes her to church each Sunday, even though this means a forty-five-minute drive to get her, a half-hour drive to the church, and then another hour and fifteen minutes to get both of them home. Her sister, Jeanette, lives only a short drive from their mother's house; she would lose only a few minutes, rather than hours, if she took on this task. But when Rita suggests that Jeanette and her husband pick their mother up, Jeanette is adamant that she can't do it because their mother sometimes keeps them waiting.

Outrageous as this seems, there is a story behind the story. On questioning, Jeanette admits that she feels she can't ask her husband to adjust his schedule to get her mother. Since Jeanette knows she can count on Rita to get their mother to church, it is far easier for her to inconvenience her sister than to risk confrontation with her husband. Her sister's anger is a price Jeanette is willing to pay to buy harmony with her husband. A reliable and sturdy older sister is often expected to pick up the slack, simply because she is so, well, reliable.

Rita's resentment may be typical of older siblings who find they are still expected to do more than their share of caretaking for parents and also for siblings who are now adults. But younger siblings have their own resentments, which often are the flip sides of their older siblings' complaints. If the older sister feels she does too much, so does the younger.

## "Hey, You Guys, Wait for Me!"

Some years ago my two older sisters helped me out. Naomi, the oldest, offered to give me a table she no longer needed. When Mimi (two years older than I) and her husband were visiting Naomi, they took the table to their own home. A few weeks later Mimi drove down to visit me and brought the table in the back of their van. Soon after her arrival Mimi and my husband (who, I might note, is an older brother) decided to bring in the table. Quick as a wink they had their coats on and were out the door. I put on my shoes and followed—but by the time I got to the porch, they were already maneuvering the table. Feeling helpless and useless as I stood on the porch, I called out, plaintively, "Hey, you guys, wait for me!"

Both Mimi and I burst out laughing. This refrain took us right back to our childhoods, when Mimi was always one step ahead. A scene leapt to mind—one I was too young to remember but that I've seen over and over in a home movie.

Soon after he got a movie camera, my father filmed us playing in Prospect Park: Mimi, at four; our neighbor Michael, who was Mimi's age; and me, just two. Michael and Mimi are happily running between two trees—first around one, then across a field and around the other. I am trying to join their game, but I'm struggling to keep up. As Mimi and Michael are dashing back on a return trip, I am running with all my might in the opposite direction, still bent on making my first loop around the distant tree.

And there you have the scene that replays again and again when you're growing up (just as my parents loved to replay that home movie): The older sibling is capable, competent, running ahead, while the younger one is awkward, incompetent, trailing behind. This constellation, forged in childhood, can resurface whenever siblings come together, no matter how old they are.

## Baby Sister's Revenge

Maureen felt incompetent compared with her older sister, Meg. Meg had always shown her how to do things and helped her do things better. If their mother was away or sick, Meg did the cooking and took over cleaning the house. As an adult Maureen gradually gained confidence and ultimately became a manager at a large pharmaceutical firm. But when she is with Meg, she begins to feel the way she did as a child: The weight of feeling helpless makes her wobble, and then she resents Meg for knocking her off balance.

Meg was visiting her younger sister. One morning both sisters headed to the kitchen for breakfast at the same time. After a few minutes, Maureen went to put up water for coffee and found the electric teakettle already on. Her older sister had beaten her to it. A small burst of anger erupted in Maureen's chest. How dare Meg take over in her kitchen while she was right there? (Had Meg gotten up before Maureen, she would not have minded her sister doing whatever she liked to prepare food for herself.) Maureen focused on the presumptuousness of Meg taking over, but I would wager that she reacted as she did because Meg's action threw her back to her childhood, when Maureen felt she couldn't do anything right and Meg seemed able to do everything. Meg might well have intended a metamessage of nonintrusion ("I won't impose by making you wait on me"), but Maureen perceived a completely different metamessage: "I'm the boss here—and everywhere. I can do things better than you."

Maureen didn't say anything about how she felt. Instead she picked on a small "faultable" she was lucky enough to spot. "Did you get the water from the tap?" she asked.

"Yes," Meg replied.

Maureen then said, "We don't drink tap water here. It has a funny taste. We use bottled water." With this she took the teakettle off its base, emptied it, filled it with bottled water, and put it back on to boil. The moment passed without further words, but inside Maureen guiltily noted that she was gleeful to have caught Meg in a mistake, because it gave her an excuse to undo her big sister's action and redo it herself.

In telling me about this, Maureen explained that she would never make a move in other people's kitchens without asking if she should, and asking how they prefer that it be done. "Shall I boil the water?" "Should I use this kettle?" "Do you prefer tap water or bottled?" Though this seems to Maureen self-evidently considerate, to some it could be as annoying as Meg's straightforward action was to her. Though Maureen sees herself as considerate, she is also making sure not to give anyone else grounds to correct her—to avoid the position of being corrected that she so often resented as a younger sibling. In other words, though she's a grown-up—a household manager at home and a business manager at work—the script from which she's reading her lines is still the one given to her as a younger sister.

## "You're Not My Mother"

When I think about this scene from Meg's point of view, Maureen's reaction seems terribly unfair. As the older, Meg was expected to take a motherlike role toward her younger sister. Now Maureen resents her for taking the role that was forced on her. And this is the case with older sisters even more than older brothers.

An example of this pattern comes from the PBS series that featured the Loud family of Santa Barbara, California. Delilah, at sixteen, is not the oldest sibling, just the oldest sister. There are two older brothers living at home: nineteen-year-old Kevin and seventeen-year-old Grant, whom we met in Chapter 6. (Lance is away.) There is also a sister one year younger (Michelle). Yet when their mother is out of town, Delilah is the one who assumes responsibility for food preparation. When Pat (the mother) returns from her trip, her husband, Bill, reports, "Oh, Delilah really took over, I'll tell you. She really loved that thing. Man, she stands right there (she's like your mother, you know), and she said, 'All right, Michelle, you set the table, and, Kevin, you cook the eggs, and, Grant, you cook the bacon, and I'll cook the toast, and, Dad, you fix the orange juice.' "

Bill believes that Delilah loved taking over; maybe she did. But maybe she just felt it was her job. How unfair it would be if Kevin, Grant, and Michelle ended up not appreciating that Delilah did the work of their mother but resented her for lording it over them. That's what happens to the older sister in many families: By being given responsibilities in taking care of the home, older sisters are often expected to act like mothers.

Parents in general, and mothers in particular, find themselves nicked by the double-edged sword of connection and control. If you care about people, you have opinions about how they should lead their lives, but expressing those opinions can come across as interfering or controlling rather than caring. Older sisters are often pressed into service as mini-moms, asked to take care of younger siblings. (Older brothers are routinely asked to teach younger siblings, and to protect them, but they are less often expected to take care of them.) Along with the responsibility of caring for younger sisters and brothers can come the habit of judging their behavior and telling them how they can do things better. When these habits continue into adulthood, older sisters can be resented for taking over and telling others what to do.

Rose, an older sister in her fifties, was telling of the strains that had attended a family gathering. "I felt vaguely unhappy the whole time," she said, "because I couldn't make everyone happy." Then she added, "I realize this is very narcissistic of me." Narcissistic—that is, self-centered—because she was worrying about everyone else? In a way, yes: Thinking it is your job to make everyone happy puts you at the center of the family. In that sense you are being self-centered. But it's a particular sort of self-centeredness when the power you seek is to make everything okay for everyone else—a benevolent dictatorship. That is what parenthood is. And that legacy is often passed on to the oldest child, especially the oldest sister.

## Taking the Family Script to Work

Family relationships provide a map that guides us through our adult lives, sometimes leading us to our goals, sometimes leading us down blind alleys or into cul-de-sacs.

Workplaces are often referred to—and experienced—as families. For one thing, co-workers often compete for the boss's affection and approval like siblings competing for their parents' attention. This was the situation at *The New Yorker* under the editor William Shawn, according to the writer Brendan Gill. Gill recalls that when he received a note from Shawn signed "With love," he felt enormously grateful, because "like everyone else on the magazine, I felt a desire, childish as it unquestionably was, to be a Shawn favorite, and even, still more childishly, to be first among his favorites."

How much this sounds like journalist and author Ana Veciana-Suarez recalling that much of her life was "spent in an effort to not disappoint" her father: "I needed to be better than he expected, better than my siblings, the outstanding among the extraordinary, the one he would notice in whatever way I could manage to get noticed." No doubt this motivation contributed to Veciana-Suarez's success as a journalist and novelist.

## Seeing the World Through Family-Colored Glasses

Our families are like filters through which we react to other situations and people throughout our lives. Students in my seminar were discussing an article by Sam Vuchinich, the sociologist who recorded dinner-table conversations in order to examine how conflicts ended. In one example two teenage sisters differed on a point of history. Jane said, "King Henry the Eighth is the one that started Protestantism," but her sister Alice disagreed: "Calvinists did that." Each argued for her view over a few turns, until Jane closed the discussion by saying, "Yeah. Whatever." A third sister then changed the subject. In commenting on the article to the seminar, I dismissed this example as being a disagreement rather than an argument. I said I didn't think it carried the emotional weight of other examples, in which family members differed about personal actions and desires.

A seminar member had a different view. "I really reacted to that example," he said. "If that conversation had taken place in my family, it would have been very emotionally loaded." He explained that among his brothers and parents, possessing knowledge and being right carries a lot of weight. Family members have staked out domains in which they are expert. Questioning their knowledge is a significant challenge; being exposed in an error is a significant humiliation.

The difference between this student's response and mine results, I suspect, from our sibling constellations: I have only sisters, he has only brothers. Status among girls and women is typically a function of rapport-talk: who is included, who is left out, and who confides in whom. Status among boys and men is typically a function of report-talk: who displays the most knowledge and expertise.

Here is an example of how this dynamic plays out in one family of brothers. Suppose they are watching a video. One brother might remark that a particular actor is the same one who played a certain role in another film. This remark will meet with a competing observation from another brother: "Yeah, but before that he had a role in this other film." A third brother might top that: "His first role was—!" The original observation sparks a competitive display of knowledge in which the brother who offers the most arcane tidbit wins, and anyone who gets the facts wrong loses. And this dynamic continues now that all the brothers are adults.

There are many brothers for whom family gatherings become competitions for expertise. The writer Michael Ondaatje describes such a set of brothers in *Running in the Family,* his memoir of returning to Sri Lanka (the former Ceylon):

> Simon was the oldest of four brothers. . . . For years [the brothers] tried but were never able to have a meal together. . . . There was nothing one could speak about that would not infringe on another's area of interest. If the subject was something as innocent as flowers, then Dr. William Charles Ondaatje, who was the Ceylonese Director of the Botanical Gardens, would throw scorn on any opinion and put the others in their place. He had introduced the olive to Ceylon. Finance or military talk was Matthew Ondaatje's area, and law or scholarship exercised Philip de Melho Jurgen's acid tongue.

Ondaatje describes a comic scene in which, every Sunday, the brothers come to their fourth brother Simon's church, with their families, intending to share lunch after the sermon. But every week their conversations become arguments, and each calls for his carriage and hustles his hungry family home before anyone has a chance to eat. The brothers' competition always turns their conversations into divisive arguments before they can have lunch, but family loyalty keeps them coming back each Sunday to try again.

## Watching Alignments, Setting Resentments

How are these alignments drawn that remain so fixed throughout our lives? Let's look at conversations that took place in families to see how children could develop both the loyalties and the resentments that last a lifetime.

Several of the conflicts Sam Vuchinich presents include sisters who defend family members, and take the heat as a result. Vuchinich offers the following example to illustrate how a mother breaks up a dispute between her son and daughter by telling them to stop squabbling. But, looking closely, we can see that the "squabbling" erupted when the sister (who is older) tried to side with and protect her mother.

The conflict begins when the mother asks, "Would it be ill manners if I smoked in front y'all?"

"Yeah. While we're eating," her husband, Duke, replies.

Her son piggybacks on his father's refusal: "You know how I feel about that."

Melissa, the daughter, then aligns with her mother against her brother. "Well, he's got a lot of room to talk," she says.

The mother responds by defending her son: "He just doesn't like people smoking around him."

Meanwhile, the son turns on his sister: "*What are you talking about?*" he demands, and repeats, "What are you talking about?"

"All your friends and everything," says Melissa, implying that he does not object to his friends smoking.

"They don't smoke around me," he says.

Then the mother verbally separates brother and sister by saying loudly, "*Melissa. Y'all.*"

Vuchinich comments that "*Y'all*" is the mother's shorthand for "*Y'all stop squabbling.*" And her injunction works; the topic turns to something else. But what struck me is how the son and daughter each aligned with the same-sex parent—and how the parents reacted. The seventeen-year-old brother aligned with his father by echoing his denial of the mother's request to smoke. The twenty-year-old daughter spoke up to side with her mother against him. But the mother showed no sign of appreciating this support; instead, she stepped in to defend her son's right to attack her. Then she singled out her daughter for disapproval by chastising her by name before including her son in a more general form of address: *"Melissa. Y'all."*

Perhaps the parents are inclined to protect the younger sibling against the older one. (Or perhaps their mother's reaction has to do with Melissa being female. If girls are expected to be peacemakers, they may be more severely sanctioned for squabbling.) In any case, the example dramatizes how alignments created by talk can favor a younger child over an older one, even when the older child was aligning with, and defending, her mother.

Vuchnich gives another example in which a daughter tries to protect a family member and gets jumped on for her efforts (though he presents the transcript simply as an example of a conflict). In this case the girl is the youngest. There is a wide age spread among these siblings: The older son is eighteen, the next son is twelve, and the daughter is only six. Yet look how fiercely she defends her middle brother against the oldest, and how fiercely her father comes down on her.

Vuchinich explains that the middle son, who has been a "source of trouble" because he hasn't been doing his chores, has left the room five minutes before. When the mother says to the father, "I thought you were going to send him to summer camp this year," the older son jumps on the bandwagon: "He needs to go to camp." He's aligning himself with her against the middle brother. Swiftly the daughter comes to her absent brother's defense: *"So do you, so shut up!"* And just as swiftly her father reprimands: *"All right!"* The son then intensifies his attack on the middle brother by adding, "A work labor camp." The daughter presses on with her defense of the absent brother, adding an attack on the one who's there: *"You too!"* she shouts.

"I told you to be quiet, didn't I?" the father intervenes. So the daughter repeats her accusation to him: "He needs to go to one too, Dad."

At this point, according to Vuchinich, the father slaps his "daughter sharply on the upper arm. There is a 6.5 second silence and a new topic of talk is started by the mother." The daughter is trying to align not with her mother but with a middle brother. But, like the daughter in the preceding example, she is trying to protect someone who has been picked on by others. And, like the other daughter, she is reprimanded for her efforts.

We cannot know what family experiences led up to these conversations. But they provide a glimpse of the shifting alignments—the alliances, the betrayals, the comparisons—created by talk among siblings and parents. In all cases age and gender both play a part, though it isn't always possible to distinguish the dual influences. It is easy to see how the sisters who are rebuked for trying to make peace might harbor resentment against the siblings who seem to be treated more leniently. Although the vast majority of conversations that take place in a family are ephemeral and soon forgotten (as I'm willing to bet these were—or would have been, if they hadn't been taped), the cumulative effect can be assumptions and habitual reactions that last a lifetime.

## Unequal Treatment

Almost any older sibling knows the feeling that the younger got preferential treatment, though sometimes it's hard to put your finger on how. You can see an example of how it happens—subtly but unmistakably—in the Australian researcher Alyson Simpson's recordings of her own family's talk.

As we saw in Chapter 5, Simpson analyzed the conversation that took place during a mundane family context: playing a board game. Her focus was issues of power, control, and "gendered subjectivity," but I was interested in the ways the older sister and younger brother were spoken to. In addition to the mother (Alyson) the family includes the father, their six-year-old daughter, Heather, and their four-year-old son, Toby. Since Heather is both the older sibling and a girl, while Toby is both the younger and a boy, it's impossible to isolate the influence of age and gender. I will focus on age—bearing in mind that gender may also be playing a role.

Let's look more closely at the ongoing conversation that included the conflicts I mentioned in Chapter 5. The family is playing a game called Babar Ups 'n' Downs, which the author identifies as a newer version of Snakes and Ladders. (It sounds like the game I played as a child called Chutes and Ladders.) Each player, represented by an animal token, throws the dice and advances his or her token the number of squares shown on the dice. The square on which a token lands directs a player how to move the token along the board.

Heather is in trouble. She is not happy with the results of her turn, and she wants to throw the dice again, hoping for a more favorable result. Her mother chastises her and gives her a lesson in following rules: "That was the luck of the chance that you threw, and that is how a game is played."

"No!" Heather protests, petulant.

"If you are going to be silly about it, Heather," her mother warns, "you can leave the game."

Heather's little brother echoes their mother: "She is being silly."

"I know she is being silly, Toby," their mother concurs. "You can't organize to win the game."

The mother accepts Toby's piggybacking on her criticism and reinforces his doing so by agreeing, repeating his echo of her words. In this way she aligns herself with little Toby as a team opposed to six-year-old Heather.

Encouraged, perhaps, by his mother's endorsement of his joining her team, Toby then picks up and repeats her threat, turning it into a command. "So leave the game!" he orders.

Mother continues to chastise her daughter: "Heather, it's a game! We've talked through this before."

"Leave the game!" Toby repeats.

At this Heather begins to cry, protesting, "It's not fair!"

The mother does not explicitly approve her son's right to order his older sister to leave the game, but neither does she reprimand him or interfere with his talking to his older sister as if he were her parent. (Toby's echo of his mother's threat is reminiscent of the earlier example in which an older brother ups the ante of his mother's comment on a troublesome younger brother: "He needs to go to camp.")

Now watch what happens when Heather tries to talk to her brother in the same way their mother might. Still playing the game, Heather shows her brother how to count. "One two three four five six," she says.

And Toby repeats, "One two three four five six."

Their mother then says, "Toby can count to six. He can count to ten. In fact he can count to ten in Greek."

The transcript alone does not make clear the spirit in which Heather counted and Toby repeated her words, but Alyson Simpson, author and mother, comments: "When Heather insists on showing Toby how to count to six, Alyson reminds her that Toby can count to ten in Greek." Looked at this way, we see Heather taking the role of mother, teaching her little brother to count. But her mother indirectly indicates she is acting improperly by informing her that Toby does not need her lesson: Not only does he know what Heather is teaching him but he knows more.

Then the mother shifts attention to the little boy, telling her husband how she learned of their son's impressive counting ability: They were browsing in a store specializing in math-related toys when Toby said, "That's ena." The mother did not immediately realize what he meant, so he repeated, "That's ena." (*Ena* is Greek for the number one.)

Mother then prompts Toby to display this knowledge for his father's benefit. "Do you remember what eight is in Greek, Toby?" she asks.

"Yes," Toby says.

"What is it?" she prompts.

Toby replies, "Otto."

"Otto," his mother repeats. "That's an easy one to remember."

At this point Heather chimes in, "Otto is." And then she tells her brother, "Count up to otto, eight in Greek. Toby?"

Heather here is aligning herself with her mother—trying to team up with her—by echoing Mother's request. But rather than appreciating her daughter's support, the mother says, "Wait a minute.

He's busy doing this." In other words, she opposes Heather and sides with Toby. This rejection is surprising, since it was the mother herself who brought up Toby's ability to count in Greek.

The game proceeds, but Heather is still taking the role of mother vis-à-vis Toby, who shows no inclination to do what his sister says. "Count up to otto in Greek," Heather tells Toby.

Toby's response is unequivocal: "No no no no."

Heather encourages him: "But Daddy would like to hear."

Heather, at six, is talking to her brother, only two years younger, as her mother would. Although this strikes me as rather charming, given Heather's age, I can imagine someone (a younger brother perhaps) finding it irritating. In any case, it is striking that the mother accepted and reinforced her four-year-old son's mimicking the role of parent to his older sister but showed no such acceptance or reinforcement of the girl's doing the same.

In the end Heather wins the game fair and square:

FATHER: Oh! Heather's won.
HEATHER: I won.
FATHER: Heather's won.

When I read these lines in Simpson's article, I thought the mother might turn this into an object lesson by saying something like, "You see? You don't have to cheat to win." But instead she says, "I don't know you deserved to after that display." Ouch.

There is nothing unusual about this conversation. It is as common as they come: a family playing a board game in the evening. But reading the words fixed in a transcript—words that were gone in a flash at the time—you can see the seeds of frustration that might be planted for both siblings. The older sister—just two years older—tries to talk to her little brother as if she were his mother. This is something the younger might well feel she has no right to do.

From the sister's point of view, her little brother is getting preferential treatment. Not only was her motherlike talk rejected while Toby's was accepted but she had been showcasing Toby for their father, whereas he had been trying to send her away. Most hurtful, the mother and the four-year-old son seem firmly aligned as a team, leaving the six-year-old sister outside the circle. (Simpson comments in her analysis that reminding Heather of the rhyme she knew, as we saw in Chapter 5, was a way to reestablish solidarity with her.)

I present this conversation not to hold this family up as a bad example. Quite the contrary, I believe it is typical of family talk. And it is conversations like these, taking place daily as we grow up—fleeting interchanges, ephemeral alignments—that set the resentments and allegiances that color our relationships with siblings throughout our lives.

It's hard to read this conversation without feeling bad for Heather. What could explain the favoritism? Heather was surely being difficult in wanting a second chance and becoming obstinate when denied. (It is clear from a remark her mother makes, "We've talked through this before," that Heather's petulance is not an isolated incident.) Perhaps the mother feels that the younger sibling needs protection whereas the older does not. Could she be trying to correct a general imbalance by which Heather is too hard on her little brother?

Perhaps the mother knows that when Heather gets Toby alone she makes life difficult for him. This is, after all, the case with many older brothers and sisters toward younger ones when they are out of their parents' view.

## "Can I Play in Your Backyard?"

The tyranny of an older brother or sister when there are no adults in sight is absolute. My father chuckles as he recalls that when I was three years old he overheard me asking my five-year-old sister, "Mimi? Can I play in your backyard?" I don't remember that, but I do remember this: Mimi and I shared a bedroom. One day she proposed a deal: Neither of us could step onto the other's side of the room without permission. Fair enough. I consented—before I realized that the door was on her side. I had agreed to become Mimi's prisoner, a contract that she enforced with glee. I can't tell you what she would have done had I simply stepped out of the room, because I never defied her. Mimi's word was law.

Older siblings know they have power, by virtue of their size, acumen, and rank, which many use to torment their younger sisters and brothers. One brother told his younger sister, at night when the pipes rattled, that there was a monster in her closet rapping on the walls. It may sound absurd to adults, but to the little girl it was real—and really frightening. An older brother bent on terrorizing a younger one was even more creative: He *became* the monster in the closet, hiding there quietly while their mother tucked the little brother into bed and turned out the light. Then the older brother began slowly pushing the closet door open. He recalls that the four-year-old "was out of bed and down the hall before he had time to scream."

Asking adults what they did to their younger siblings—or what their older sisters or brothers did to them—yields a panoply of cruelties that can be hair-raising. A brother closed the hide-a-bed with his little sister in it, and she remained trapped until their parents came home. Another used his little brother's feet for target practice to see how close he could throw darts without hitting him. He knew he had reached the limit of his skill when a dart got stuck in his brother's shin. And woe to the little boy who had *two* older brothers: "We used to put him in a laundry hamper," recalls the middle brother about the youngest, "and send him down the stairs. We thought that was great." The curve in the stairway, which the hamper hit hard, made the trip more treacherous—and more fun to watch.

Although both sisters and brothers can make life miserable for younger siblings, it's more often (though not exclusively) brothers who devise physical tribulations rather than (or in addition to) psychological ones. When Karen's parents asked her brother Victor what he had been doing, he answered, "I was playing with Karen in the backyard." They had no idea what activities were hidden in that innocent word *play.*

Four years older, Victor had constructed a sledding course for Karen. (He never hazarded it himself.) He hosed down the sloping surface of their backyard in the dead of winter and waited until it turned into a smooth, swift layer of ice. If Karen made the course, she went careening over a stone wall to fall three feet into the neighbor's yard. If she missed the tricky curve, she was thrown down a hill, which she could not climb up without her brother's help. Knowing this, he liked to leave her there for extended periods of time. I asked Karen, now an adult, whether she blamed him for this play. "I didn't blame him," she said. "I worshiped him." This more or less captured how I felt about my sister Mimi.

Mimi and her high school friend Davina recently asked me, guiltily, if I had forgiven them for the cruel things they did to me. In particular, did I hold it against them that they blindfolded me and forced me to eat cat food? They are surprised that I bear no grudge. In fact, I don't remember. What I recall is that Mimi and Davina—mischievous and daring where I was timid—protected me against threatening boys. At summer camp, when Mimi and Davina took everyone's shoes, tied the laces at random, and mixed them all up in a mound, they left my shoes alone. I recall my gratitude for their public protection more than my distress at their private torments.

For many older siblings the right to mistreat—even abuse—younger siblings in private goes along with an obligation to protect them from outsiders. Curt, whose brother John beat him so badly that he remarks, "I'm sure a psychiatrist would allow me to say I was an abused child," recalls that John "beat the shit out of some kid who was like ragging me. And this was John, who'd rag on me much worse than this kid was." In light of the connection-control grid, both childhood memories of being mistreated (or of mistreating) and of being protected (or of protecting) can contribute to the sense of being linked forever as members of a family.

The man who, as a child, hurtled down the stairs in a hamper bears no grudge against his brothers. It's not that he enjoyed the ride, but the fright and the bruises were a price worth paying to be included in his older brothers' play. "He really wanted to be with us most of all," says the middle one now. "He used to slip notes under Richie's door asking if he could spend time with him."

The desire for company can go both ways, though older siblings typically are better at masking it. A man says of his younger brother, with whom he shared a room as a child, "I remember after 'lights out' he would say 'Good night,' and I would say 'Bad night,' which really bothered him, so I loved to do it. But now I realize that I did it because I wanted him to stay up and talk to me.

He probably wanted to stay up too, because he wouldn't relax until I said 'Good night.' " So the older brother's slightly sadistic pleasure at the younger one's misery was, in a way, a ritual through which each could prolong the other's company before sleep. It was a power maneuver, for sure, but also a connection maneuver.

The guilt of the older sibling is, in many cases, deeper than the resentment of the younger, perhaps because, as adults, older siblings realize how helpless their younger siblings were, or because they have a greater appreciation of the harm they may have done. Or perhaps older siblings simply are driven by a deeper, more lasting motivation: resentment of the arrival of a child who unseats them as the center of their parents' attention, and, adding insult to injury, who becomes the beneficiary of preferential treatment.

## Institutional Power, Interactional Power

Yet siblings don't have to be younger to be favored, nor do they have to be older to be tyrants. A thirteen-year-old girl was telling me about her family. "There's a chain of command," she said. "If my little sister wants something, she asks me, then Dad, then Mom. Mom is the boss." So the younger sister is at the bottom of the chain of command. But this does not mean she is powerless. Not at all. The older sister explained, "She can get anything she wants because she has the power of the tantrum." By screaming and crying uncontrollably, the younger usually ends up getting what she wants.

What the youngest can't get by institutional power—authority given by virtue of rank—she gets by interactional power: by throwing a tantrum. Younger siblings have many ways of creating interactional power. In my mother's family the youngest of her three older brothers terrorized everyone with his explosive temper. Another means of achieving interactional power is just the opposite: refusing to talk. And this too can be used to override the institutional power of age. A woman recalls that, although she was younger than her sister, she exerted great power over her because she liked being alone, whereas her sister wanted company. Refusing to talk to her would drive her sister mad.

Silence can be the most devastating form of interactional power, and, like any linguistic strategy, it can become a kind of familylect—a way of speaking (or not speaking) that is passed down, picked up, and shared by other family members. In his memoir J. D. Dolan writes that refusing to speak was his father's preferred means of expressing disapproval. He had stopped speaking to his older sister for three years, even while they lived in the same house. He had stopped speaking to his older brother for twenty years. And he stopped talking to his oldest daughter, Joanne, when she returned home one night later than he allowed.

John, Dolan's oldest brother, learned the same tactic. He sided with Joanne and stopped talking to his father. And years later John stopped talking to J.D. When their paths cross on a visit home, J.D. finds himself feigning weakness to get his brother to talk: When his neck aches slightly, he surprises himself by saying, "I think I'm getting arthritis," though he knows he's not. Without looking at him John says, "It's probably not arthritis, it'll get better," and walks out.

"I truly hated my brother at that moment," Dolan writes, "and I hated myself for the shameless ploy, the cheap appeal for sympathy I'd used to even *try* to talk to him." His brother's silence had the power to make Dolan speak in a way that he felt wasn't true to himself. And that is eloquent testimony to how silence can be a tool of interactional power in a family.

## The Younger's Revenge

Phyllis thought her daughter was being a little temperamental. She heard eight-year-old Carrie, who was busy at the computer, call out to her fourteen-year-old brother, "Jason, c'mere! It's too hard. I can't do it!" Jason kindly went to her rescue, but the next thing Phyllis heard was, "He's breathing in my face!" This seemed nonsensical and unfair: First Carrie called her brother to help, then she got angry because he responded to her call. But "breathing in my face" was her way of saying he was getting too close. And getting too close was a way of saying he was doing too much: She was trying to draw a picture of herself on the computer, and she wanted him to show her how to do it, not do it for her, as he was doing. And, to add insult to injury, he had drawn her fat!

Older brother, younger sister: Because he is older he is expected to help, and usually he does. But the sister is also a sitting duck for an older boy's pranks—or genuinely mean-spirited victimization. Yet parents' sympathies are not always automatically with the younger sibling, especially since they can't know what goes on when they are not there.

"She's a bitch!" a mother said of her seven-year-old daughter, Laurie. "So are her friends!" As evidence she told me this: "We were visiting my sisters, and the kids were playing in a corner. Laurie started to cry, like she always does, to get me to come over and punish her brother. But one of my sisters had been watching; Laurie had provoked him!"

This scenario reminded me of the tactics of a baboon in Shirley Strum's book *Almost Human*. (Though baboons are not people, the dynamics of their interactions can shed light on human behavior, as I think they do here.) Olive, a young female, had been attacked by Toby, an adolescent male, when they were alone, and she could not defend herself against him. Later that day Olive again found herself in Toby's vicinity, but this time they were not alone. Her older brother Sean was nearby. Eyeing the two males, Olive raised a ruckus, screaming her head off as if Toby had attacked her—which he had, only not on that occasion. On *this* occasion Sean sprang to her defense, roundly beating Toby. It's possible that little Laurie was doing something like this, provoking her brother, yes, but provoking him to do in the earshot of adults what he probably did routinely when they were alone and she was defenseless. And the sense of injustice that Laurie might feel could color her relationship with her brother—and with others—throughout her life.

## "You Got Away with Murder"

My first husband, who was Greek, had an uncle—his father's older brother—whom he had never seen, and whom his father had not seen since their teens. They had been among the more than a million Greeks expelled from their homeland in Smyrna (now Izmir), Turkey, in 1922. During the chaos of expulsion, the family was separated: The older brother ended up on a boat that took him to Algeria, from where he eventually immigrated to the United States to make his home in New York. The younger brother escaped with their parents on a boat that took them to the Greek island of Crete, where he remained, married, and raised his children—and where I was living when I met my first husband.

When I made a trip back to New York to visit my own family, my future-ex-husband asked me to visit his uncle. I did. The uncle seemed glad to meet me. After a few questions about his brother's family, he began telling me stories from their childhood. But they were not affectionate, sentimental reminiscences. They were stories that bristled with resentment about how his younger brother had been their parents' favorite, and how as a child he, being older, was blamed for everything, while his brother got away with murder and was blamed for nothing. I was astounded by how deep that childhood pain must have been, to remain the primary remembrance of a brother he had not seen in forty-five years.

This gnawing sense of injustice is common among older siblings. Adults often see younger siblings as defenseless creatures who cannot be blamed for their mischief and expect older ones to exercise limitless self-restraint. It comes down to perceptions of power: Weaker ones can't be blamed for exercising power because they are perceived as not having any. But those who are perceived as having it can't honorably use it, except against an equally powerful foe: picking on someone your own size. That may be why Heather's mother saw no need to protect Heather against Toby but did intervene to protect Toby from Heather.

My oldest sister, Naomi, had to have her front tooth capped when she was twelve because it broke when she lunged to stop her younger sister (Mimi, not me) from falling off the bed where they were playing. It's parallel to the situation in international affairs: Stronger countries, like the United States, are expected to sustain losses in helping out weaker countries. As the weaker ones, younger siblings are regarded as incapable of inflicting serious damage. As the stronger ones, older siblings are expected to keep their power in check. What is maddening to them, I think—and ironic—is that the perception of them as too powerful to retaliate leaves them defenseless in the presence of adults.

## Do You Get the Picture?

With parents the arbiters of fights and the granters of favors, it is inescapable that children compete for their attention and approval. Earlier I discussed a conversation among three adult sisters and their mother at a restaurant. Let's return to that conversation, because it includes a brief exchange that reflects a flash point in the lives of adult siblings: whose photographs their parents have displayed.

The sisters all have children of their own: Yvonne has a daughter named Susie; Marian has a daughter named Corrie; and Olga has a son, Tommy, and a daughter, Jill. At one point Yvonne (the youngest) remarks to the mother, "You have pictures of all your daughters on the wall." But the middle sister, Marian, sets her straight: "No, she has one of Susie, that's it." Hearing her daughter's name, Yvonne points out that if this is so, it simply rights a previous imbalance: "You didn't have one of Susie. For a long time there was only one of Corrie." The oldest sister, Olga, then mentions her son: "You had one of Tommy, I think." Marian, with the voice of the most recent authority, declares that her own and Olga's children no longer reign: "Tommy and Jill and Corrie are down."

Photographs—how many their parents have, and which they display—are scrutinized by children as if they were a bar graph showing who is loved most. The youngest of three, I can still recall the desolate feeling I got when, as a child, I spent hours looking at the old photographs my parents kept in a drawer. Picture after picture showed a beaming child—the first child, my oldest sister. There was Naomi at seven on a pony at the Brooklyn Zoo. Naomi at six in her cowgirl outfit. Naomi at five, at four, at three. A whole separate album held one after another baby picture of Naomi—and under each one my father had written a couplet, a little poem! There were even some pictures of my sister Mimi. But in the whole drawer—and, believe me, I searched—there were so few pictures of me, it felt like proof positive that my parents didn't love me as much.

A mother of two who was herself the youngest of two recalls that she had borne a grudge against her parents for having so many photographs of her sister and so few of her—until she found herself replicating the pattern. "I even yelled at a colleague," she said: " 'Do you realize you have sixteen pictures of your son and only one of your daughter?' I vowed never to be that person—and now I am that person." Whenever she might take a photo of the little one, she explained, the older one was acting up, or he had to be driven to a soccer game, or the younger one had fallen asleep. She finally understood that parents of more than one child take diminishing numbers of photographs because they have more work to do, not because they love later children less. But this doesn't change the metamessages younger children perceive when they tally the photos they find.

Though adult children don't normally rummage through their parents' drawers, they do scan the walls and furniture tops of their homes and offices to take stock of the photographs on display as a measure of how siblings rate in their parents' affections. And when adult children have children of their own, photographs of grandchildren become stand-ins in a kind of competition by proxy.

A woman feels hurt when she sees that her parents have put on display a handsome new photo of her nephew at his high school graduation, because it displaced the older framed picture of her own daughter at a ballet recital. A middle sister, to her chagrin, finds herself counting snapshots on her parents' walls to test her impression that there are fewer of her family than of her siblings'. In stepfamilies, too, the photograph test becomes a measure of affection: A man's second wife is hurt when she finds in his office more photos of his daughter from his first marriage than of the stepdaughter that came from hers.

Ellen, who had been living abroad for a number of years, came to visit her parents soon after her return to the States. Among the surprises awaiting her were the photographs of her brother that had sprouted on every surface like weeds after a rainy spring. Ellen knew that her brother had received many awards and recognitions in recent years, but somehow she didn't expect each one to be represented by a photograph in their parents' home. Unsettled by her reaction, she retreated to the den for the night. As she pulled open the couch to prepare her bed, she saw yet one more large photo of her brother right above the couch—ready to hang over her head as she slept. In a fit of pique Ellen turned the photo to face the wall. She knew it was silly, but each photo of her brother seemed to be taking a chunk of her parents' attention and affection away from her.

For children growing up, parents and other adults are the world. Children who have siblings must negotiate their way through the inroads and byways made by brothers and sisters. As grown-ups trying to find our way, we're still clutching the maps we collected as kids. And the photographs we find are signposts on the same old maps.

## My Brother's Keeper

Sibling relationships are a paradigm of the affection that can grow with caretaking.

Bambi Schieffelin, an anthropologist who worked among the Kaluli people of New Guinea, observed the central role played by the sibling relationship—especially the relationship between an older sister and a younger brother—as captured in the Kaluli word *ade.* A Kaluli mother will encourage an older sister to share with, give to, nurture, and care for her younger brother by using the term *ade* to invoke the relationship and the obligations that go along with it. The term can refer to both older and younger siblings in relation to each other, and it can take the place of a name or pronoun. So, for example, Schieffelin recorded a mother saying to an older sister, "Don't disturb *ade*" (who is asleep), and "Give half to *ade*" (referring to a banana). She also recorded a mother using the term to encourage a younger brother to seek help from his older sister: "Go be carried by *ade*."

The *ade* relationship is about obligations associated with the older sibling role (especially older sisters) and rights that accrue to the younger (especially younger brothers, but in some cases younger sisters as well). It is also about compassion and human connection. Mothers use the term to teach older children to share, give, and nurture because they "feel sorry for" a younger, less capable child. And the feelings associated with the relationship run deep. "On ceremonial and funerary occasions," Schieffelin writes, "people sing about 'having no *ade*,' which is extremely powerful in evoking sadness and weeping."

Having younger siblings for whom you are responsible, and older siblings who are responsible for you, becomes a metaphor for being connected, for not being alone in the world. Thus the sibling relationship captures the way family members are situated on the connection-control continuum: Taking care of siblings creates closeness, and being close entails rights and obligations that limit freedom but are emblematic of the sense of belonging that is family. (In another part of the world, the South Pacific kingdom of Tonga, anthropologist Susan Philips notes that a sister has a "traditional right to ask for and receive anything under the control of her brother, whether this be food, material possessions, or money for her children's school tuition.")

Before we leave the concept of *ade*, it's worth noting that although the term refers most often to the relationship between an older sister and a younger brother, Schieffelin also heard it used to refer to pairs of brothers or pairs of sisters. But she never heard it used with brothers over six years of age, whereas she heard mothers use the term in encouraging cooperation among sisters into their teens, and she heard women use it into adulthood when seeking help or objects from a sister. In other words, it is older sisters in particular who are encouraged to care for and share with younger siblings—just as older sisters in the United States often find themselves in the role of mini-mom.

## Brothers and Sisters Forever

*Ade* seems like a good word to capture the lifelong relationship between Bessie Delany and her older sister, Sadie. At the age of 103, Sadie said, "So I told Bessie that if she lives to 120, then I'll just have to live to 122 so I can take care of her." She explained, "Neither one of us ever married and we've lived together most all of our lives. . . . She is my right arm. If she were to die first, I'm not sure I would want to go on living because the reason I am living is to keep *her* living."

Siblings don't have to be unmarried to remain devoted to each other. As a child I loved to visit my great-aunts Gertrude and Anna, who lived together. Gertrude had lived all her life with Anna and Anna's husband and son, except for the year she herself was married, until her young husband died. (Of course they continued living together after Anna's husband died, many years later.) Anna's son once commented to me, "My mother and my aunt Gertrude were married to each other." He meant that only the word *marriage* could capture their lifelong devotion. In this family it was the younger sister, Anna, who took care of her older sister. Gertrude was a scholar who had been educated in Europe before the family immigrated to America. Anna was a businesswoman who had mastered the ways of the New World. Those were the skills she drew on in looking after her older sister. I didn't know them when they were young, but I can still see them, both old, holding hands and supporting each other as they crossed the street.

As Gertrude and Anna showed, the closeness of sisters and brothers can last a lifetime. But so can the scars left by a sibling's words. My father, at ninety-two, still hesitates when asked to smile for a photograph, recalling that his older sister always whispered to him, when they were having their pictures taken, "Keep your mouth closed. You look ugly when you smile." Part of the reason older siblings can be so tough on younger ones is that they are close enough to know just which points of weakness will really get to them. The older can zero in on a younger's fear of being fat or having to wear glasses. And, given that an older child always knows more and can do more, just about any older sister or brother can ridicule a younger one for being stupid.

Dustin, whose intelligence sparkles through every word he speaks, recalls a conversation he had with a summer camp counselor when he was nine. The counselor happened to comment that Dustin was smart. He told her, earnestly, that she had made a mistake: "No," he said, "I'm stupid."

Surprised, she asked, "Don't you get good grades in school?"

"Oh, yes," he said, "the best. But that doesn't mean anything."

Nothing his counselor said could budge Dustin from the conviction he knew to be fact: He was stupid.

Where did Dustin get this idea, against all the evidence of his young life? Easy. From his older brother, Allen. Wherever Dustin turned in the house, he found handwritten notes with the same message: "Dustin is a dope." Allen would repeat this every chance he got. He sang it in the descending notes of the first three strings of the guitar: "Dustin—is—a dope." As he tells me this, Dustin sings the words in those descending notes. "In a way I knew Allen was teasing," he says. "I knew he was just calling me names. But in another way I did actually feel stupid." It was many years, almost into adulthood, before it occurred to Dustin that his brother's teasing, name-calling judgment was not the truth.

## It's the Past That Keeps Changing: Reframing to Reshape Sibling Relationships

Nothing can change the past. Having grown up as an only child; an oldest child; a younger, youngest, or middle—these influences will always be with us, shaping how we speak to others and how we react when they speak to us. Yet from another point of view, as a historian once put it, the present is always the same. It's the past that keeps changing. We can change the past by changing our interpretation of it. And this reframing can change its effects.

Pauline recalls that her father always felt cut out of the family circle; the core, he claimed, consisted of his wife and her sisters. Her father complained that when he walked in, the room went silent. Because they stopped talking when he appeared, he was sure the sisters were talking about him. Pauline had assumed her father was right about this, but in retrospect she could see another interpretation. Women doing rapport-talk tend to fall silent when anyone walks in, not because they are talking about that person in particular but because rapport-talk is about personal topics, and therefore private. The silence was probably not a specific rejection of her father, though she could understand why he thought it was.

Reframing also provided Pauline a new interpretation of what she had always taken to be her mother's neglect. Pauline's mother had been given responsibility for her younger sisters while their mother worked. After she married and had two daughters of her own, Pauline's mother continued to put her own sisters—and, by proxy, her sisters' children—ahead of her own family, which was (she felt) just an extension of herself. Pauline recalls that her mother once bought two dresses, one for her and one for her cousin Marny, daughter to her mother's youngest sister. Her mother gave Marny first choice—and Marny said she wanted both. So both is what Marny got, and Pauline got none. Though she still felt slighted when she thought about it, Pauline reframed her interpretation of this past event as having to do less with her mother's feelings for her than with the responsibility her mother had been assigned as the older sister.

E-mail opens up new pathways for siblings to communicate, and new pathways can result in reframing, or changing old patterns. Kira, in her forties, used to talk to her brother on the telephone maybe twice a year. Now that they are on e-mail, they exchange messages at least weekly, sometimes as often as four times in a day. And e-mail has given her the channel—and the courage—to confront him when he hurts her feelings, which he does often. In the past, if he said something to hurt her, she would withdraw to lick those wounds. Now she tells him, on e-mail, "You hurt my feelings," and he—just as quickly as he hurt her—apologizes. One time, for example, he wrote, "Sorry, I was a jerk. I'm still trying to grow up." With the hurt behind her, she can happily return to "talking" to him by e-mail. What a contrast to the past, when the memory of her brother's put-down would linger, preventing her from picking up the phone to call.

Kira said of her brother, "I'm nineteen months older, and he can wound me quicker than anybody." Siblings can do that because they loom so large in our minds and our hearts. Our place in the sibling constellation affects the way we talk to each other throughout our lives. Understanding how it does so provides insight that makes possible reframing, by which we can change the way we interpret what our siblings say, or change the way we speak, to reshape and improve relationships with our brothers and sisters.

NINE

# In-Laws and Other Strangers

## Mixing Families, Mixing Talk

THE FIRST COMMENT that Arthur's mother made about the woman he would marry was, "Grace talks more than we do."

*We*—that small word that builds ramparts around a family, separating "us" from those outside—the alien "them." Arthur's parents, of Swedish and English extraction, have what I call a high-considerateness style. In this style a speaker's first obligation is not to impose on others. Grace, influenced by her French Canadian mother, has what I call a high-involvement style, by which a speaker's first obligation is to show interest and enthusiasm. Her mother-in-law's observation identified a speck of conversational style difference around which would grow a pearl of mutual understanding that took Arthur and Grace many years to develop.

Offering bouquets of talk to show goodwill and interest is self-evidently loving to some, annoyingly intrusive to others. If too much talk can irritate, too little can wound. When Mildred calls her son's home, her back figuratively stiffens if her daughter-in-law answers the phone. In a typical exchange, when Jill answered, Mildred said, "Hello, Jill. How are you?" Jill replied, "Fine, thanks. Here's Harvey." Mildred felt Jill was treating her callously, even cruelly, and said so to her son, who made her case to Jill, who found it baseless.

"I answered politely," Jill said. "What's wrong with saying 'Fine, thanks'? What does she want?" It wasn't what Jill said that was hurtful but what she neglected to say—something greeting-like, such as, "Oh, hello, Mildred. How have you been?" Mildred expected a more enthusiastic, more effusive reaction—anything to imply that Jill was glad to hear from her, anything to keep the conversation going a few minutes before handing the phone over. It wasn't the message of "Fine, thanks" that was hurtful but what Mildred perceived as a metamessage that Jill was curtailing their conversation—getting rid of her as quickly as possible.

Dolores complains to Burt, "Your parents have no interest in me. They never ask about what I do. Sometimes I think they see me as part of the woodwork."

"Of course they're interested," Burt reassures her. "They'd be happy if you told them about your work."

"I can't just start talking if they don't ask," Dolores protests. She is no more convinced by his account of his family's intentions than he is by her account of hers. When her parents offer him just the kind of interest she is looking for in his parents, his reaction is not appreciation but irritation.

"I feel under attack when your family gets going," he says. "They fire so many questions at me, I don't know where to start answering."

"Start anywhere," she tells him. "You don't have to answer them all; just pick one and start."

Though they think they're talking about what kinds of people their parents are, and how their in-laws feel about them, Dolores and Burt are actually caught in the web of what I call conversational style differences. And like the fly that gets more enmeshed in a spiderweb each time it flails to get free, your efforts to make things better can make them worse when you talk to someone with a different style. The very reason Dolores's parents' questions come so rapid-fire when they talk to Burt is that he hesitates in answering—which he does because he's taken aback by the pace of the questions. He needs them to slow down. But they don't know this, so they try harder to find the question that will get him talking—efforts that result in his feeling assaulted and backing off. For their part, Burt's parents have decided that Dolores prefers not to talk about herself. They make extra efforts not to intrude, to respect what they perceive as her reticence, a preference for privacy.

Dolores and Burt's marriage was forged from different metals: she is an outgoing New Yorker whose Jewish grandparents emigrated from Poland and Russia; he is a reserved Minnesotan whose Scandinavian descent goes further back but is no less influential. The resulting alloy is—for the most part—strengthened by their differences. Though occasionally frustrating, his quiet calm is comforting to her, and, though occasionally overwhelming, her outgoing charm is engaging to him. But without the foundation of romantic love, their families react to their styles with puzzled disapproval rather than indulgent fascination.

## Conversational Style at Home

"Wouldn't this be a better world if we all just said what we mean?" I am often asked. My answer is, We do. We do say what we mean. But we say it in our own conversational styles. This works fine when we talk to someone whose conversational style is relatively similar to ours, but it creates confusion when we talk to someone whose style differs.

*Conversational style* is my term for the many ways of talking that determine how we say what we mean: how fast or slowly, how softly or loudly we speak; with what intonation or musical lilt; how relatively direct or indirect we are when making requests, offering advice, expressing concern, and so on; what we tell stories or jokes about; how we get to the point; our preference for or avoidance of confrontation, sarcasm, irony, interruption; and many other subtleties of talk.

Conversational style tends to be invisible. We draw conclusions not about ways of speaking but about the person who spoke. We don't walk away from a conversation thinking, "Gee, that was awkward. I guess you expect a half second shorter pause than I do between conversational turns, so it was hard for me to get the floor." Instead, we walk away with a negative impression of the other person's intentions ("She doesn't like me"; "He didn't give me a chance to talk"); character ("He's a self-centered boor"; "She's too shy to talk to"); or abilities (I once heard a young, fast-talking professor say about a world-famous scholar who tended to speak slowly, "He's not very bright"). Our own good intentions we take for granted.

We develop our conversational styles growing up, as we learn to talk. The rightness of our ways of speaking seems self-evident and natural, but they are influenced by the social distinctions that determine whom we hear and talk to—ethnic background, the part of the country where we or our parents grew up, and class differences all affect the ways of speaking that come to seem the obvious ways of being a good person.

I have written books about this subject, showing how, as the original subtitle of the book *That's Not What I Meant!* puts it, "conversational style makes or breaks your relations with others." Yet nowhere are the effects of style differences more troubling than in the family, where so much rides on our relationships. Saying one thing and having it taken to mean another is frustrating no matter whom you are talking to. But when the person who misreads your intentions is your partner in life, the person you look to as a bulwark against the world, or the family near and dear to the person you love—then the ramifications are deeply painful.

There may have been a time when people tended to marry within a homogenous community, but more and more of us now marry or live with others from slightly or very different cultures—which can mean someone from a different ethnic background, class background, or geographic region. When parents raise children in a different part of the country—or the world—than they themselves grew up in, conversational style differences can be the source of frustration across generations. All this moving around, and the cross-cultural relationships that come with it, means that the most intimate conversations—talk at home—are prey to confusions growing out of conversational style differences. When your extended families get into the picture, the importance of conversational style comes home with a vengeance.

## Where Stereotypes Come From

In principle, we all greet and meet each other with open minds, judging each person as an individual. But more often than we would like to admit, we judge others with reference to the social groups we see them as representing. When conversational style differences lead to negative impressions, it is hard to avoid drawing conclusions not only about the individual who spoke a certain way but about the whole group we associate that individual with. In other words, ways of talking lead to mutual stereotyping.

One of the basic conversational style differences that lead to mutual stereotyping is something as simple as rate of speech. This emerges in the following story from Finnish folklore, about someone from a region of Finland known as Häme.

> A Häme man enters a neighbor's house, sits for quite a while before the neighbor asks why he has come, and then says that he came to tell him that his house is burning.

Finnish linguists Jaakko Lehtonen and Kari Sajavaara tell this story not to reinforce negative stereotypes about people from Häme but to illustrate that the slower rate of speech that typifies people from that region has led to images about them that have entered folklore.

All over the world speakers from some geographic regions tend to speak more slowly than those from others. And in every one of those countries that I know of, people from the slower-speaking regions are stereotyped as stupid, and those from the faster-speaking regions are stereotyped as aggressive. Lehtonen and Sajavaara note that this is the case in Germany with the slower-speaking East Frisians, in French attitudes toward Belgians, among the Swiss toward residents of Bern or Zurich, and, as we saw, among Finns toward their compatriots from Häme—even as Finns themselves are stereotyped as slow and dull by neighboring Swedes.

In the United States you can see this in stereotypes of southerners as polite but dull and New Yorkers as brash and aggressive. The fast-talking professor who misjudged a slower-speaking colleague as "not very bright" had been born and raised in New York City, where quickness of mind is equated with quickness of speech. The world-famous scholar she misjudged had been born and raised in New England, where speaking slowly connotes not dullness but thoughtfulness.

## It's All Relative

Differences in conversational style are always relative, never absolute. It's a matter not of some people being fast talkers and others being slow but of how fast or slow a speaker is in relation to others in the same conversation. The same person can be a bulldozer in one conversation and unable to get a word in edgewise in another. Thus Lehtonen and Sajavaara note that Finns have a hard time finding their way into Swedish conversations, but Swedes have the same problem when talking to Americans.

My colleague Ron Scollon grew up in Detroit; I grew up in Brooklyn. When I talk to Ron, I have to count to seven after it seems to me he has nothing to say; otherwise, I inadvertently interrupt him. Suzanne Scollon, who is married to Ron, is Hawaiian of Chinese descent; she expects longer pauses than he does. When they talk to each other, it's Suzanne who protests, "Don't interrupt me," and "You're asking me another question before you've given me a chance to answer the first one." Ron and Suzanne Scollon worked among Athabaskan Indians in Alaska. When Suzanne talked to Athabaskans, she became the conversational steamroller, as Athabaskans are comfortable with longer silences than she could tolerate.

But the story doesn't end there. The Scollons invited me to a workshop in Alaska, after which they sent me on a bush flight to an Athabaskan village just inside the Arctic Circle named Fort Yukon. They were curious about how someone like me, who thinks friendly verbosity is next to godliness, would fare as a stranger in a setting where people do not talk to those they don't know. Ron Scollon later assigned my book *Conversational Style* to students at the University of Alaska, Fairbanks, and asked them on a midterm exam, "Deborah Tannen spent a day in Fort Yukon. What do you think she experienced there?" Most students answered correctly that I was unnerved when no one would talk to me. (After several hours of failed attempts to spark conversations,

I broke down and called the local American missionaries.) But a student who came from a region even farther north than Fort Yukon—from the northernmost village in the Arctic Circle—wrote: "People in Fort Yukon talk so fast, she probably fit right in."

Because conversational style tends to be invisible, few people think of their reactions as resulting from pacing and pausing, or from differences in their tolerance (or need) for silence. The conclusions they come away with are about each other as people—or the group of people they associate each other with.

## Now in the Family

Conversational style differences can be alluring when people first meet, especially if there is a romantic attraction. When people live together over time, such differences can cause frustration as well as fascination, even if they have lots of time to work them out. But these different habits for using language to show your intentions and say what you mean become especially problematic when extended families get together. The situation is aggravated when people are getting to know each other—as extended families have to do.

A couple, for example, were excited about their siblings meeting each other. But when his sister Leslie and her brother Gary first met, Leslie's way of showing interest in Gary had the opposite effect of what she intended. She asked a series of questions meant to send a metamessage of enthusiasm and casualness. The metamessage Gary perceived is what led me to call this way of showing interest *machine-gun questions*.

Leslie began by asking Gary where he had traveled from: " 'r you from Chicago?"

Gary answered hesitantly and minimally: "Yeah."

"Whaddya do there?" Leslie followed up.

"I'm uh—uh a lawyer," he answered—and stopped there.

"What kind of law?" she asked. "Contract law? Litigation?"

"I do uh—um contract law," he replied.

Leslie knew something was wrong. She was asking these questions in a high-pitched tone and clipped syntax that to her implied,

"I'm being casual and friendly. Answer whatever you like." Her questions were not designed to get specific answers, just to show interest. She was being kind by giving him the floor, assuming people like to talk, especially about themselves. The truth is, Leslie already knew (because her brother had told her) where Gary was from and what he did, but asking these questions seemed to her the obviously nice way to show that she was eager to get to know him.

Gary, however, didn't feel drawn out by Leslie's questions; he felt hemmed in, as if she were grilling him. For one thing, Gary does not like to talk about himself. For another, the high-pitched, clipped character of the questions caught him off guard. The metamessage he perceived was not casualness and friendliness but aggressive attack. It was the rapid-fire pace that made him hesitant—so he stumbled and seemed inarticulate, even when talking about his own job. This gave their conversation an odd rhythm. Instead of question-answer-pause, question-answer-pause, it was question-pause. Answer-question-pause.

This imbalance is an example of complementary schismogenesis, which I described in Chapter 4. Leslie and Gary were both reacting to the other's way of speaking, which was driving each of them to more and more exaggerated forms of their habitual styles. The speed of Leslie's questions caused Gary to hesitate, and his hesitation made her try harder to find the right question to get him going. This is typical of what happens when styles differ: since you don't think of changing your style, whatever you do to make things better makes them worse. That is why complementary schismogenesis is a mutually aggravating spiral.

Gary and Leslie didn't realize that they were reacting, in part, to each other's behavior. Neither did the members of a Norwegian American family who hosted a nephew from Norway one summer. They found him sullen and uncommunicative, even as he was writing home to his parents that he thought he'd lose his mind because his American aunt never stopped talking. The irony is that both the aunt and the nephew were more talkative and more taciturn, respectively, in reaction to each other. His aunt was talking more and more in a desperate attempt to encourage her nephew to open up and talk—to say *something*. It didn't occur to her that if she allowed the air to fill with silence, he would begin to speak. And he didn't realize that it was his own silence that was making her talk with ever more urgency.

## What's a Good Topic?

Not only the pacing of conversation, but also what people talk about and how, can cause confusion when families of different backgrounds meet. Like hors d'oeuvres, conversational openers are offered to whet the interactional appetite, but if it's a cuisine you're not used to, they can just as easily make you gag.

People who grew up in different countries often have very different ideas of what topics are appropriate for friendly conversation with someone you're just getting to know. Linguist Heidi Byrnes explains that for Germans, among the best topics to get a conversation going are politics and religion, and the best way to enjoy such topics is to argue about them. Most Americans regard it as unthinkable to discuss religion or politics with someone they just met, partly because they regard these matters as too personal, and partly because these topics are likely to lead to arguments—a type of conversation most Americans want to avoid with someone they just met. In a way this shows how arguments express both control (they seem too competitive) and connection (arguing seems too intimate to do with a stranger).

Byrnes found that American exchange students tended to clam up when challenged by German students in the host country about politics or religion. The result? The German students concluded that Americans have no opinions, and the American students concluded that Germans have no manners. The same thing can happen between families, where one side thinks it's really fun to argue about politics, and the other thinks the only thing worse than talking politics is arguing with someone you barely know.

A British woman who married an American encountered this sort of short circuit, on a smaller scale, when their families got together. Her relatives found their new American family embarrassingly self-revealing as they raised personal topics with in-laws they had only recently met. Her mother was shocked when his mother talked about her frustrations with her husband, for example. On the other side, his parents felt they couldn't get to know their new British kin, who seemed so reserved and cold that they could find no ground on which to meet. From the perspective of the connection continuum, the British family found the Americans behaving in a way that was too close for comfort given the context of new acquaintanceship, and the Americans found their new British kin too distant given the context of family.

The British relatives assumed it was something particular (and peculiar) about their new in-laws that drove them to speak about personal topics with people they didn't yet know well. But this is a habit widespread among Americans that surprises many non-Americans. Some find it endearing; others find it objectionable. For example, a European who had lived in America for a long time tried to explain to a fellow European that when Americans ask personal questions of new acquaintances they are trying to show interest and establish rapport. But the European thought he knew what was *really* going on. He kept repeating, "The point is, Americans are rude." To him, ways of speaking were ipso facto evidence of character. Taking for granted that his assumptions about ways of speaking are self-evidently right, and drawing conclusions about intentions, he just couldn't (or wouldn't) accept the idea of conversational style.

Such misjudgments are unfortunate in any situation, but when the people you are misjudging (or those who are misjudging you) are family members, the unfortunate consequences of conversational style differences have literally come home to roost. Realizing that what's going on is not necessarily evidence of bad character or bad intentions, in-laws can come to appreciate the efforts of their new kin, even if they don't always find them easy to enjoy.

## Cross-Culture in the Same Culture

These examples come from families where partners were born and grew up in different countries, in some cases speaking different languages. But all families are like cross-cultural experiences in that each partner was born into a particular family—and every family is, in a way, a nation unto itself, with its own customs and ways of speaking. In *You Just Don't Understand* I wrote in detail about how simply growing up male and female is, in a sense, growing up in different worlds, and results in different conversational styles. By the same token, sometimes what seem like the same backgrounds are nonetheless slightly different, because of ethnic, regional, or class influences, or just because each family develops a unique style.

Even partners who are ostensibly from "the same culture" can have different ideas of how to show interest. Several years ago I was interviewed by a journalist who offered her own complaint: "This always happens when my husband and I get together with friends," she said. "Whenever I start to tell a story—even an incident that happened to me—my husband takes over. He'll interrupt, and add details, until he's telling it instead of me. I get really angry at him, because he doesn't think I can tell a story myself."

I offered an explanation: "Maybe he isn't trying to tell it *for* you. He may be trying to tell it *with* you."

"That's what he says," she replied with conviction. "But I tell him storytelling is not a team sport."

I explained that, for high-involvement speakers, it is. If being a good conversationalist means demonstrating your involvement, then talking along is much nicer than sitting quietly while a loved one tells about something. That would be a failure of involvement. A partner who cares will show that caring by taking part. Maybe (just maybe) her husband ends up taking over because she backs off, leaving him alone on the field. It sounded to me like the journalist had a high-considerateness style while her husband had a high-involvement style.

In explaining these patterns, I mentioned that this conversational style clash often erupts between high-involvement speakers, such as Italians, Armenians, African Americans, Russians, or New Yorkers, and high-considerateness speakers, such as German Americans, Irish Americans, midwesterners, Scandinavians, or New Englanders. "Well," the journalist said, "we're both from New York and we're both Jewish."

I asked, "Is your family German Jewish, and his Russian or Polish?"

The answer was yes. That explained it. His family's talking habits had been shaped by the East European influence, hers by the Northern European style.

Another couple who thought they had the same background found their styles were different enough to cause conflict with in-laws. The coming holidays revived old irritations for Maria, a first-generation Mexican American from south Texas, and her husband, Eduardo, a second-generation Mexican American from California. Maria was happy to invite her in-laws for Christmas, but she resented that her mother-in-law always brought just about all the fixings for Christmas dinner, which she had cooked in advance. This seemed to imply that Maria was incapable of cooking dinner.

Maria tried to let her mother-in-law know how she felt. "You shouldn't go to all that trouble," she'd say. "I bought lots of food and was planning to cook it myself."

Eduardo's mother would always assure her that she was happy to cook and bring food. Maria could save what she'd bought to prepare on another day. Finally, Maria told her directly that *she* preferred to do all the cooking. Her mother-in-law accepted this, but Maria was angry that she had been forced to be rude. She complained to Eduardo, "Why do I have to spell everything out for her?"

Maria had to spell everything out not because Eduardo's mother was bent on making her uncomfortable but because she genuinely missed Maria's meaning, since Eduardo's family tended to be more direct. The differences could have been a matter of personal or family style, but they also might have resulted from ethnic influences. Although both Maria and Eduardo are Mexican American, the Texas community in which Maria grew up was more ethnically monolithic, whereas Eduardo's California community was more ethnically mixed. Furthermore, Eduardo's family was one generation further from natives of Mexico.

If Maria was discomfited by the need to be more direct with her mother-in-law, she was also critical of the way Eduardo spoke to her mother. For example, he responded honestly when his mother-in-law asked if he would drive her to visit some other relatives on Christmas Day. "There won't be time for that," Eduardo explained, to Maria's (and her mother's) horror. Dismissing a request out of hand seemed callous to them; he should at least have expressed willingness to consider it, perhaps by saying, "I'd like to help you out. Let's see how the day goes. We'll see if we can manage it." He still could refuse when the time came (his tentativeness would have prepared her for that), but at least he would have showed that he made an effort to consider her request.

Changing ways of speaking is difficult—unless you think of it as style rather than personal character. We all feel that talking a certain way defines us as a certain kind of person; talking differently reveals a different sort of person. The reason Maria resented having to tell her mother-in-law directly not to cook and bring food is that *she* feels like a rude person when she does. And Eduardo feels like a hypocrite saying he's going to try to do something that he knows perfectly well he won't be able to do. If they think of themselves as accommodating to a different conversational style, they can talk differently to their in-laws without feeling they have compromised themselves.

## "Why Do You Do That, Mom?"

When parents raise their children in a different region than the one they grew up in, parent and child can end up with different ideas about polite and right ways of talking: The parents take for granted the norms they learned growing up, while the children absorb the norms of the place where *they* are growing up. Since conversational style is invisible, children judge their parents' characters, not their style.

Vincent always cringed when he was with his mother in a store and she wanted to ask a question, like "Where is the shoe department?" or "What time does the store close?" Typically, she'd approach the nearest salesperson and pop the question—even if that salesperson was busy serving another customer. Often the question would spark a chilly response, like "I'll take care of you as soon as I finish with this customer." His mother would grumble about the rude salesperson, but Vincent thought his mother got just what she deserved: It was her own fault for interrupting. Neither Vincent nor his mother realized that the fault lay with a regional conversational style difference.

In New York City, where Vincent's mother grew up and lived as a young woman, it is considered perfectly polite to interrupt an ongoing service encounter to ask a brief question—anything that can be answered in a single turn. Because the question-answer exchange takes only a moment, it seems self-evident to New Yorkers that the *polite* thing to do is help the customer out rather than keep her waiting needlessly. How illogical, this thinking goes, if someone needs only a moment of your attention, to make her wait while you engage in an extended interaction with someone else. That's high-involvement logic, in which the show of connection to others takes priority.

In Virginia, however, where Vincent was growing up, a high-considerateness style applies in this situation. The rights of the person who got there first trump those of all other customers, regardless of how much or little time is required to help them out. In this view, cutting in between customer and salesperson engaged in a conversation is rude. To Vincent's mother, as to many high-involvement speakers, asking a quick question is no more an interruption than whispering to the person beside you at a dinner table, "Please pass the salt." Only someone rude and self-centered would expect you to go without salt on your food while a long conversation takes its course.

One of the frustrations of moving to a new country, or a different part of the same country, is finding that your antennae are off: People react badly when you think you've been polite, or you just don't get the reaction you expected. When the person misjudging you is your child (or, conversely, when you feel your parent is behaving badly in public), you need an understanding of conversational style to know what adjustments might prompt a better response—and to reassure yourself that the parents and children you love are good people after all.

## Put Your Best Foot Forward—or in It

When families get together, even the most innocent conversational moves can carry weight, especially when in-laws are trying especially hard to please, or to make a good impression. When families are made up of partners from different cultures, the opportunities for inadvertently offending in-laws are endless.

Questions or comments run the risk of seeming to make a request. I encountered this pitfall with my Greek in-laws, my first husband's parents. During an early visit to their home in Crete, I asked, trying to make friendly conversation, "Gee, I haven't seen any grapes since arriving. I always associated Greece with grapes." From that day forward every meal was followed by grapes—large purple ones, with pits. The reason I had not seen them before was that they were out of season—hence sour, and hard to come by. Though I didn't like them, I felt obliged to eat them because my new in-laws, eager to provide whatever I wanted, had interpreted my casual observation as an indirect request, and had gone out of their way to scrounge them up.

Complimenting would seem a surefire way of making a good impression, but with cultural differences even praise can offend. In India when people compliment one of your possessions, etiquette requires you to give it to them, so complimenting becomes a way to ask for things. This makes comprehensible the reaction of a woman who arrived from India to visit her son in America and meet her new American daughter-in-law.

Helping her mother-in-law unpack, the young woman, eager to please, did her best to be attentive and nice: She oohed and aahed over the lovely saris and handcrafted jewelry her husband's mother brought forth from her suitcase. The mother-in-law was appalled. "What kind of woman did he marry?" she complained to her daughter. "She wants everything!"

Cultural rituals for exchanging compliments can be subtle and varied. In *The Joy Luck Club,* Amy Tan shows how a well-meaning young American man offends his fiancée's Chinese mother by taking literally her ritual put-down of her cooking:

As is the Chinese cook's custom, my mother always made disparaging remarks about her own cooking. That night she chose to direct it toward her famous steamed pork and preserved vegetable dish, which she always served with special pride.

"Ai! This dish not salty enough, no flavor," she complained, after tasting a small bite. "It is too bad to eat."

This was our family's cue to eat some and proclaim it the best she had ever made. But before we could do so, Rich said, "You know, all it needs is a little soy sauce." And he proceeded to pour a riverful of the salty black stuff on the platter, right before my mother's horrified eyes.

Because he didn't know—couldn't know—the subtleties of Chinese conversational rituals, the hapless young man put his foot in his mouth, along with the food, throughout the dinner. First he offended by taking too much food: He helped himself to a full portion of shrimp and snow peas the first time it was offered, when "he should have taken only a polite spoonful, until everybody had had a morsel." Later he offended by taking too little: He politely refused seconds when he should have shown his appreciation by "taking small portions of seconds, thirds, and even fourths."

## Arguing for Fun

When you sit down to meals that are the main events of most holiday gatherings, you have to worry not only about what you eat but also about how you talk as you eat. In many families, arguing is a sign of conversational breakdown to be avoided at all costs. In other families, arguing, along with playful insults, is a kind of dynamic opposition that is regarded as fun. That is the case in a family described by one of my students:

Our family's favorite pastime is insulting each other and arguing. A fairly typical conversation between me and my brothers and sister is who is the stupidest or most annoying one of us. My father would say something like, "The table needs to be set." This would spark an argument between us kids. We would order each

> other to do it directly and try to give definite reasons why we couldn't when ordered to do the task.

The student notes, though, that the dynamic opposition occurs between peers: among her siblings, or among her father and his brothers, but not across generations. This is important to keep in mind, as everything said in a family is placed somewhere on the connection-control grid. Hierarchy and closeness have to be properly balanced. Someone coming into a family where this style reigns might decide to match their playful insults—and misstep badly by trying it out on the father instead of a brother.

Anyone whose family does not regard arguing as fun can be shocked—even scared—by such display. Charlotte, who grew up in the Midwest, recalls the first time she found herself in the midst of a family dinner at the Boston home of her Italian American husband, Tony. She thought she had fallen into a family feud as the voices flew about her head and the hands with them. She could barely believe Tony's reassurance that they were just having a great time together.

When Tony visited Charlotte's home, he was the one in for a surprise. He kept waiting for the conversation to bring everyone together in one big talking hydra head, but, the entire evening, people talked only one-on-one to someone next to them. This meant the conversation was different in every way: The volume was lower; more information was exchanged; there was less joking and laughter; and there was no raucous storytelling in which the whole table might come together as audience. Not only did this strike Tony as less fun but it didn't fit his image of family as a unity created by the many voices becoming one.

## What to Do After Dinner Is Done

Families also have different ideas of how to clean up and what to do next. Sometimes these differences reflect apportionment of men's and women's roles. The modern man who gets up to help the women clear the table may embarrass the older generation in a family where the men stay put—or retreat to the living room to read the papers or watch TV. And the modern woman who does not expect to wait on her husband—or her father-in-law—hand and foot might offend the older generation, who assume it is her obligation to do so.

In one extended family the men and boys all troop outside to play baseball while the women gravitate to the kitchen, where the conversation interests them more and they clean up as they talk. Of course there are always women who prefer to go out and play baseball, and men who find the women's conversation more interesting than the game. A typical scene following dinner in another family finds the father and one brother-in-law retired to the living room, reading; another brother-in-law working in the yard or garage; while around the table, still sitting and talking, are all the women—and one man, who prefers sitting and talking with the women.

In yet another family a gathering includes two brothers, a sister, their parents, and their spouses and children. The immediate family all get along—but their spouses are another story. It's like a meeting of the United Nations, each obeying rules of protocol that are unfamiliar to the others. A particular object of mutual criticism is child rearing. The Italian daughter-in-law is effusively affectionate with her children, smothering them in her wide embrace, plastering their faces with adoring kisses. At this her Irish American sister-in-law recoils: Where is the discipline? How will these children develop backbone and respect? Surely all that physical affection is not normal or healthy.

At the same time, the Irish American disciplinarian is being frowned upon by the Japanese sister-in-law, who thinks she is way too strict with her poor little children, who should be allowed to run and express themselves without being stomped on. So of course the way the Japanese sister-in-law lets her child run around is the object of disapproval by everyone else.

## "They're Not Like Us"

In A. R. Gurney's play *The Dining Room,* an elderly woman is explaining to her grandson the fine details of serving dinner that were observed in her day. When her grandson asks about finger bowls, she replies, "Oh yes. Our side of the family always used finger bowls between the salad and the dessert."

"Our side of the family"—how loudly those words echo. Because "our side" used finger bowls, the comment implies, "we" were higher class, more estimable, more admirable. Us and them. Nothing reverberates more insistently than intimations that one clan is higher class, more refined, than the other.

Americans rarely talk about class differences, as those in many other countries do. But even in the United States class differences exist and may result in different ways of speaking and acting. Like all conversational style differences, you don't really see them until a difference causes a problem—and then they may seem to be flashing in neon lights. Sometimes an encounter with in-laws makes you look at your family in a way you never did before—and if there are differences in class or culture, the view can be deeply troubling, especially if your family's style is not the norm in the part of the country where you live. That is what happened when Sylvia's brother and sister-in-law visited her in Washington, D.C., on their way from a vacation in Florida to their home in New York City.

Sylvia and her husband took her brother Harry and his wife, Rebecca, to a new upscale restaurant. As the two couples entered the restaurant, a waiter approached and offered a table in the front room. Sylvia asked whether there wasn't a table available in the more pleasant, recently redecorated back room. He said there wasn't, so they began seating themselves at the table they'd been assigned.

Rebecca, however, walked on into the back room to have a look. She spied an available table and returned to ask permission to claim it. With permission granted, the party proceeded to the back room. As the rest of the party were seating themselves, Rebecca came noisily behind them, waving the menus she had rescued from the first table. Already they were attracting attention, breaking local codes of politeness that require diners to accept the table they are given without question and not wave their arms (let alone menus) in everyone's full view.

Soon after they were seated, Sylvia's brother Harry lit up a cigarette; he was immediately told by a passing waitress that they were in the no-smoking room. He formed his face into an expression of good-natured disappointment and shrugged in a gesture of resignation. "But he'll need an ashtray to put it out," Sylvia called after the waitress as Harry reached down to the floor at his side and crushed the cigarette under his foot. Sylvia winced and automatically glanced at the surrounding faces in time to see the woman at the table behind them recoil in disgust and moral judgment—which she expressed with her whole body, including an exaggerated roll of her head and eyes, displayed for the man sitting opposite her.

Sylvia could see that this stranger felt Harry was despicable. And she understood why. This woman clearly felt, as Sylvia herself did, that the restaurant's green tile floor was private space, deserving of the same consideration as the floor of a person's home. But Harry felt it was public space, like the cement floor of a subway station. Harry's back was to the woman; even if he had been scanning the room for a reaction—which he wasn't, since he didn't feel he had done anything unusual—he could not have seen her. And that may have been why the woman felt free to display her disgust for the benefit of her companion. But it also was on display for Sylvia, who thereby got a glimpse of how her brother appeared to people from a different background—people like her husband's family.

Sylvia experienced the pain of seeing someone she loved become the object of scorn, knowing that his goodness was invisible to these others, blocked by their misinterpretation of his actions. Sylvia knows that Harry is kind to the point of weakness. Had he heard of some personal misfortune the woman sitting behind him had suffered, he would have felt deeply for her. He would not for the life of him hurt anyone. But the scowling woman did not know this.

Conversational style differences can have the same effect. A way of speaking that seems innocuous, or downright friendly, to the person using it can be interpreted as offensive by someone who learned different conversational norms. When the people drawing unfair conclusions are strangers in a restaurant, their misjudgment is insignificant. But when they are members of your own family, the damage is serious. With more and more families blended from different backgrounds, opportunities abound to feel misjudged—or to feel that your relatives are misjudged. This adds to the urgency of understanding how conversational style works.

## Working It Out

Couples who have lived together for years often find that they have adapted to their different styles, becoming in small ways more like each other. It's as if their marriages are stews that have been cooking so long the flavors have merged and become delicious. But their relationships with each other's families—let alone the families' relationships with each other—haven't cooked long enough, so they're still tough.

Some couples simply give up trying to bring their extended families together. For example, Vicky and Zack tried for years to invite both his family and hers to their home for the holidays, but it never went well. Her garrulous southern relations overwhelmed his midwestern kin, who backed off, secretly thinking Vicky's family were loud and ill-mannered—while the southerners were thinking that Zack's relatives were awfully dull and withdrawn.

Complementary schismogenesis set in. One side felt it was rude to talk along while another voice was going, so they patiently waited for a pause in which they could step in. But the other side were doing their best to avoid any pauses, which to them would be a sign that the conversation was flagging. The more the midwesterners backed off, the more effort the southerners had to expend to fill what they perceived as potential lulls. The result: conversational meltdown, with each side blaming the other. In the end Zack and Vicky decided to invite one side of the family for Christmas, the other for Thanksgiving.

Frustrations can sometimes be solved fairly easily once style differences are identified as the culprits. Some flare-ups can be avoided by minor adjustments. For example, the husband who tries to take part in his wife's stories may learn to hold back, or the wife may learn to accept and appreciate his participation rather than clamming up at the first sign of vocalization from him. But even if neither changes, just knowing that they have different conversational styles will release them from the cycle of hurt and blame—hurt caused by feeling misunderstood or not respected and blame for each other or the relationship.

Grace, whose mother-in-law initially remarked, "She talks more than we do," learned to get along well with her in-laws by modulating (though it feels to her like cramping) her customary speaking style. She now glances at her watch when she begins to speak, to make sure she does not dominate the conversation. She tones herself down if she gets too excited: She reminds herself to lower her pitch and speak more softly. "Although I have become much more adept at this," Grace commented, "it is like having to learn a foreign language. It does not come naturally to me, so I have to be somewhat more self-conscious to succeed at it."

Although Grace has succeeded, hers is a bittersweet victory, because it means she has to be self-conscious and guarded in just the setting where we all feel we should theoretically be most natural and unguarded—the inner sanctum, the family. Yet Grace sees this as a boon. Having learned that not everyone regards her exuberant, expressive style as charming, and having learned how to modulate it when she wants to, she finds that she can communicate better with co-workers, clients, and friends whose styles are different from hers.

Dolores and Burt did eventually solve the problem of her feeling that his family wasn't interested, and his feeling overwhelmed by her family's rapid-fire questions. She decided to try Burt's suggestion and just started telling her in-laws about her work, unasked. To her amazement they listened attentively, asked follow-up questions, and told Burt how pleased they were that Dolores was finally opening up. And Burt pushed himself to jump into conversations while someone else was talking—and was amazed that they sometimes (not always) stopped speaking, giving him the floor—and their ears.

# Coda

## Talking Families

Family members are our greatest source of comfort and our greatest source of pain. They see our strongest points, as we wish them to, but they also see our faults. And sometimes they are looking at us so close up that they see faults where others would see strengths.

This is one of the ironies of family: Each of us looks to our family as a haven in a hostile world, a refuge from the harsh judgments of strangers who do not have our best interests at heart. Yet the very people from whom we most want approval are also our harshest critics.

But there is hope. Talk is the hope, just as talk is the minefield we traverse to reach the safety of family. Both the pain and the comfort are played out in words exchanged—fleetingly, in the throwaway conversations we have as we go about our daily lives, and intensively, as we try to talk things out. So the best way to begin untangling the threads—bolstering the comfort and minimizing the hurt—is to understand the workings of talk, through which the comfort, the hurt, and the untangling are all carried out.

The first step in turning talk from a liability to a balm is separating messages (the meaning of the words spoken) from metamessages (what it means to you that those you love say these words in this way—or what you think it means to them). Be clear about which you are reacting to, and be explicit once you have figured it out. Don't waste time—and emotional capital—arguing about the message if it is the metamessage that really got your goat.

The next step is understanding, and balancing, the needs for connection and control that drive all our conversations. When two people are close, each person's actions and words have resounding impact on the other. Just knowing about that impact means you're not completely free to do as you please. The double meanings of connection and control can result in sharply divergent interpretations of the same behavior, so bearing this in mind can help. If you feel yourself bristling at what seems like a control maneuver—trying to limit your freedom—consider that it might also be a connection maneuver—trying to get close. At the same time, if you intend something as a connection maneuver, bear in mind that it might be interpreted as a control maneuver.

For example, the father who tries to learn everything about rap music in order to be closer to his son might understand why his son doesn't thank him but instead resents the incursion into his territory. And the grown daughter who is offended when her mother tells her how to improve the decoration of her home might console herself by considering that her mother is simply fulfilling what she sees as a requirement to help her children—even after they no longer need her help on a daily basis.

Many parents of adult children feel, "I can't even open my mouth," because whatever they say is taken as criticism. They might resolve to join the Biting Tongue Club. Realizing that their comments carry extra weight, they can make an extra effort to refrain from offering advice, or even making helpful suggestions that could be taken as criticism.

Reframing is what makes all this possible. If your grown children seem to take every chance remark as criticism, it is not that they no longer care what you think but that they care very much. Because they want your approval so badly, they become attuned to any hint—any metamessage—of disapproval. By reframing, you can modulate your reactions, thinking differently about another person's ways of talking.

Reframing also can mean talking differently to get better results. For example, let's say a woman and a man are locked in battle over apologies. She demands one, and he refuses to provide one. Without an apology, she feels he doesn't care about having hurt her, so she can't move on. He resists admitting fault because he feels justified in what he did, and he senses that apologizing would open him to future humiliation.

By reframing, either could break this impasse. If he reframes his understanding of apologies, he could say "I'm sorry" to acknowledge the result of his actions—as an expression of regret that he caused inconvenience or pain to someone he loves. If she reframes her understanding of apologies, she could give up her insistence on hearing those specific words. Instead, she might become attuned to other ways that he shows he regrets the pain he caused her, and other types of evidence that he is willing to make changes to avoid hurting her again.

Reframing can be enhanced by metacommunicating, talking about ways of talking. Thus two people deadlocked about an apology could discuss the metamessages involved in the original offense, as well as the metamessages of saying, "I'm sorry."

By metacommunicating, both can talk about the different ways these metamessages are placed on the connection-control grid. Part of the reason their argument is never resolved is that they are focusing on different axes of the grid. His sense that, by demanding he apologize, she is trying to humiliate him means he is focused on the control continuum, between hierarchy and equality. Her concern that not apologizing implies he doesn't care means she is focused on the connection continuum, between closeness and distance. Once this difference is clarified they can focus their negotiations on addressing both their concerns: his about being pushed around or put down, and hers about being pushed away or dismissed.

In all these ways understanding what drives conversations can help improve relationships within the family.

Among the patterns driving conversations, and causing frustrations, are gender differences. Understanding gender patterns can also lead to small changes with big results. For example, we saw a pattern in how girls and women, as compared to boys and men, tend to sit when they talk casually or personally. Whereas women and girls typically face each other directly and keep their gazes fixed on each other's faces, boys and men tend to sit at angles—or parallel—and look away, glancing at each other intermittently. Knowing this, a mother who wants her son to tell her what's going on in his life might find she learns more by taking him somewhere in the car, just the two of them, than by sitting him down across the kitchen table and asking him questions.

Sometimes you won't get other-sex family members (or family members from a different culture) to act just like you, but understanding why they don't is helpful in itself. Here's an example.

Ida loves her women's book group, which meets every other week. The women in her group talk as much about their lives as about the books they read. At one meeting they never got to the book at all. When the meeting began, one woman asked another how her mother was doing and learned she had died. The group spent the entire evening discussing death and dying—consoling the member who had lost her mother but providing comfort and connection to the others as well.

Eager that her husband, Bernie, enjoy the same pleasure, Ida encourages him (he might say she nags him) to join a group of men. Finally, he locates some men who meet regularly for lunch, and he begins attending their lunches. But like the proverbial horse to water, Bernie just doesn't seem to be getting from his group what Ida gets from hers. After each lunch she asks what they talked about, and he reports that the conversation remained impersonal. She asks why he didn't tell them about this or that matter on his mind, and he says it just didn't come up. Sometimes he announces with satisfaction, "Well I learned something today." But her disappointment deepens when he reports some interesting piece of information he had not previously known.

Good as her intentions are, Ida is trying to get Bernie to interact with men the way women typically interact with each other. Understanding that men's and women's friendships tend to proceed differently, she could relieve him of the feeling that he is disappointing her, and relieve herself of the conviction that there is something lacking in him.

With such small re-framing, there is comfort simply in understanding why people you love are talking (or behaving) the way they do—and why it is so different from the way you would have spoken or acted in a similar situation.

Linguist A. L. Becker captures the complexity of conversation in two axioms proposed by the Spanish philosopher José Ortega y Gasset. He quotes Ortega:

> Two apparently contradictory laws are involved in all uttering. One says, "Every utterance is deficient"—it says less than it wishes to say. The other law, the opposite, declares, "Every utterance is exuberant"—it conveys more than it plans and includes not a few things we would wish left silent.

Exuberance and deficiency complicate every conversation we have in the family. What we say is deficient in that there are innumerable assumptions, implications, and unstated yearnings that underlie our words, but because they are unstated, those we talk to miss many of them entirely.

At the same time what we say is exuberant: Metamessages we might have wished to conceal come leaking through, or the people we talk to hear metamessages we really did not send, because of their own experiences, assumptions, and associations.

Talk in the family is an ongoing balancing act between exuberance and deficiency, as we try to fill in meanings we intended that did not come across and dispel meanings others gleaned that we did not intend. We can never completely avoid these exuberances and deficiencies, since each of us comes to conversation with a unique history of relationships and a unique position in the family. But understanding the mechanisms of talk—from metamessages and alignments to the connection-control grid to processes of framing and reframing—can provide a lens through which to see where the confusion originated, and a language with which to begin repairs.

A woman said of her sister, "We can talk all day about absolutely everything. We have a shared history, shared concerns, and a shared conversational style." When it goes well, talk among family members can be one of the most pleasurable experiences around: What ease lies in the smooth shifts from important topics to trivial ones, a similar sense of humor, voices comfortably overlapping or just as comfortably silent, mutual interests that ensure the person you are talking to will not be bored or indifferent. You laugh at inside jokes and tell stories that everyone knows but still finds hilarious. Understanding how talk works in families means that more conversations at home will offer this reward—and, through such conversations, strengthen the most important relationships in our lives: those in the family.

# Notes

### PREFACE

xviii Framing is a concept that derives from Erving Goffman, *Frame Analysis,* and Gregory Bateson, "A Theory of Play and Fantasy," in *Steps to an Ecology of Mind.* I have written about framing in many articles and books. For general audiences, see Chapter 5, "Framing and Reframing," in *That's Not What I Meant!;* for scholarly audiences, see my essays in the book I edited, *Framing in Discourse,* and my essay "The Sex-Class Linked Framing of Talk at Work," in my book *Gender and Discourse.*

### CHAPTER ONE: "I CAN'T EVEN OPEN MY MOUTH"

6 Phyllis Richman, *Who's Afraid of Virginia Ham?* pp. 36–38.

7 The terms *message* and *metamessage* come from Gregory Bateson's essay "A Theory of Play and Fantasy," in *Steps to an Ecology of Mind.* I discuss these terms and concepts in more detail in earlier books, especially *That's Not What I Meant!* and *You Just Don't Understand.*

11 *connection and control* This duality is related to the forces of status and connection that I discuss in *You Just Don't Understand* and what I call power and connection in *Talking from 9 to 5.* For scholarly audiences, see "The Relativity of Linguistic Strategies: Rethinking Power and Solidarity in Gender and Dominance," in my book *Gender and Discourse.*

17 The conversation between the people I call Evelyn and Joel was taped by the couple themselves, as part of the Sloan-supported research project I describe in "Author's Note" by which both parents carried tape recorders for a week, recording all the conversations they felt comfortable recording.

20 The couple I call Molly and Kevin were also volunteers in the Sloan-supported research project.

### CHAPTER TWO: "WHO DO YOU LOVE BEST?"

29 I discuss the idea of alignment in several essays for scholarly audiences. See especially my chapters in the book I edited, *Framing in Discourse.*

31 Katherine Russell Rich, *The Red Devil,* pp. 30–31.

40 *their mother, Miriam, was not Jewish* Margaret Salinger, *Dream Catcher,* p. 20.

41 Eudora Welty, *One Writer's Beginnings,* pp. 20–21.

43 John Osborne, *Look Back in Anger,* p. 65.

44 Salinger, *Dream Catcher,* pp. 19, 147, and 115.

45 J. D. Dolan, *Phoenix,* p. 42.

46 Adeline Yen Mah, *Falling Leaves,* pp. 56 and 57.

47 Charles Randolph-Wright's play *Blue* was performed at Arena Stage in Washington, D.C., during the 1998–99 season. When this book went to press, it was not yet available in print.

49 Jane Shapiro, *The Dangerous Husband,* p. 48.

50 Mary Catherine Bateson, *Full Circles, Overlapping Lives,* p. 101.

53 Samuel Vuchinich, "The Sequential Organization of Closing in Verbal Family Conflict," p. 128.

54 Shari Kendall, "The Interpenetration of (Gendered) Spheres," pp. 154–155.

56 Mah, *Falling Leaves,* p. 34.

58 Diana Friedman, "My Not-So-Wicked Stepmother," *Newsweek,* June 19, 2000, p. 11.

61 Joe DiPietro, *Over the River and Through the Woods,* pp. 35 and 29.

62 Mah, *Falling Leaves,* p. 144.

62 Dolan, *Phoenix,* p. 54.

### A BRIEF INTERLUDE I: "GO AHEAD, TREAT ME LIKE A STRANGER"

64 Art Spiegelman, *Maus: A Survivor's Tale,* p. 159. I found this reference in Angelika Bammer, "Mother Tongues and Other Strangers: Writing 'Family' Across Cultural Dialects," p. 99.

65 Jaber Gubrium and James Holstein, "Family Discourse, Organizational Embeddedness, and Local Enactment," p. 76.

## CHAPTER THREE: FIGHTING FOR LOVE

67 *a Ukrainian proverb* Thanks to Alla Yeliseyeva.

68 *the desires for connection and for control* In *Talking from 9 to 5* (especially Chapter 7, "Talking Up Close: Status and Connection"), I discuss the relationship between these two dimensions in more detail.

70 For a more academic discussion of the grid diagram, see "The Relativity of Linguistic Strategies: Rethinking Power and Solidarity in Gender and Dominance" in my book *Gender and Discourse.*

71 Danzy Senna, "The Color of Love," *O: The Oprah Magazine,* May–June 2000, pp. 117–120. The quotations are from pp. 118 and 120.

73 Diane Rehm told this anecdote on her NPR radio program, *The Diane Rehm Show,* March 31, 2000. The context was an interview with the author Mary Catherine Bateson.

77 Samuel Vuchinich, "The Sequential Organization of Closing in Verbal Family Conflict," p. 132. I have regularized the spelling of words because nonstandard spelling can be distracting to read.

80 Frank E. Millar, L. Edna Rogers, and Janet Beavin Bavelas, "Identifying Patterns of Verbal Conflict in Interpersonal Dynamics," pp. 236–237. I am making rather more of this example than the authors do. They present it to illustrate how a couple can "bypass" each other—a term and concept they borrow from Neil Postman, *Crazy Talk, Stupid Talk,* p. 155. In addition, this is one of several examples the authors cite to illustrate that "many interpersonal conflicts are not resolved and settled" (p. 237).

80 Janice Moulton, "A Paradigm of Philosophy: The Adversary Method," p. 156. According to Moulton, this understanding of the Socratic method, identified with the *elenchus,* actually entails a misunderstanding. The elenchus, she writes, "shakes people up about their cherished convictions so they begin philosophical inquiries with a more open mind" rather than proving them wrong. I discuss this at greater length in my book *The Argument Culture.*

84 Vuchinich, "Sequential Organization of Closing," p. 133.

87 Winston Groom, "Being a Father," p. 32.

## CHAPTER FOUR: "I'M SORRY, I'M NOT APOLOGIZING"

100 The National Public Radio spot "The Apology Line" was produced by Tammy Van Donselaar for WAMU in Washington, D.C., and aired on March 24, 1995.

103 Gregory Bateson introduced the term and concept *complementary schismogenesis* in several of the essays collected in *Steps to an Ecology of Mind.* In particular, see "Culture Contact and Schismogenesis" and "Bali: The Value System of a Steady State." Bateson identified two types of schismogenesis, symmetrical and complementary, in broad cultural patterning such as "dominance-submission, succoring-dependence, exhibitionism-spectatorship, and the like" (p. 109). As far as I know, the idea of applying this notion to everyday conversation is my own. I discuss it in more detail in several books, especially *That's Not What I Meant!* (for general audiences) and *Conversational Style* (for scholarly audiences).

103 Elinor Ochs, Carolyn Taylor, Dina Rudolph, and Ruth Smith, "Storytelling as a Theory-Building Activity," pp. 52–54. I am making rather more of this example than the authors do. They present the excerpt to illustrate that a co-narrator (in this case Jon) can contest the version of events presented by an initial teller (in this case Marie).

108 *"When you believe in the propriety . . ."* Steven Levy, "I'm Stunned That This Judgment Was Entered," *Newsweek,* June 19, 2000, p. 31. (Excerpts of a telephone interview with Microsoft executive Steve Ballmer.)

108 *Judge Thomas Penfield Jackson . . . "left little doubt . . ."* Jared Sandberg, "Microsoft's Six Fatal Errors," *Newsweek,* June 19, 2000, p. 23.

108 *"They had a very detailed presentation . . ."* Nicholas Economides, professor at the Stern School of Business at New York University, quoted in David Streitfeld, "Courting Defeat: Did the Giant Slay Itself?" *Washington Post,* June 8, 2000, pp. A1, A21. The quotation is from p. A21.

108 *"We shouldn't have pissed off the judge"* Sandberg, "Microsoft's Six Fatal Errors," p. 23.

110 Faye and Kenny were volunteers in my Sloan-supported research project.

113 Sue Silverman, *Because I Remember Terror, Father, I Remember You,* pp. 240–241.

116 Leonard J. Marcus and Barry C. Dorn, "Mediation Before Malpractice Suits?" *Newsweek,* March 27, 2000, p. 84.

117 *A caller to a talk show* The radio talk show was Leonard Lopate's *New York & Company* on WNYC in New York City.

118 Robin Lakoff, "Nine Ways of Looking at Apologies." The book is still in press, so no page number was available when this book went to press.

## CHAPTER FIVE: "SHE SAID," "HE SAID"

127 Celia and Lou are pseudonyms for speakers whose conversation was taped by volunteers in my Sloan-supported research project.

134 *his comments . . . in breath groups* Laying out spoken dialogue in poetic lines is a convention practiced by many linguists who analyze conversation. As I discuss in my book *Talking Voices: Repetition, Dialogue, and Imagery in Conversational Discourse,* this convention captures in print the rhythmic chunking that is organic to spoken language. Maureen Taylor identified this excerpt from Bill Loud's conversation and transcribed it in this way in a term paper written for my seminar.

136 *I conducted a research project* I was helped by Patricia O'Connor, whose children and their friends participated. I remain grateful to her and all the participants and their parents.

138 "that *would be the women's Viagra*" *Newsweek,* June 19, 2000, p. 19.

138 The quotation from David Reimer comes from *As Nature Made Him,* by John Colapinto, pp. 179–180.

139 *A training video that I made* The video, *Talking 9 to 5,* was made by and is available from ChartHouse International, Burnsville, MN (1-800-210-9TO5/1-800-210-9865, www.charthouse.com).

142 Alyson Simpson, " 'It's a Game!': The Construction of Gendered Subjectivity." Quotations are from pp. 198, 220, and 221.

143 Joan Silber, "The Dollar in Italy," *In My Other Life,* pp. 125–139; the quotation is on p. 134.

145 Sandra Petronio is quoted in Mary Geraghty, "Strategic Embarrassment: The Art and Science of Public Humiliation," *Chronicle of Higher Education,* April 4, 1997, p. A8.

145 Jean Berko Gleason, "Sex Differences in Parent-Child Interaction." Gleason also cites Louise Cherry and Michael Lewis, "Mothers and Two-Year-Olds: A Study of Sex Differentiated Aspects of Verbal Interaction."

146 James Matisoff, *Blessings, Curses, Hopes, and Fears: Psycho-Ostensive Expressions in Yiddish,* p. 58. The Yiddish expression is *Oy, vos far a mieskayt!* Although I grew up hearing my Russian Jewish mother say what sounded to me like "kunnahurra" whenever she praised a child, I had no idea, until reading Matisoff's book, that the Yiddish expression she was using is *kein eyn hora*—literally, "no eye," that is, no evil eye.

147 J. D. Dolan, *Phoenix,* pp. 53–54.

148 Elinor Ochs and Carolyn Taylor, "Family Narrative as Political Activity." Quotations are from pp. 310, 313, 326, 312, 326, 329, and 327.

155 The study in which I explore the greater tendency of Greeks and Greek Americans, both male and female, to use indirectness when making requests is entitled "Ethnic Style in Male/Female Conversation." First

published in 1982, it is reprinted as a chapter in my book *Gender and Discourse.*

159 Samuel Vuchinich, "The Sequential Organization of Closing in Verbal Family Conflict," p. 129. I present examples of conversations in which a sister tries unsuccessfully to get her voice heard in my book *You Just Don't Understand,* pp. 133–135 and 137.

## CHAPTER SIX: "YOU GUYS ARE LIVING IN THE PAST"

163 The distinction between socializing *with* children (that is, enjoying their company) and socializing them (teaching them what they need to know in order to function in adult society) is made by Shoshana Blum-Kulka in *Dinner Talk,* a study of dinner-table conversations in Jewish American, American Israeli, and Israeli households.

167 The example of Denise, Jim, and Anna was tape-recorded and analyzed by a student in one of my classes.

174 *parents are hurled back to their own teenage years* Linda Lehr and John Anning helped me understand this perspective.

175 "Different Tunes," in *The Peggy Seeger Songbook,* pp. 230–238.

177 Karin Aronsson and Ann-Christin Cederborg, "A Love Story Retold: Moral Order and Intergenerational Negotiations." Quotations are from pp. 87, 94, 95, 100, 96, and 98.

180 *an Australian family that was televised* According to David Lee ("Frame Conflicts and Competing Construals in Family Argument"), the series, entitled *Sylvania Waters,* was a joint production of the Australian Broadcasting Corporation and the British Broadcasting Corporation, and aired in Australia in 1992 and in Britain in 1993. The central couple, Noeline Baker, a New Zealander, and Laurie Donaher, an Australian, had lived together for most of the previous thirteen years and were planning to get married. Michael, fifteen, was the only one of their several children from previous marriages who lived with them at the time of filming. I have changed the spelling of the man's name to Larry from Laurie to make it easier for American readers to identify the speaker as male.

186 *Karen's own history played a role* Karen Wilson made this comment in a telephone conversation. I am grateful to her for taking the time to discuss this example with me, and for her and her family's permission to use their words.

187 *The conversation we'll look at next* The conversation between Bill and their son Grant was analyzed, separately, by two students in seminars I taught: Shu-Ching Susan Chen and Pornpimon Supakorn. Although my analysis differs from theirs, I am grateful to them for identifying and transcribing the segments.

197 *Pat begins with a question* The conversation between Pat and Lance Loud was also analyzed by Pornpimon Supakorn for her seminar paper. Although my analysis differs from hers, I am grateful to her for identifying and transcribing the segment.

201 Candice Carpenter told this anecdote at "The Global Community of Women," a conference organized by the Women's Center of Vienna, Virginia, March 11, 2000.

### A BRIEF INTERLUDE II: "CALL ME BY MY RIGHTFUL NAME"

205 Micah Perks, *Pagan Time.* Page references were not available when this book went to press.

206 David Reimer appeared on *The Oprah Winfrey Show* on February 9, 2000.

207 Donna Williams, *Somebody Somewhere,* p. 89.

207 Sue Silverman, *Because I Remember Terror, Father, I Remember You,* pp. 93–94 and 196.

### CHAPTER SEVEN: "I'M STILL YOUR MOTHER"

212 Sarah Vowell, "American Goth," in *Take the Cannoli,* pp. 210–219; quotations are from pp. 210, 211, 212, 213, 215–216, 216, and 217.

215 Amy Tan, *The Joy Luck Club;* quotations are from pp. 196, 199, 200, and 201.

216 "Welcome to Kindergarten, Mrs. Johnson," lyrics by Marta Kauffman and David Crane, in *A . . . My Name Is Alice: A Musical Review,* by Joan Micklin Silver and Julianne Boyd, pp. 21–24.

216 Andrea DeCapua and Lisa Huber, " 'If I were you . . .': Advice in American English," p. 127.

217 The couple I call Sheila and Dan, who were volunteers in my research project, recorded the conversation themselves.

218 Stephanie Coontz, *The Way We Never Were,* p. 210.

219 Nicole Wise, "Parents Shouldn't Be on Call All the Time," *Newsweek,* August 7, 2000, p. 15.

219 Hildred Geertz, *The Javanese Family,* p. 22.

220 Stephen Fellner, "Epiphanies," *Poet Lore* 94:4.16–17 (Winter 1999–2000).

220 Shari Kendall, "The Interpenetration of (Gendered) Spheres," pp. 138 and 148.

225 Jane Bernstein, "My Real Father," pp. 177–178.

226 These lines from *An American Love Story* were identified by Alla Yeliseyeva in a term paper written for a seminar I taught.

226 Jeffrey Solomon's play *MotherSON* was unpublished when this book went to press, but information about it is available at the Web site mother-son.com.

227 *According to Shari Kendall* Kendall made this comment in a personal communication.

229 Diane Rehm, *Finding My Voice,* pp. 22–23.

231 Liz Lochhead, *Perfect Days,* pp. 18, 19, and 20.

232 *In Taiwan a teenage boy who lost his family* Brook Larner, "The Night Heaven Fell," *Newsweek,* October 4, 1999, pp. 48–49. The teenager is identified as Xu Yan Wu.

233 Rehm, *Finding My Voice,* p. 19.

233 Mark Mathabane was a guest on *The Diane Rehm Show,* August 28, 1989, on the publication of his book *Kaffir Boy in America.*

234 John Steinbeck, *The Grapes of Wrath,* p. 100. Elisa Everts called my attention to this quotation.

234 *A woman who called in to a talk show The Diane Rehm Show,* May 16, 2000. The context was an interview with the author Jayne Anne Phillips.

234 Karen Henwood, "Women and Later Life," p. 307.

235 Sue Silverman, *Because I Remember Terror, Father, I Remember You,* pp. 238 and 240.

238 Jenny Cook-Gumperz, "Gendered Contexts," pp. 189–190.

239 Jacki Lyden, *Daughter of the Queen of Sheba,* pp. 197 and 188.

245 Judy Carter's joke is quoted in Murray S. Davis, *What's So Funny?,* p. 281.

## CHAPTER EIGHT: "HELP ME—GET OUT OF MY WAY"

248 Joan Silber, "What Lasts," in *In My Other Life,* pp. 203–223. Quotations are from pp. 218 and 210.

250 *Bessie Delany said of her older sister* Sarah Delany and A. Elizabeth Delany, with Amy Hill Hearth, *Having Our Say,* p. 9.

250 J. D. Dolan, *Phoenix,* pp. 34 and 102.

257 Brendan Gill is quoted in "The Love Boat," by Russell Baker, *New York Review of Books,* March 23, 2000, pp. 4–6; quotation is on p. 4.

258 Ana Veciana-Suarez, "Mi Papi," p. 132.

258 *Jane said, "King Henry the Eighth . . ."* This example comes from Samuel Vuchinich, "The Sequential Organization of Closing in Verbal Family Conflict," pp. 123–124.

259 Michael Ondaatje, *Running in the Family,* p. 67.

260 *"Would it be ill manners . . ."* This example comes from Vuchinich, "Sequential Organization of Closing," p. 125.

261 *"I thought you were going to send him . . ."* This example comes from Samuel Vuchinich, "Starting and Stopping Spontaneous Family Conflicts," pp. 592–593.

262 Alyson Simpson, " 'It's a Game!': The Construction of Gendered Subjectivity." The dialogue quoted is from pp. 198, 216–219, and 221.

270 Dolan, *Phoenix,* p. 45.

271 Shirley Strum, *Almost Human,* pp. 133–134.

275 Bambi Schieffelin, *The Give and Take of Everyday Life,* pp. 120, 124, 126, 127, and 113.

276 Susan U. Philips, "Constructing a Tongan Nation-State through Language Ideology in the Courtroom," p. 238.

277 Delany and Delany, *Having Our Say,* p. 5.

278 *It's the past that keeps changing* I heard this from Ruth Wodak in a paper she presented at the American Anthropological Association meeting, Chicago, IL, November 1999. She tells me that her source is the historian Peter Burke. In an essay entitled "History as Social Memory," Burke notes, "It is becoming commonplace to point out that in different places and times, historians have considered different aspects of the past to be memorable (battles, politics, religion, the economy, and so on) and that they have presented the past in very different ways (concentrating on events or structures, on great men or ordinary people, according to their group's point of view)" (p. 99).

## CHAPTER NINE: IN-LAWS AND OTHER STRANGERS

283 The cross-cultural differences in conversational style that are the subject of this chapter have been the focus of my research for many years. I discuss them in most detail in *That's Not What I Meant!* as well as the book for scholarly audiences *Conversational Style.*

285 Jaakko Lehtonen and Kari Sajavaara, "The Silent Finn," p. 198.

287 *machine-gun questions* I write about this in *Conversational Style.*

296 Amy Tan, *The Joy Luck Club,* p. 197.

299 A. R. Gurney, *The Dining Room,* p. 32.

### CODA: TALKING FAMILIES

307 A. L. Becker, *Beyond Translation,* p. 5.

# References


Aronsson, Karin, and Ann-Christin Cederborg. 1997. "A Love Story Retold: Moral Order and Intergenerational Negotiations." *Semiotica* 114:1/2.83–110.

Bammer, Angelika. 1994. "Mother Tongues and Other Strangers: Writing 'Family' Across Cultural Dialects." In *Displacements: Cultural Identities in Question,* ed. by Angelika Bammer, 90–109. Bloomington, IN: Indiana University Press.

Bateson, Gregory. 1972. *Steps to an Ecology of Mind.* New York: Ballantine.

Bateson, Mary Catherine. 2000. *Full Circles, Overlapping Lives: Culture and Generation in Transition.* New York: Random House.

Becker, A. L. 1995. *Beyond Translation: Essays Toward a Modern Philology.* Ann Arbor: University of Michigan Press.

Bernstein, Jane. 2000. "My Real Father." In *Father: Famous Writers Celebrate the Bond Between Father and Child,* ed. by Claudia O'Keefe, 172–183. New York: Pocket Books.

Blum-Kulka, Shoshana. 1997. *Dinner Talk: Cultural Patterns of Sociability and Socialization in Family Discourse.* Mahwah, NJ: Erlbaum.

Burke, Peter. 1989. "History as Social Memory." In *Memory: History, Culture and the Mind,* ed. by Thomas Butler, 97–113. Oxford: Basil Blackwell.

Byrnes, Heidi. 1986. "Interactional Style in German and American Conversations." *Text* 6:2.189–206.

Cherry, Louise, and Michael Lewis. 1976. "Mothers and Two-Year-Olds: A Study of Sex-Differentiated Aspects of Verbal Interaction." *Developmental Psychology* 12:4.278–282.

Colapinto, John. 2000. *As Nature Made Him: The Boy Who Was Raised as a Girl.* New York: HarperCollins.

Cook-Gumperz, Jenny. 1992. "Gendered Contexts." In *The Contextualization of Language,* ed. by Peter Auer and Aldo Di Luzio, 177–198. Philadelphia: John Benjamins.

Coontz, Stephanie. 1992. *The Way We Never Were: American Families and the Nostalgia Trap.* New York: Basic Books.

Davis, Murray S. 1993. *What's So Funny? The Comic Conception of Culture and Society.* Chicago: University of Chicago Press.

DeCapua, Andrea, and Lisa Huber. 1995. " 'If I were you . . .': Advice in American English." *Multilingua* 14:2.117–132.

Delany, Sarah, and A. Elizabeth Delany, with Amy Hill Hearth. 1993. *Having Our Say: The Delany Sisters' First 100 Years.* New York: Kodansha.

DiPietro, Joe. 1999. *Over the River and Through the Woods.* New York: Dramatists Play Service.

Dolan, J. D. 2000. *Phoenix: A Brother's Life.* New York: Alfred A. Knopf.

Edelman, Hope. 1995. *Motherless Daughters: The Legacy of Loss.* New York: Delta.

Ervin-Tripp, Susan, Mary Catherine O'Connor, and Jarrett Rosenberg. 1984. "Language and Power in the Family." In *Language and Power,* ed. by Cheris Kramarae, Muriel Schulz, and William M. O'Barr, 116–135. Beverly Hills: Sage.

Geertz, Hildred. 1989 [1961]. *The Javanese Family: A Study of Kinship and Socialization.* Prospect Heights, IL: Waveland Press.

Gleason, Jean Berko. 1987. "Sex Differences in Parent-Child Interaction." In *Language, Gender, and Sex in Comparative Perspective,* ed. by Susan U. Philips, Susan Steele, and Christine Tanz, 189–199. Cambridge: Cambridge University Press.

Goffman, Erving. 1974. *Frame Analysis.* New York: Harper & Row.

Groom, Winston. 2000. "Being a Father." In *Father: Famous Writers Celebrate the Bond Between Father and Child,* ed. by Claudia O'Keefe, 29–35. New York: Pocket Books.

Gubrium, Jaber F., and James A. Holstein. 1993. "Family Discourse, Organizational Embeddedness, and Local Enactment." *Journal of Family Issues* 14:1.66–81.

Gurney, A. R. 1982. *The Dining Room.* New York: Dramatists Play Service.

Henwood, Karen L. 1993. "Women and Later Life: The Discursive Construction of Identities Within Family Relationships." *Journal of Aging Studies* 7:3.303–319.

Hochschild, Arlie Russell. 1989. *The Second Shift.* New York: Ballantine.

Hrdy, Sarah Blaffer. 1999. *Mother Nature: A History of Mothers, Infants, and Natural Selection.* New York: Pantheon.

Kendall, Shari. 1999. "The Interpenetration of (Gendered) Spheres: An Interactional Sociolinguistic Analysis of a Mother at Work and at Home." Ph.D. dissertation, Georgetown University.

Kim, Elizabeth. 2000. *Ten Thousand Sorrows: The Extraordinary Journey of a Korean War Orphan.* New York: Doubleday.

Lakoff, Robin. 2001. "Nine Ways of Looking at Apologies." In *Handbook of Discourse Analysis,* ed. by Deborah Schiffrin, Deborah Tannen, and Heidi E. Hamilton. Cambridge, MA: Basil Blackwell.

Lee, David A. 1997. "Frame Conflicts and Competing Construals in Family Argument." *Journal of Pragmatics* 27.339–360.

Lehtonen, Jaakko, and Kari Sajavaara. 1986. "The Silent Finn." In *Perspectives on Silence,* ed. by Deborah Tannen and Muriel Saville-Troike, 193–201. Norwood, NJ: Ablex.

Lochhead, Liz. 1998. *Perfect Days.* London: Nick Hern Books.

Lyden, Jacki. 1997. *Daughter of the Queen of Sheba.* Boston: Houghton Mifflin.

Mah, Adeline Yen. 1997. *Falling Leaves: The Memoir of an Unwanted Chinese Daughter.* New York: Broadway Books.

Matisoff, James A. 2000 [1979]. *Blessings, Curses, Hopes, and Fears: Psycho-Ostensive Expressions in Yiddish.* Stanford: Stanford University Press.

Millar, Frank E., L. Edna Rogers, and Janet Beavin Bavelas. 1984. "Identifying Patterns of Verbal Conflict in Interpersonal Dynamics." *Western Journal of Speech Communication* 48.231–246.

Moulton, Janice. 1983. "A Paradigm of Philosophy: The Adversary Method." In *Discovering Reality,* ed. by Sandra Harding and Merrill B. Hintikka, 149–164. Dordrecht, Holland: Reidel.

Ochs, Elinor, and Carolyn Taylor. 1992. "Family Narrative as Political Activity." *Discourse & Society* 3:3.301–340.

Ochs, Elinor, Carolyn Taylor, Dina Rudolph, and Ruth Smith. 1992. "Storytelling as a Theory-Building Activity." *Discourse Processes* 15.37–72.

Ondaatje, Michael. 1982. *Running in the Family.* New York: Vintage.

Ortega y Gasset, José. 1957. *Man and People* [*El Hombre y la Gente*], trans. by Willard R. Trask. New York: W. W. Norton.

Osborne, John. 1975. *Look Back in Anger.* London: Faber & Faber.

Perks, Micah. 2001. *Pagan Time.* Washington, D.C.: Counterpoint Press.

Philips, Susan U. 2000. "Constructing a Tongan Nation-State Through Language Ideology in the Courtroom." In *Regimes of Language: Ideologies, Polities, and Identities,* ed. by Paul V. Kroskrity, 229–257. Santa Fe, NM: School of American Research Press.

Postman, Neil. 1976. *Crazy Talk, Stupid Talk: How We Defeat Ourselves by the Way We Talk—and What to Do About It.* New York: Dell.

Rehm, Diane. 1999. *Finding My Voice.* New York: Alfred A. Knopf.

Rich, Katherine Russell. 1999. *The Red Devil.* New York: Crown.

Richman, Phyllis. 2001. *Who's Afraid of Virginia Ham?* New York: HarperCollins.

Salinger, Margaret A. 2000. *Dream Catcher.* New York: Washington Square Press.

Schieffelin, Bambi B. 1990. *The Give and Take of Everyday Life: Language Socialization of Kaluli Children.* Cambridge: Cambridge University Press.

Seeger, Peggy. 1998. *The Peggy Seeger Songbook: Warts and All: Forty Years of Songmaking*. New York: Oak Publications.

Shapiro, Jane. 1999. *The Dangerous Husband*. New York: Little, Brown.

Silber, Joan. 2000. *In My Other Life: Stories*. Louisville, KY: Sarabande Books.

Silver, Joan Micklin, and Julianne Boyd. 1985. *A . . . My Name Is Alice: A Musical Review*. New York: Samuel French.

Silverman, Sue William. 1999. *Because I Remember Terror, Father, I Remember You*. Athens: University of Georgia Press.

Simpson, Alyson. 1997. " 'It's a Game!': The Construction of Gendered Subjectivity." In *Gender and Discourse*, ed. by Ruth Wodak, 197–224. London: Sage.

Spiegelman, Art. 1986. *Maus: A Survivor's Tale*. New York: Pantheon.

Steinbeck, John. 1939. *The Grapes of Wrath*. New York: Viking.

Strum, Shirley C. 1987. *Almost Human: A Journey into the World of Baboons*. New York: W. W. Norton.

Tan, Amy. 1989. *The Joy Luck Club*. New York: Ballantine.

Tannen, Deborah. 1984. *Conversational Style: Analyzing Talk Among Friends*. Norwood, NJ: Ablex.

Tannen, Deborah. 1986. *That's Not What I Meant! How Conversational Style Makes or Breaks Relationships*. New York: Ballantine.

Tannen, Deborah. 1989. *Talking Voices: Repetition, Dialogue, and Imagery in Conversational Discourse*. Cambridge: Cambridge University Press.

Tannen, Deborah. 1990. *You Just Don't Understand: Women and Men in Conversation*. New York: Ballantine.

Tannen, Deborah. 1994. *Talking from 9 to 5: Women and Men in the Workplace: Language, Sex and Power*. New York: Avon.

Tannen, Deborah. 1996. *Gender and Discourse*. New York: Oxford University Press.

Tannen, Deborah. 1998. *The Argument Culture: Stopping America's War of Words*. New York: Ballantine.

Tannen, Deborah, ed. 1993. *Framing in Discourse*. New York: Oxford University Press.

Veciana-Suarez, Ana. 2000. "Mi Papi." In *Father: Famous Writers Celebrate the Bond Between Father and Child*, ed. by Claudia O'Keefe, 122–134. New York: Pocket Books.

Vowell, Sarah. 2000. *Take the Cannoli: Stories from the New World*. New York: Simon & Schuster.

Vuchinich, Samuel. 1987. "Starting and Stopping Spontaneous Family Conflicts." *Journal of Marriage and the Family* 49.591–601.

Vuchinich, Samuel. 1990. "The Sequential Organization of Closing in Verbal Family Conflict." In *Conflict Talk*, ed. by Allen Grimshaw, 118–138. Cambridge: Cambridge University Press.

Welty, Eudora. 1984. *One Writer's Beginnings*. Cambridge, MA: Harvard University Press.

Williams, Donna. 1992. *Nobody Nowhere: The Extraordinary Autobiography of an Autistic*. New York: Times Books.

Williams, Donna. 1994. *Somebody Somewhere: Breaking Free from the World of Autism*. New York: Times Books.

Williams, Donna. 1996. *Like Color to the Blind: Soul Searching and Soul Finding*. New York: Times Books.

Wodak, Ruth, and Muriel Schulz. 1986. *The Language of Guilt: Mother-Daughter Relationships from a Cross-Cultural Perspective*. Amsterdam: John Benjamins.

# Index


Acknowledgment, as apology, 112–14, 116–17, 118
*Ade,* concept of, 275–77
Adolescents, 161–202
  aikido approach of, 196–98, 202
  and assumptions, 169–70, 172–73, 181, 182–85, 190, 192–93
  attempts to communicate with, 128–33, 167–75, 182–202
  and connection-control balance, 162–65
  and dating, 167–75
  deny-everything approach of, 195–96
  drawing away from parents, 128–31, 133–36, 161–62, 174–75, 180
  in family hierarchy, 69
  and framing, 167–68, 173, 178, 180–81, 196
  and generation gap, 164, 169
  isolating alignments of, 167–70, 180
  listening to, 194, 196, 201
  and metamessages, 182–83
  in mother-daughter relationships, 128–36, 175–80
  and parents' alignment, 185–88, 191, 194–95, 201
  peer pressure on, 163–64
  protection of, 162, 167, 170–74, 178, 202
  and reframing, 198–202
  self-naming of, 203
Adoption, 66
Adult children, *see* Children, adult
Advice:
  connection and control in, 19, 24
  double meaning of, 6, 15, 125, 162
  and implied incompetence, 23–24, 61
  to mothers, 216–17
  by older sibling, 252–53
Age:
  aging parents, 59–61, 239–41
  and change, 244–45
  and control acts, 220
  and family hierarchy, 68
  and insight, 214–15
Aggression, of boys, 142, 159
Aikido approach, 196–98, 202
Alfred P. Sloan Foundation, xxv
Alignment, 29–66, 79
  and adolescents, 167–70, 180, 183, 185–88, 191, 194–95, 201
  and apologies, 114–15
  in communication, 225–28
  conflicting, 47–48
  and criticism, 34
  and family as fortress, 30–31, 65

Alignment (*cont'd*)
favoritism in, 47, 56–57, 258, 262–66, 269
individuals excluded by, 34, 37–39, 40, 44–46, 58–59, 63, 114–15
information withheld or revealed in, 41, 47–48
and listening, 194, 195, 201
in men's friendships, 33
and metamessages, 34
mother-child, 38–39
of parents, 34, 41–44
with pets, 49–52
physical, gender differences in, 136–38
and revealing secrets, 31–33, 39–41
shifting, 30, 47–48, 53–55, 58–59, 62–63
of siblings, 260–62
and spying, 46–49
stealthy nature of, 44
vs. strangers, 64–66
use of term, xx, 29–30, 66
and ventriloquizing, 51–53
within the family, 33–66
in women's friendships, 33
Allo-mothers, 218
*Almost Human* (Strum), 271
Alzheimer's disease:
family not recognized in, 65
gender difference in response to, 146–47
*American Family, An* (TV), xxvi, 131–33, 155, 187–98, 256
*American Love Story, An* (TV), xxvi, 128–31, 170–74, 186, 225
*A . . . My Name Is Alice* (musical), 216, 232
Anger:
apology as dissolver of, 97–98
expression of, 72, 93
and saying good-bye, 88
Anning, Emily, 162, 167, 201–2
Anning, John, 201–2
Apologies, 95–123
acknowledgment as, 112–14, 116–17, 118
admission of fault in, 109–10, 119
admit-no-fault, 108–9
and alignment, 114–15
anger dissipated with, 97–98
in arguments, 90, 92–93
child's wish for, 113–14
complementary schismogenesis in, 103, 108, 109, 119
as connection maneuvers, 96–97
contrition in, 109–10, 119
as degradation ritual, 114–16
in e-mail messages, 279
explanation in, 110
kiss and make up in, 120–23
litigation vs., 117
men's handling of, 100–103, 117–20, 305
mutual aggravation in, 103–5
need for, 95, 109, 115
negotiation of, 110–12, 120
as power maneuvers, 96
power of, 97–98, 116, 117
and Socratic method, 104–5
tone of, 105–6
trust restored through, 97
truth as beside the point in, 115–16
women's demand for, 98–100, 109, 117–20, 305
Apology Line, 100
Arguments, 67–94
about arguments, 88–90
apologies in, 92–93
avoidance of, 17
benefits of, 71–72, 296–97
for closeness, 90–91, 93–94
communicating through, 67, 76
communication barriers in, 77–78
complaint-countercomplaint, 104–5
conflicting opinions in, 76
and connection-control grid, 68–71, 74, 90, 93–94, 289, 297
and conversational style, 289–90, 296–97
and daily pressures, 20, 85
fair fighting in, 91–94
family dynamics in, 67
for fun, 296–97
with in-laws, 85–88
making vs. having, 93
mediation in, 116–17
personal histories brought to, 73–75

raising one's voice in, 77–78
real issues in, 75–76, 83–85
refusal to continue, 78
sarcasm in, 77, 78, 81, 84, 92, 93, 103
silence vs., 76
Socratic method of, 80–83, 92
sore spots in, 73–75
timing in, 79, 88
Aronsson, Karin, 177, 179
*As Nature Made Him* (Colapinto), 205–6
Assumptions, 307
and adolescents, 169–70, 172–73, 181, 182–85, 190, 192–93
and experience, 169, 170, 183
and framing, 173, 181, 184–85
as seemingly self-evident, 169
and work ethic, 192–93
Australian Broadcasting Commission, xxvi
Autism, 206–7

Baker, Noeline, xxvi
Ballmer, Steve, 108
Bateson, Gregory, xviii, 103
Bateson, Mary Catherine, 50
Bavelas, Janet Beavin, 80, 81
*Because I Remember Terror, Father, I Remember You* (Silverman), 113–14, 235
Becker, A. L., 146, 148, 307
Bernstein, Jane, 225, 226
Birth order, 249–53
*Blue* (Randolph-Wright), 47, 48
Blum-Kulka, Shoshana, 147–48
British Broadcasting Corporation (BBC), xxvi
Byrnes, Heidi, 289

Caring and criticizing, double meaning of, 5–6
Carpenter, Candice, 201
Carter, Judy, 245
Cederborg, Ann-Christin, 177, 179
Children:
adult, *see* Children, adult
alignment of parent and, 34, 37–39, 44–46
apologies wanted by, 113–14
approval sought by, 163, 216, 304
communication of parents and, 136–38, 217, 226, 304
comparisons with, 222–23
and favoritism, 47, 56–57
and grandparents, 24–27
in hierarchical position, xix, 11, 148–49
information inadvertently revealed by, 48–49
and inheritance, 56–58
parental judgment of, 148–52, 214
parents aligned against, 34, 41–44
parents judged by, 26, 164, 293
as parents' redeemers, 231–32
and pets, 50–51
at play, 237–39
praise of, 146
pre-adolescent, 162–65
stepchildren, 47, 56–57
tantrums of, 269
world of, 275
Children, adult:
and aging parents, 59–61, 239–41
alignment of, vs. parents, 34
battles over inheritance, 56
and family hierarchy, 68
living at home, 27
and mothers, 210–16, 231–32, 304; *see also* Mother-daughter relationships; Mothers
return to dependency by, 62
visits to parents from, 27, 62
with younger siblings, 253
Class differences, 299
Closeness-distance continuum, 69, 211, 305
Colapinto, John, 205–6
Coleman, Willette, 100
Comfort, giving, 237–39
Communication:
about absent individuals, 35–36
about money, 156–58
about relationships, 10–11, 127–31, 133
about troubles, 126–27
with adolescents, 128–33, 167–75, 182–202
alignment in, 225–28
in arguments, *see* Arguments

Communication (*cont'd*)
between parents, 131–36
in context, 74–75
e-mail changes in, 227–28, 279
eye contact and, 137
facial expressions in, 18
gender differences in, *see* Gender patterns
by high-considerateness speakers, 281, 291–92, 294
by high-involvement speakers, 160, 281, 291–92, 294
indirect, 16, 152–56, 244
interrupted, 159–60
lack of, 127
and metacommunication, 8–9, 28
mother as center of, 225–28
of parents and children, 136–38, 226, 304
power created in, 11–12
pressure in, 35
repetition in, 84
self-evident meanings in, 17–19
seminars on, xxvii
silence in, 76, 270
tone used in, 18, 77, 105–6
and trust, 34–35
ventriloquizing in, 51–53
words used in, *see* Words
Comparisons:
across generations, 223–25
hurtful, 222–23
overreaction to, 222
Competition:
of being right, 258–59
and connection, 139–42
gender patterns in, 139–44
photographs as instrument of, 273–75
of siblings, 56, 249, 259–60, 273–75
Complaint-countercomplaint matches, 104–5
Complementary schismogenesis:
in apologies, 103, 108, 109, 119
in conversational style, 199, 288–89, 301
use of term, 103
Complimenting, 295
Conflicts, *see* Arguments
Connection:
with adolescents, 167
apologies and, 96–97
closeness vs. distance in, 69, 211, 305
and competition, 139–42
and control, 11–13, 15–17, 19, 24, 28, 92; *see also* Connection-control grid
of family members, 11–12, 30, 65–66, 70
gender differences in, 139–42
and grandparents, 25, 61
and joking, 146–47
vs. strangers, 64–66
use of term, xviii–xix
*see also* Alignment
Connection continuum:
closeness-distance in, 69, 211, 305
use of term, xix, 69–70
Connection-control grid, 68–71
and adolescents, 162–65
and arguments, 74, 90, 93–94, 289, 297
balance in, 304, 307
and conversational style, xix–xx, 297
and in-laws, 86–88
and metacommunicating, 305
and mothers, 211–12, 214, 236–39, 257
and siblings, 257, 268–69, 276
Contrition, 109–10, 119
Control:
acts of, 220
and advice, 19, 24
apologies as maneuvers of, 96
and connection, 11–13, 15–17, 19, 24, 28, 92; *see also* Connection-control grid
and decisions, 157
drive toward, 68
and hierarchy, 68–71, 148–50, 152, 157
and judgments, 11, 14, 16–17, 148–52
in money issues, 157–58
by policing, 10–11
and protection, 55
use of term, xviii–xix

Control continuum:
hierarchy-equality in, 69, 211, 305
use of term, xix, 68–69
Conversational rituals, shared, xvii, xxiii–xxiv, 99–100
Conversational style, xvi, 281–302
after dinner, 297–98
and arguments, 289–90, 296–97
complementary schismogenesis in, 199, 288–89, 301
and connection-control grid, xix–xx, 297
in cross-cultural relationships, 284–86, 290–93, 295–96
development of, 284
gender patterns in, 125–26, 291, 305–6
high-considerateness vs. high-involvement, 281, 291–92, 294
at home, 283–84, 301–2
of in-laws, 281–83, 287–89, 290, 293, 295–302
as invisible, 283–84
pacing of, 288–89
power created via, 11–12
regional differences in, 293–94
relative differences in, 286–87
social distinctions in, 284, 299–301
of spouses, 301–2
stereotypes from, 284–86
topics in, 289–90
understanding, 303
use of term, 283
*Conversational Style* (Tannen), 286
Cook-Gumperz, Jenny, 238
Coontz, Stephanie, 218
Corrections, *see* Criticism
Criticism:
acknowledged validity of, 26
and alignment, 34
and biting one's tongue, 246–47, 304
breaking cycle of, 201–2
caring and, 5–6
cumulative effect of, 8–9, 13–15, 19
history of, 13–15, 16, 19, 211
inferences of, 4, 15–17, 26–27
and judgments, 18, 149–50
love and, 6–9
from mothers, 104, 210–14, 241–42, 263
from older siblings, 253
piggybacking by younger brother, 263
point of view in, 14–15
reframing of, 212–14
Cross-cultural relationships:
and conversational style, 284–86, 290–93, 295–96
within families, 290–93
Cursing, 77, 78

*Dangerous Husband, The* (Shapiro), 49–50
Dating, 167–75
*Daughter of the Queen of Sheba* (Lyden), 239–40
Daughters, *see* Mother-daughter relationships
DeCapua, Andrea, 216
Decisions:
alternative suggestions to, 16
and control, 157
Delany, Bessie and Sadie, 250, 277–78
Dennis the Menace, 49
Deny-everything approach, 195–96
"Different Tunes" (Seeger), 175–77
*Dining Room, The* (Gurney), 298–99
Dinner-table conversations:
alignments in, 53–55, 260–62
arguments in, 77–78, 84
and birth order, 252–53
and class differences, 298–301
taping of, xxvi, 220
*Dinner Talk* (Blum-Kulka), 148
DiPietro, Joe, 61
*Divorce American Style* (film), 8–9
Dolan, J. D., 45–46, 62, 147, 250–51, 270
"Doorknob complaints," 79
Dorn, Barry, 116–17
*Dream Catcher* (M. Salinger), 40, 44–45

Edelman, Hope, 234–35
E-mail, communication patterns changed via, 227–28, 279
"Epiphanies" (Fellner), 220
Ervin-Tripp, Susan, 220
"Evil eye, the," 146
Exaggeration, 77–78, 92

Examples:
sources of, xxv–xxvii
tape recorder used in, xxvii
Excuses, in arguments, 90, 122–23
Eye contact, 137

Facial expressions, interpretation of, 18
*Falling Leaves* (Mah), 46–47, 56–57
Family, 303–8
alignment in, *see* Alignment
allure of, 3
apologies in, *see* Apologies
breaking rules in, 75
closeness implied by, 11–12, 16, 65–66, 232
as community of speech, xvii, xxiii–xxiv, 99–100
control and connection in, 11–13, 15–17
conversational style in, 283–84, 301–2
coordinating tasks in, 20–23
criticism from, 5–6, 13–15, 16, 19
cross-cultural relationships within, 290–93
eating together, 12–13
as filter, 258
financial burden of, 136
forms of, xxii–xxiii
as fortress, 30–31, 65
gossip within, 33–36
as haven, 303
hierarchical nature of, xix, 11–12, 68–71, 87, 107, 148–50, 152, 157
and importance of being right, 258–60
and in-laws, 85–88
judgments from, 11, 148–52, 303
layers of meanings in, xvi–xvii
living together, 20
mother-child relationship as center of, 232
neglect of, 75
as opposite of strangers, 64–66
overreactions to, 4, 222–23
pain caused by, 4, 6–8, 307
paradox of, 27–28, 29
policing activities of, 10–11
power in, 11
private language of, xxiv, 270
revealing secrets of, 31–33, 39–41, 48–49, 228–29, 230
shared history in, 4, 211
shared responsibility in, 20–23
taking for granted, 75
and workplace, 257–58
Familylect (family dialect), unique, xxiv, 270
Family presentation, 228–29
Family reunions, 29
Fathers:
e-mail and communication with, 227–28
as family judge, 147–52
as object of respect, 219
as silent, 225–27
*see also* Parents
Favoritism, 262–66
and inheritance, 56–57
and older siblings, 269
and stepchildren, 47, 56–57
in workplace, 258
*see also* Alignment
Fellner, Stephen, 220
Fighting, *see* Arguments
*Finding My Voice* (Rehm), 229
Fox, Jennifer, xxvi, 128, 226
Framing:
and adolescents, 167–68, 173, 178, 180–81, 196
and assumptions, 173, 181, 184–85
and reframing, 198–202, 304–5
socializing vs. caretaking frame, 163
use of term, xviii, 163, 167
Friedman, Diana, 58
Friendships:
gender patterns in, 33, 306
with parents, 245–46
*Full Circles, Overlapping Lives* (M. Bateson), 50

Gates, Bill, 108
Geertz, Hildred, 219
Gender patterns, 124–60
and apologies, *see* Apologies
in arguments, *see* Arguments
in being right, 259

in competition, 139–44
in connection, 139–42
in conversational style, 125–26, 291, 305–6
in friendships, 33, 306
and indirectness, 152–56
in joking, 146–47
in making judgments, 148–52
and money, 156–58
norms in, 142–44
of parents and children, 136–38, 217
in parents' talk, 131–36
power lines or connection lines in, 147–52
in rapport-talk vs. report-talk, 124–25, 259
and siblings of opposite sex, 158–60
in talk about personal relationships, 127–31, 133
in teasing, 143–46
in troubles talk, 126–27, 151
when kids leave, 133–36
Generation gap, 164, 169
Gerrity, Thomas P., 141
Gilbert, Craig, xxvi
Gill, Brendan, 257–58
Glaser, Gonen, 101
Gleason, Jean Berko, 145, 159
Goffman, Erving, xviii
Gordon, Cynthia, 237
Grandparents:
and connection, 25, 61
and grandchildren, 24–27
*Grapes of Wrath, The* (Steinbeck), 234
Greeks and Greek Americans, communication styles of, 145, 155–56, 219, 234, 272, 295
Groom, Winston, 87
Gubrium, Jaber, 65
Gurney, A. R., 298–99

Henwood, Karen, 234–35
Hierarchy, family:
children in, 11, 148–49
in connection-control grid, 68–71, 157
gender patterns in, 150, 152
parents in, 11, 107, 148–50, 152
and power struggle, 87
siblings in, xix, 11–12, 249
spouses in, 157
and use of name, 107
Hierarchy-equality continuum, 69, 211, 305
High-considerateness style, 281, 291–92, 294
High-involvement style, 160, 281, 291–92, 294
Hochschild, Arlie, 218
Holstein, James, 65
Hrdy, Sarah Blaffer, 218
Huber, Lisa, 216
Humor, use of, 146–47, 217

Immigration concerns, 240
Incompetence, implication of, 23–24, 61
Indirectness, gender patterns in, 152–56
Individual, point of view of, xxiii
Inheritance, battles about, 56–58
In-laws:
arguments about or with, 85–88
and connection-control grid, 86–88
conversational style differences of, 281–83, 287–89, 290, 293, 295–302
Insults:
in arguments, 80, 82, 92
playful, 144–46
from teenagers, 178, 182–83
Italian Americans, use of teasing by, 145
*"It Will End Up in Tears . . ."* (Glaser), 101

Jackson, Thomas Penfield, 108, 109
Johnston, Alexandra, 252
Joking, 146–47
*Joy Luck Club, The* (Tan), 215–16, 295–96
Judgments:
and control, 11, 14, 16–17, 148–52
and criticism, 18, 149–50
from family members, 11, 148–52, 303
gender patterns in, 148–52
from parents, 26, 148–52, 214

Judgments (*cont'd*)
right to make, 17, 150
from siblings, 252–53, 257
in stereotyping, 285–86

Kaluli people of New Guinea, 275–76
Kendall, Shari, xxv, 54, 55, 220–21, 227
Ketcham, Hank, 49
*Kid, The* (film), 101
Kim, Elizabeth, 242–43

Lakoff, Robin, 118
Lee, David A., xxvi, 180–81, 184
Lehr, Linda, 163–64
Lehtonen, Jaakko, 285, 286
Listening:
and alignment, 194, 195, 201
and comfort, 235
and eye contact, 137
Litigation, 117
Lochhead, Liz, 231
*Look Back in Anger* (Osborne), 43–44
Loud family, xxvi, 131–36, 155, 187–98, 256
Love:
allure of, 3
consuming, 243
and criticism, 9
Loyalty, conflicts of, 230
Lyden, Jacki, 239–40

Machine-gun questions, 287–89
Macovski, Albert, 164–65
Mah, Adeline Yen, 46–47, 56–57, 62
Marcus, Leonard, 116–17
Marx, Joshua, 28
Mathabane, Mark, 233–34
Matisoff, James, 146
*Maus* (Spiegelman), 64
Meanings:
literal, 17–19, 303
word vs. heart, 7
Mediation, 116–17
Men:
apologies handled by, 100–103, 117–20, 305
friendships of, 33, 306
older brothers, 271
passing judgment, 148–52
and report-talk, 124–25, 225, 259
Messages:
literal meanings of, 17–19, 303
and metamessages, xvii–xviii, 6–9, 10, 14–15, 19, 28, 211, 303–4
*see also* Communication
Metacommunication, 8–9, 28
arguments avoided via, 93
and reframing, 305
use of term, 8
Metamessages:
adolescents and, 182–83
alignment and, 34
as difficult to pinpoint, 8
focus on, 9
of incompetence, 23
and messages, xvii–xviii, 9, 10, 14–15, 28, 211, 303–4
pain from, 6–8, 307
of rapport in joking, 146
in secrets, 229, 230
and shared history, 16, 19
in tone of voice, 18, 77, 105–6
use of term, xvii
Microsoft Corporation, 108, 109
Millar, Frank, 80, 81
Money, communication about, 156–58
Mother-daughter relationships:
and adolescence, 128–36, 175–80
alignment in, 38–39, 225–26
as central to family, 232
and connection-control grid, 236–39
and criticism, 210–14, 241–42
daughters' roles in, 210–16, 231–32, 239–41, 242–43, 245–47
as friendship, 245–46
mothers' roles in, 216–19, 232–35, 245–47, 304
and reframing, 212–14
*Motherless Daughters* (Edelman), 234–35
Mothers, 209–47
adult children as caretakers for, 59–61, 239–41
authority of, 215, 304
and biting one's tongue, 246–47, 304
blame assigned to, 216–18
changing, 243–45

children as redeemers for, 231–32
closeness sought by, 214–15, 235
as communication central, 225–28
and comparisons, 223–25
and connection-control grid, 211–12, 214, 236–39, 257
consuming love from, 243
criticism from, 104, 210–14, 241–42
and daughters, *see* Mother-daughter relationships
doing it better than, 242–43
expectations of, 218–19
family secrets kept by, 228–30
as friends, 245–46
images of, 232–33
insights into, 214–15
invisibility of, 219–20
leaning on strength of, 233–35
loyalty to, 230
many faces of, 220–22
overreactions of, 222–23
power of, 211–12, 215–16, 220
and reframing, 212–14
solace of, 232–33, 235, 236–37
thanks from, 240–42
*see also* Parents
*MotherSON* (Solomon), 226–27
"My Yiddishe Mama" (song), 232

Nagging, 198–99
Names:
and hierarchy, 107
and identity, 203–8
nicknames, 190
use of, 203–8
Negotiation, of apologies, 110–12, 120
*Newsweek*, 137–38, 218–19
*Nobody Nowhere* (Williams), 206

Ochs, Elinor, 103, 148–52
O'Connor, Mary Catherine, 220
Older siblings, *see* Siblings, older
Ondaatje, Michael, 259–60
*One Writer's Beginnings* (Welty), 41–42
Opinions, conflicting, 76
Ortega y Gasset, José, 307
Osborne, John, 43–44
*Over the River and Through the Woods* (DiPietro), 61–62

*Pagan Time* (Perks), 205
Parents:
adolescent children drawing away from, 128–31, 133–36, 161–62, 174–75, 180
adult children's visits to, 27, 62
aging of, 59–61, 239–41
alignment of, with adolescent children, 185–88, 191, 194–95, 201
alignment of child and, 34, 37–39, 44–46
alignment of children vs., 34, 41–44
in caretaking frame, 163, 174, 176
children judged by, 26, 148–52, 214
communication of children and, 136–38, 217, 226, 304
communication patterns between, 131–36
criticism inferred from, 5, 26–27
death of, 56
and favoritism, 47, 56–57, 262–66, 269
friendships with, 245–46
gender-specific roles of, 133–36, 217
and generation gap, 164, 169
as grandparents, 24–27
in hierarchical position, 11, 107, 148–50, 152
judged by their children, 26, 164, 293
opinions of, 24–27
power of, 11, 273
as repositories of our childhoods, 245
undercutting authority of, 55
*see also* Mothers
Peer pressure, 163–64
*Perfect Days* (Lochhead), 231
Perks, Micah, 205
Petronio, Sandra, 145
Pets:
alignment with, 49–52
and children, 50–51
as easy objects of affection, 51
ventriloquizing of, 51–52
Philips, Susan, 276

*Phoenix* (Dolan), 45–46, 62, 147, 250–51, 270
Photographs, and competition, 273–75
Point of view:
  in criticism, 14–15
  of individual, xxiii
Police, family members as, 10–11
Popcorn, making, 20–23
"Portrait, The" (song), 232
Power, *see* Control
Praising, 146, 163–64
Pressures:
  in communication, 35
  daily, 85
Privacy, in taped conversations, xxvii
Protection:
  of adolescent children, 162, 167, 170–74, 178, 202
  and control, 55
  incompetence implied in, 24, 61
Public Broadcasting System (PBS), xxvi

Questions:
  as interest or intrusion, 282
  machine-gun, 287–89
  as request, 295

Randolph-Wright, Charles, 47
Rapport-talk, 124–25, 126, 127, 150–52, 259
Rate of speech, 285–87
Raymond, Alan and Susan, xxvi
*Red Devil, The* (Rich), 31–32
Reframing:
  e-mail used in, 279
  to end impasse, 198–202, 304–5, 306–7
  and metacommunication, 305
  of mother's criticism, 212–14
  of sibling relationships, 278–80
  use of term, xviii, 304–5
Rehm, Diane, 73–75, 229, 233
Reimer, David, 138, 205–6
Relationships:
  of *ade,* 275–77
  ambivalence in, xvii
  communicating about, 10–11, 127–31, 133
  in connection-control grid, 70–71, 211
  history of criticism in, 14, 16, 19, 211
  as map for future, 257
  mother-child, as central to family, 232
  mother-daughter, *see* Mother-daughter relationships
  mutual obligations in, 68–69
  power struggles in, 68
  severing contact in, 36
  of siblings as special, 248, 275–78
Repetition, 84, 194
Report-talk, 124–25, 127, 225, 259
Resistance, signs of, 20–23
Responsibility:
  acceptance of, 112, 117, 119
  sharing of, 20–23
Reynolds, Debbie, 8–9
Rich, Katherine Russell, 31–32
Richman, Phyllis, 6
Rivalry, *see* Competition
Rogers, L. Edna, 80, 81
Role-play, by children, 237–39
Rosenberg, Jarrett, 220
Rudolph, Dina, 104
Ruiz, Jesse, 141
Rumors, damaging, 35
*Running in the Family* (Ondaatje), 259–60

Sajavaara, Kari, 285, 286
Salinger, Doris, 40, 44–45
Salinger, J. D., 40, 44–45
Salinger, Margaret (Peggy), 40, 44–45
Salinger, Miriam, 40
Sarcasm, in arguments, 77, 78, 81, 84, 92, 93, 106, 182
Schieffelin, Bambi, 275–76
Schulz, Muriel, 245
Schwartz, Delmore, 70
Scolding, 237–39
Scollon, Ron, 286
Scollon, Suzanne, 286
*Second Shift, The* (Hochschild), 218
Secrets:
  children's inadvertent telling of, 48–49

family alignments and, 31–33, 39–41
keeping, 228–29
metamessages in, 229, 230
revealing to extended family members, 31–32
revealing to outsiders, 32–33, 229, 230
Seeger, Peggy, 175–77
Self-censorship, in taped examples, xxvii
Self-confidence:
and apologies, 98, 100
and family hierarchy, 150
Self-evident meanings, 17–19
Self-identity, 208
Senna, Danzy, 71–72
Shapiro, Jane, 49–50
Shawn, William, 257–58
Sherman, Scott, 154, 155
Shurtleff, Michael, 203
Siblings, 248–80
*ade* relationships of, 275–77
alignment of both parents vs., 34
alignments of, 260–62
being right, 258–60
betrayal of trust of, 48
birth order of, 249–53
competition of, 56, 249, 259–60, 273–75
conflicting alignments of, 47–48
on connection-control grid, 257, 268–69, 276
excluded in alignments, 37–39, 40, 58–59, 114–15
and family secrets, 39–41
and favoritism, 47, 56–57, 262–66, 269
hierarchical relationships of, xix, 11–12, 249
and inheritance, 56–58
interactional power of, 269–70
of opposite sex, 158–60
reframing relationships of, 278–80
rivalry among, 56
shared history of, 307–8
sore spots hit by, 73, 277–78, 280
special relationships of, 248, 275–78
twins, 249
in workplace relationships, 257–58
*see also* Siblings, older; Siblings, younger
Siblings, older:
as caretakers, 253, 256–57, 268
guilt of, 269
idolized by younger, 70
judgments passed by, 252–53, 257
milestones reached by, 59
power of, 11, 266–69, 272–73, 277–78
younger siblings resented by, 272–73
Siblings, younger:
of adult children, 253
catching up, 254
interactional power created by, 269–70
milestones reached by, 59
older siblings idolized by, 70
older siblings resented by, 254–57, 265, 269, 270–71
power of, 269–70, 272
as victims, 271
Silber, Joan, 143, 248
Silence:
vs. arguments, 76
of father, 225–27
interactional power created by, 270
Silverman, Sue, 113–14, 207, 235
Simpson, Alyson, 142–43, 262, 264–66
Sims, Bill, xxvi, 128, 170, 186
Sinhala, 249
Sloan, Alfred P., Foundation, xxv
Smith, Ruth, 104
Socratic method:
and apologies, 104–5
in arguments, 80–83, 92
Solace, double meaning of, 235–37
Solomon, Jeffrey, 226–27
*Somebody Somewhere* (Williams), 206
Sore spots, 73–75
Spiegelman, Art, 64
Spouses:
arguments between, *see* Arguments
broken promises of, 83–85
conversational style of, 301–2
hierarchical relationship of, 157
policing activities of, 10–11
sore spots of, 73–75
Spying, and alignments, 46–49

Steinbeck, John, 234
Stepchildren, and favoritism, 47, 56–57
Stereotypes, cross-cultural, 284–86
Strangers:
 as counterpoint to family, 64–66, 74
 meanings of word, 64, 65
Strum, Shirley, 271
Suggestions, 13–19
*Sylvania Waters* (TV), xxvi

Taciturnity, 281–82, 285, 301
*Talking from 9 to 5* (Tannen), 153–55
Tan, Amy, 215–16, 295–96
Tantrums, 269
Tape recorder, use of, xxvii
Taylor, Carolyn, 103–4, 148–52
Taylor, Maureen, 133–34
Teasing, 143–46
Teenagers, *see* Adolescents
Telling Your Day, 147–52
*Ten Thousand Sorrows* (Kim), 242–43
*That's Not What I Meant!* (Tannen), 284
Timing, importance of, 79, 126
Tone:
 in apologies, 105–6
 insulting, 77
 vs. literal meanings, 18
Topic, 289–90
Troubles talk, 126–27, 151–52
Trust:
 apologies and, 97
 betrayal of, 48
 networks of, 34–35
Truth:
 alignments and, 35
 and anger, 72
 as beside the point, 115–16
 motives for telling, 35
 need to know, 35
Twins, 249; *see also* Siblings

Van Dyke, Dick, 8–9
Veciana-Suarez, Ana, 258
Ventriloquizing, 51–53
Volubility, 281, 285, 301
Vowell, Sarah, 212–14
Vuchinich, Sam, 53, 77–78, 84, 159–60, 258, 260–62

Wash, Julie, 138
Welty, Eudora, 41–42
*"Where did you go?" "Out." "What did you do?" "Nothing,"* 138
*Who's Afraid of Virginia Ham?* (Richman), 6–8
Williams, Donna, 206–7
Willis, Bruce, 101
Wilson, Cicily, 30
Wilson, Karen, xxvi, 128, 170, 186
Wise, Nicole, 219
Wodak, Ruth, 245
Women:
 apologies demanded by, 98–100, 109, 117–20, 305
 friendships of, 33, 306
 mothers and daughters, *see* Mother-daughter relationships
 as older siblings, 252–53
 polite requests of, 74
 and rapport-talk, 124–25, 150–52, 259
 self-confidence of, 98, 100, 150
 sisters, 248–49, 254–56, 307–8
Work ethic, 192–93
Workplace, as family, 257–58

Yeliseyeva, Alla, 128, 170
Yelling, 77–78
Yom Kippur, 95, 123
*You Just Don't Understand* (Tannen), xxi, 127, 291
Younger siblings, *see* Siblings, younger

*Also by Deborah Tannen and available from Virago*

# YOU JUST DON'T UNDERSTAND
## Women and Men in Conversation

*Deborah Tannen*

'Tannen combines a novelist's ear for the way people speak with a rare power of original analysis . . . fascinating' Oliver Sacks

Why do so many women feel that men don't tell them anything, but just lecture and criticise? Why do so many men feel that women nag them and never get to the point? In this pioneering book Deborah Tannen shows us how women and men talk in different ways, for profoundly different reasons. While women use language to make connections and reinforce intimacy, men use it to preserve their status and independence.

# TALKING FROM 9 TO 5
## Women and Men at Work: Language, Sex and Power

*Deborah Tannen*

'Deborah Tannen confirms that what is true in the bedroom is also true in the boardroom . . . men and women speak different languages' *Observer*

Deborah Tannen looks at the role played by talk 'from 9 to 5', focusing in particular on the differing conversational rituals that typify men and women. Those common among men involve opposition such as banter, joking and playful put-downs; common among women are ways of maintaining the appearance of equality, avoiding boasting and downplaying authority. Arguing that no one style is superior, Tannen shows that when conventions are taken literally, there are negative results for both sides. She illuminates the different ways men and women make decisions, ask for information and delegate; then shows how these styles affect how we are judged in the workplace. *Talking from 9 to 5* is a brilliantly incisive book that offers powerful new ways of understanding what's really going on at work.

# THE ARGUMENT CULTURE
## Changing the Way We Argue

*Deborah Tannen*

Why do we see everything as either/or, for or against? In the media, in politics, in our classrooms and courtrooms, issues are taken up in adversarial debate between opposite extremes rather than discussed and explored. This pervasive warlike atmosphere encourages us to believe that opposition is the best way to get anything done: the best way to explore an idea is to set up a debate; the best way to settle disputes is litigation; the best way to show you're really thinking is to criticise and attack. Tannen once again brilliantly identifies a mode of communication – the argument culture – that is getting in the way of understanding and needlessly polarising us.